STAR WARS

PRINCESS LEIA

D0565773

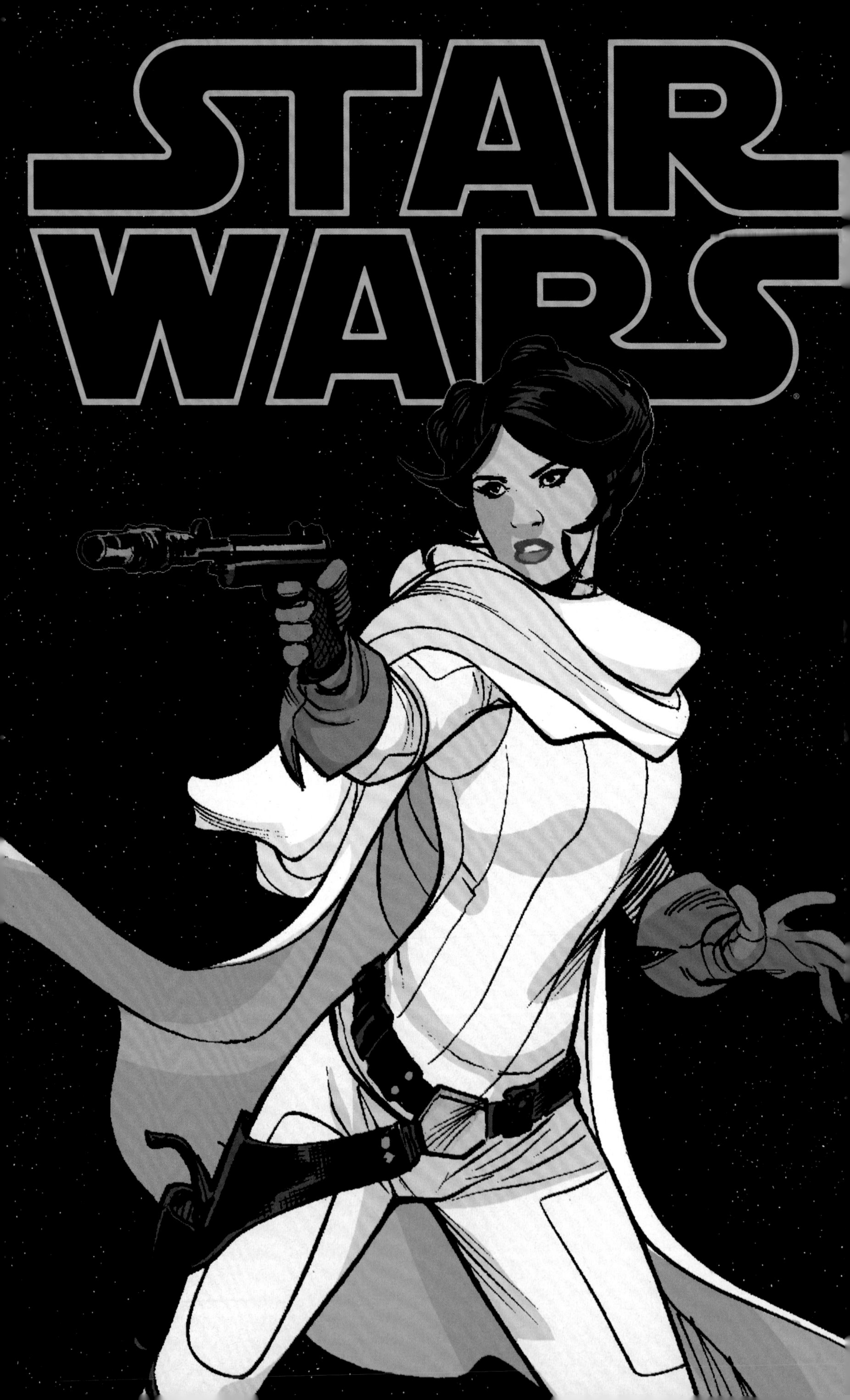
STAR WARS

PRINCESS LEIA

Writer	**MARK WAID**
Artist	**TERRY DODSON**
Inker	**RACHEL DODSON**
Colorist	**JORDIE BELLAIRE**
Letterer	**VC's JOE CARAMAGNA**
Cover Art	**TERRY DODSON & RACHEL DODSON**
Assistant Editors	**HEATHER ANTOS & CHARLES BEACHAM**
Editor	**JORDAN D. WHITE**
Executive Editors	**C.B. CEBULSKI & MIKE MARTS**

Editor in Chief	**AXEL ALONSO**
Chief Creative Officer	**JOE QUESADA**
Publisher	**DAN BUCKLEY**

For Lucasfilm:

Creative Director	**MICHAEL SIGLAIN**
Senior Editors	**JENNIFER HEDDLE, FRANK PARISI**
Lucasfilm Story Group	**RAYNE ROBERTS, PABLO HIDALGO, LELAND CHEE**

Collection Editor	**JENNIFER GRÜNWALD**
Assistant Editor	**SARAH BRUNSTAD**
Associate Managing Editor	**ALEX STARBUCK**
Editor, Special Projects	**MARK D. BEAZLEY**
Senior Editor, Special Projects	**JEFF YOUNGQUIST**
SVP Print, Sales & Marketing	**DAVID GABRIEL**
Book Designer	**ADAM DEL RE**

STAR WARS: PRINCESS LEIA. Contains material originally published in magazine form as PRINCESS LEIA #1-5. First printing 2015. ISBN# 978-0-7851-9317-3. Published by MARVEL WORLDWIDE, INC., a subsidiary of MARVEL ENTERTAINMENT, LLC. OFFICE OF PUBLICATION: 135 West 50th Street, New York, NY 10020. STAR WARS and related text and illustrations are trademarks and/or copyrights, in the United States and other countries, of Lucasfilm Ltd. and/or its affiliates. © & TM Lucasfilm Ltd. No similarity between any of the names, characters, persons, and/or institutions in this magazine with those of any living or dead person or institution is intended, and any such similarity which may exist is purely coincidental. Marvel and its logos are TM Marvel Characters, Inc. **Printed in Canada.** ALAN FINE, President, Marvel Entertainment; DAN BUCKLEY, President, TV, Publishing and Brand Management; JOE QUESADA, Chief Creative Officer; TOM BREVOORT, SVP of Publishing; DAVID BOGART, SVP of Operations & Procurement, Publishing; C.B. CEBULSKI, VP of International Development & Brand Management; DAVID GABRIEL, SVP Print, Sales & Marketing; JIM O'KEEFE, VP of Operations & Logistics; DAN CARR, Executive Director of Publishing Technology; SUSAN CRESPI, Editorial Operations Manager; ALEX MORALES, Publishing Operations Manager; STAN LEE, Chairman Emeritus. For information regarding advertising in Marvel Comics or on Marvel.com, please contact Jonathan Rheingold, VP of Custom Solutions & Ad Sales, at jrheingold@marvel.com. For Marvel subscription inquiries, please call 800-217-9158. **Manufactured between 8/28/2015 and 10/5/2015 by SOLISCO PRINTERS, SCOTT, QC, CANADA.**

10 9 8 7 6 5 4 3 2 1

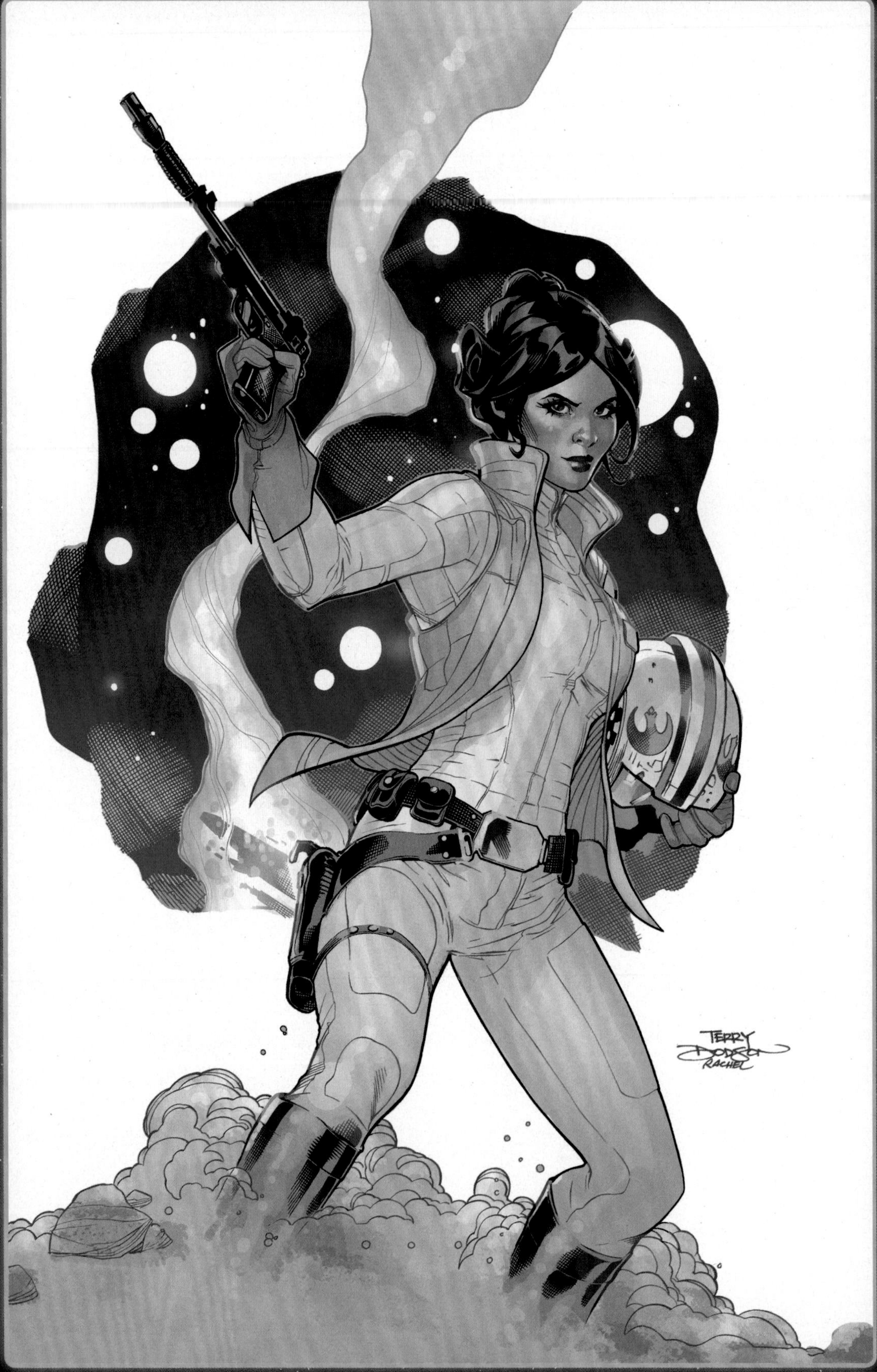
TERRY
DODSON
RACHEL

PRINCESS LEIA

It is a time of both hope and mourning within the Rebellion. While on a secret mission to deliver stolen plans for the Death Star to the Rebel Alliance, PRINCESS LEIA ORGANA was captured by the Galactic Empire and forced to witness the battle station's power as it destroyed her home planet of Alderaan.

With the help of a farmboy pilot and a fast-talking smuggler, Leia escaped her captors and completed her mission. Using the plans, the Alliance was able to destroy the Empire's ultimate weapon.

Having proven themselves a formidable enemy to the Empire, the rebels are in more danger now than ever, leaving them with little time to celebrate their triumph, or lament their loss....

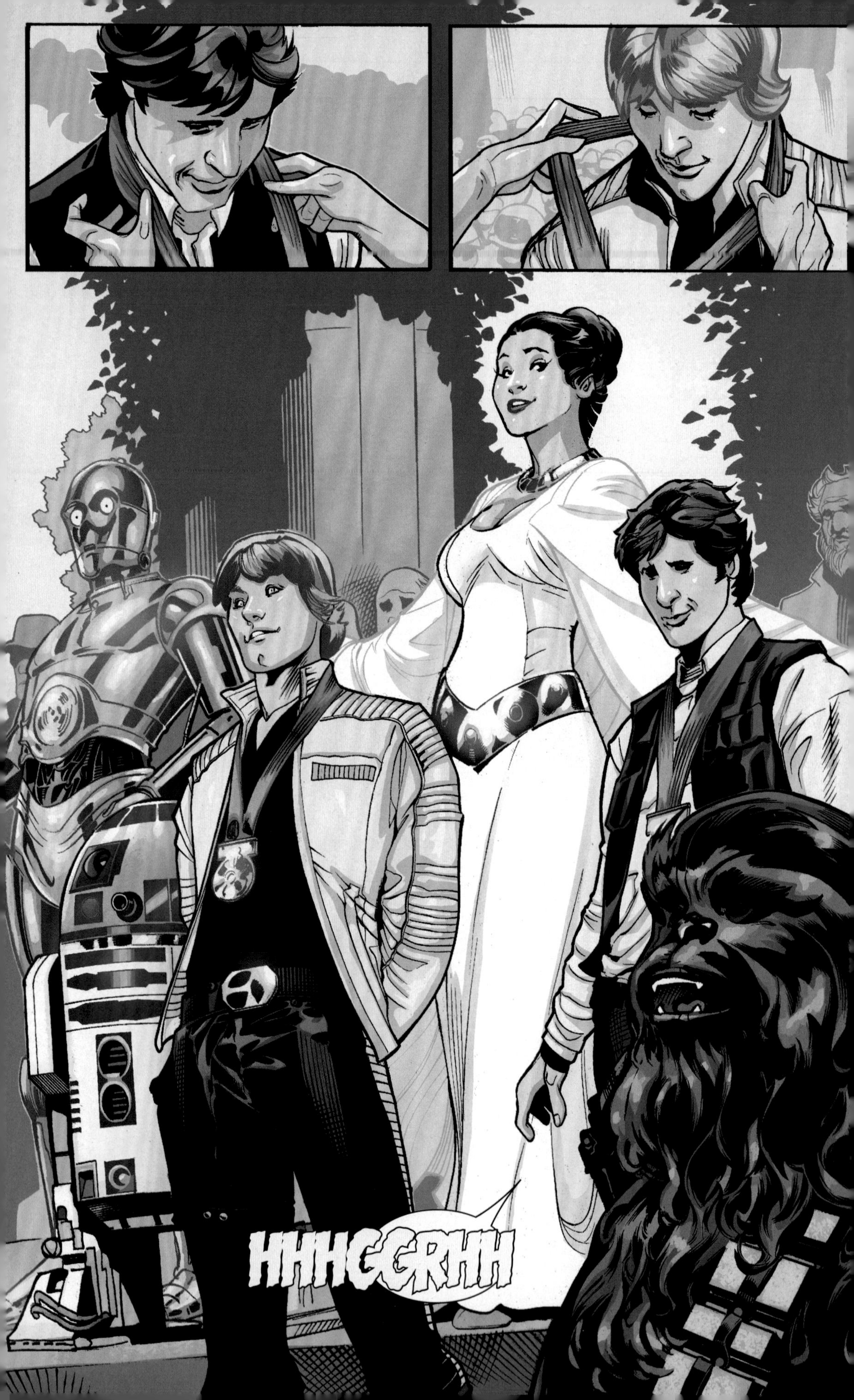
HHHGGRHH

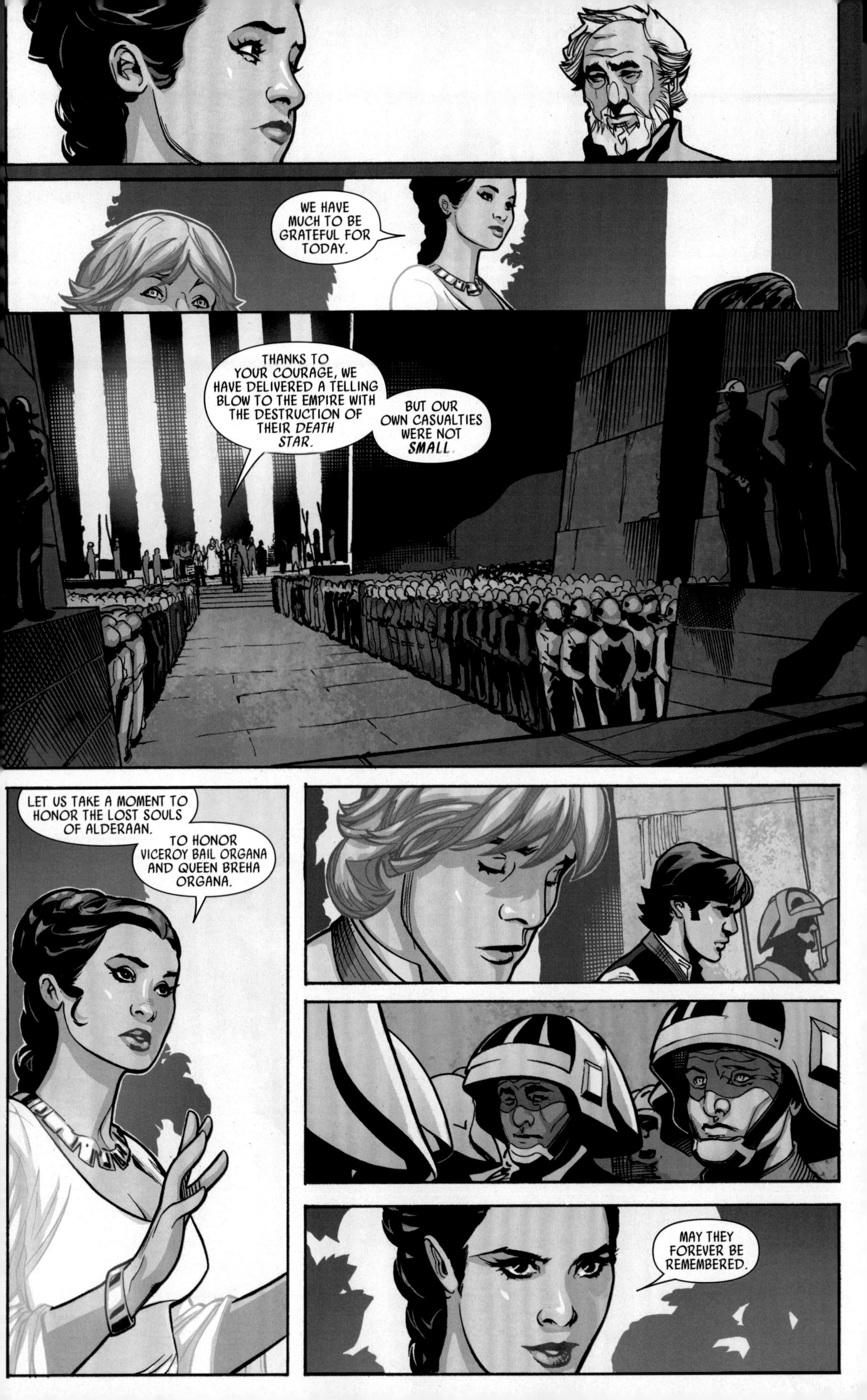
WE HAVE MUCH TO BE GRATEFUL FOR TODAY.
THANKS TO YOUR COURAGE, WE HAVE DELIVERED A TELLING BLOW TO THE EMPIRE WITH THE DESTRUCTION OF THEIR DEATH STAR.
BUT OUR OWN CASUALTIES WERE NOT SMALL.
LET US TAKE A MOMENT TO HONOR THE LOST SOULS OF ALDERAAN.
TO HONOR VICEROY BAIL ORGANA AND QUEEN BREHA ORGANA.
MAY THEY FOREVER BE REMEMBERED.

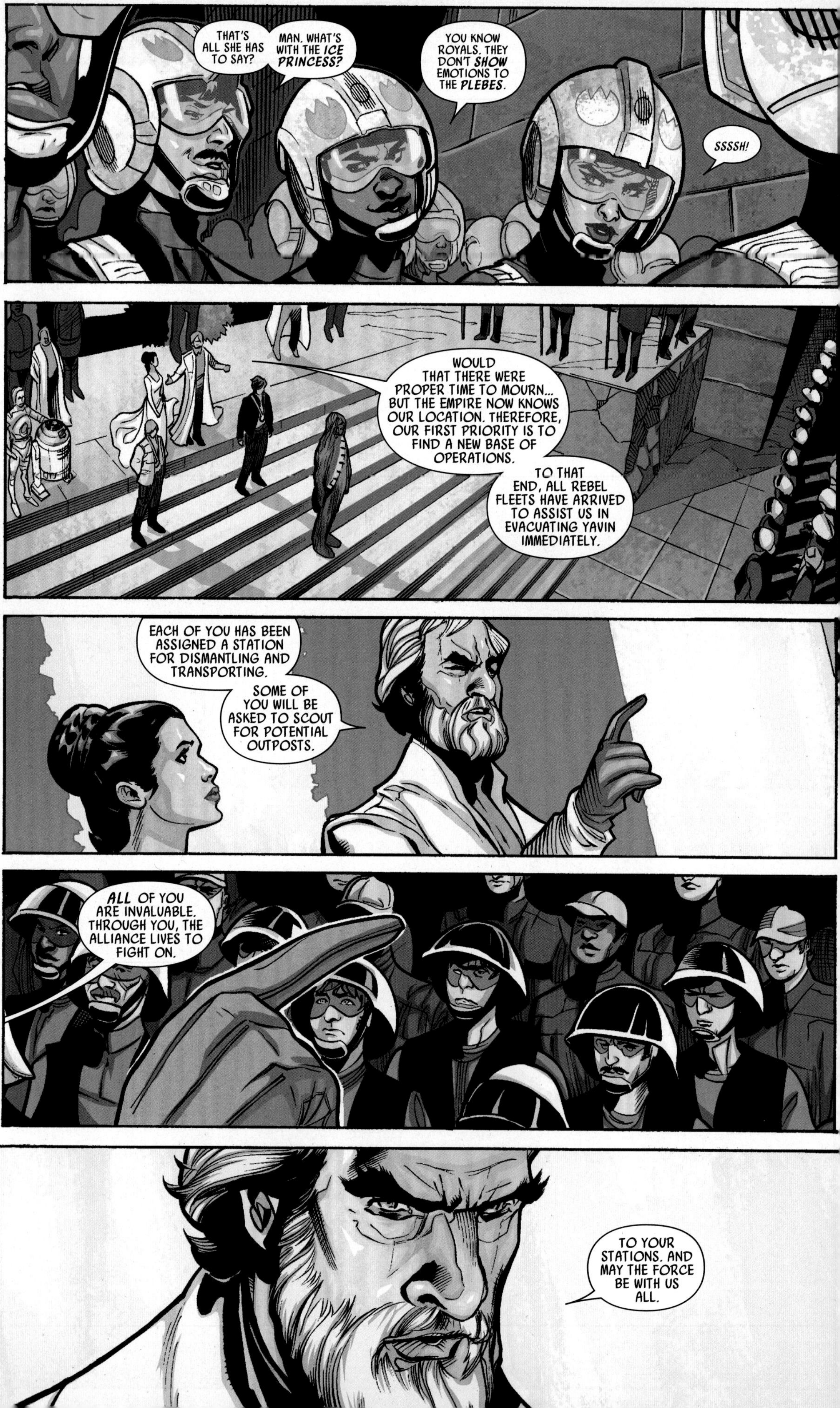
THAT'S ALL SHE HAS TO SAY?
MAN. WHAT'S WITH THE ICE PRINCESS?
YOU KNOW ROYALS. THEY DON'T SHOW EMOTIONS TO THE PLEBES.
SSSSH!
WOULD THAT THERE WERE PROPER TIME TO MOURN... BUT THE EMPIRE NOW KNOWS OUR LOCATION. THEREFORE, OUR FIRST PRIORITY IS TO FIND A NEW BASE OF OPERATIONS.
TO THAT END, ALL REBEL FLEETS HAVE ARRIVED TO ASSIST US IN EVACUATING YAVIN IMMEDIATELY.
EACH OF YOU HAS BEEN ASSIGNED A STATION FOR DISMANTLING AND TRANSPORTING.
SOME OF YOU WILL BE ASKED TO SCOUT FOR POTENTIAL OUTPOSTS.
ALL OF YOU ARE INVALUABLE. THROUGH YOU, THE ALLIANCE LIVES TO FIGHT ON.
TO YOUR STATIONS. AND MAY THE FORCE BE WITH US ALL.

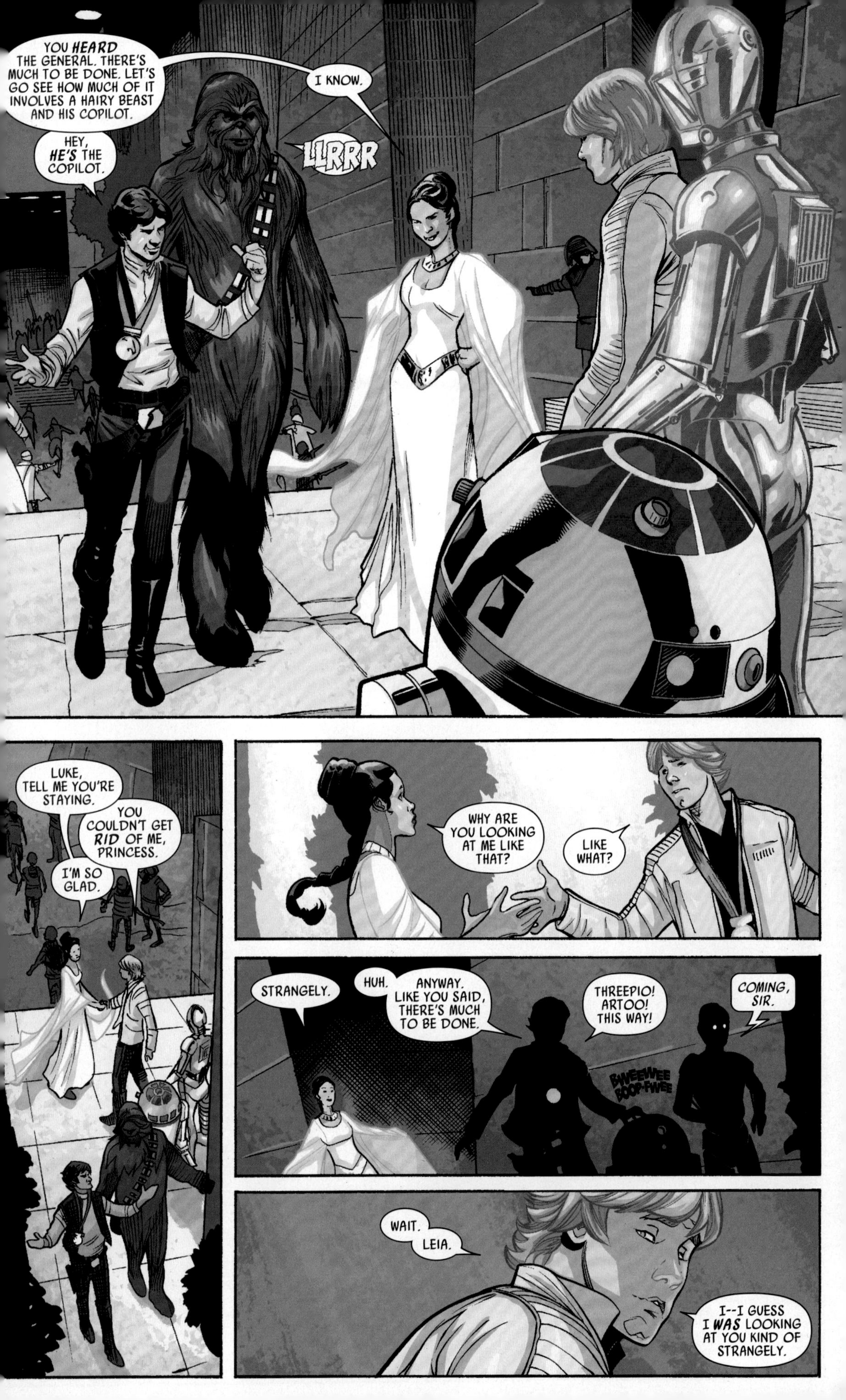
YOU HEARD THE GENERAL. THERE'S MUCH TO BE DONE. LET'S GO SEE HOW MUCH OF IT INVOLVES A HAIRY BEAST AND HIS COPILOT.
I KNOW.
HEY, HE'S THE COPILOT.
LLRRR
LUKE, TELL ME YOU'RE STAYING.
YOU COULDN'T GET RID OF ME, PRINCESS.
I'M SO GLAD.
WHY ARE YOU LOOKING AT ME LIKE THAT?
LIKE WHAT?
STRANGELY.
HUH.
ANYWAY. LIKE YOU SAID, THERE'S MUCH TO BE DONE.
THREEPIO! ARTOO! THIS WAY!
COMING, SIR.
BWEEWEE BOOP-FWEE
WAIT.
LEIA.
I--I GUESS I WAS LOOKING AT YOU KIND OF STRANGELY.

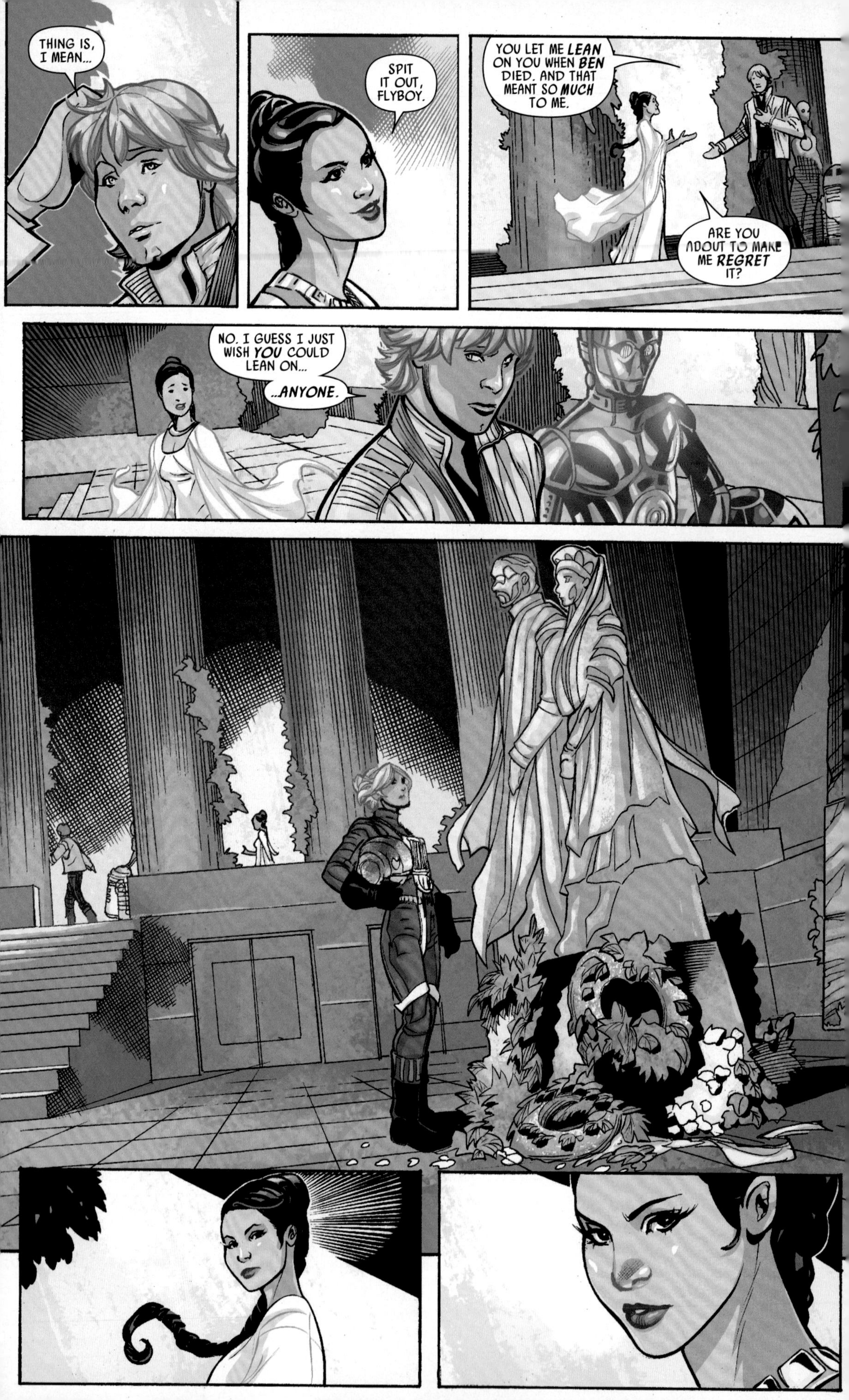
THING IS, I MEAN...
SPIT IT OUT, FLYBOY.
YOU LET ME LEAN ON YOU WHEN BEN DIED. AND THAT MEANT SO MUCH TO ME.
ARE YOU ABOUT TO MAKE ME REGRET IT?
NO. I GUESS I JUST WISH YOU COULD LEAN ON...
...ANYONE.

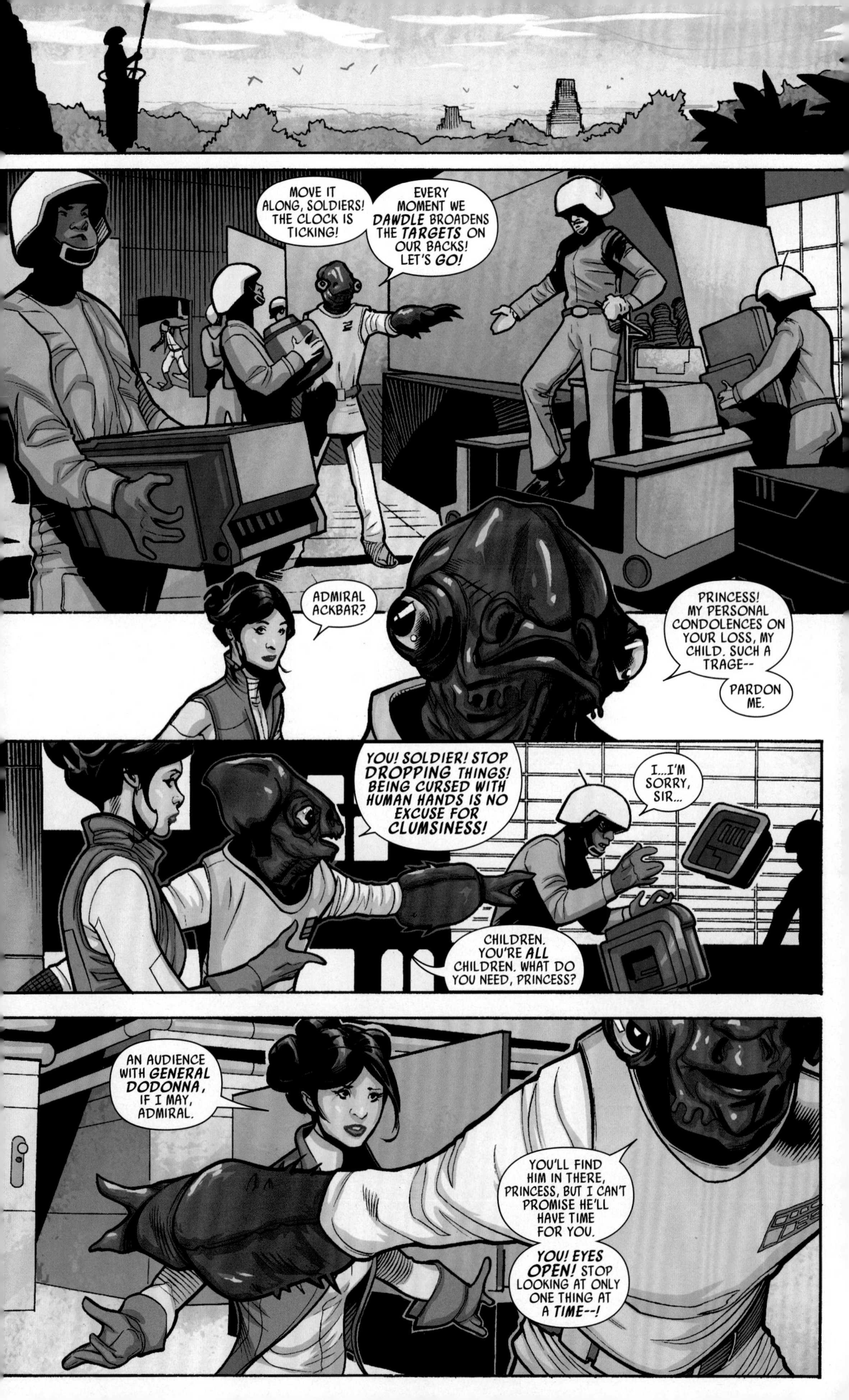
MOVE IT ALONG, SOLDIERS! THE CLOCK IS TICKING!
EVERY MOMENT WE *DAWDLE* BROADENS THE *TARGETS* ON OUR BACKS! LET'S *GO!*
ADMIRAL ACKBAR?
PRINCESS! MY PERSONAL CONDOLENCES ON YOUR LOSS, MY CHILD. SUCH A TRAGE--
PARDON ME.
YOU! SOLDIER! STOP DROPPING THINGS! BEING CURSED WITH HUMAN HANDS IS NO EXCUSE FOR CLUMSINESS!
I...I'M SORRY, SIR...
CHILDREN. YOU'RE *ALL* CHILDREN. WHAT DO YOU NEED, PRINCESS?
AN AUDIENCE WITH *GENERAL DODONNA*, IF I MAY, ADMIRAL.
YOU'LL FIND HIM IN THERE, PRINCESS, BUT I CAN'T PROMISE HE'LL HAVE TIME FOR YOU.
YOU! EYES OPEN! STOP LOOKING AT ONLY ONE THING AT A *TIME--!*

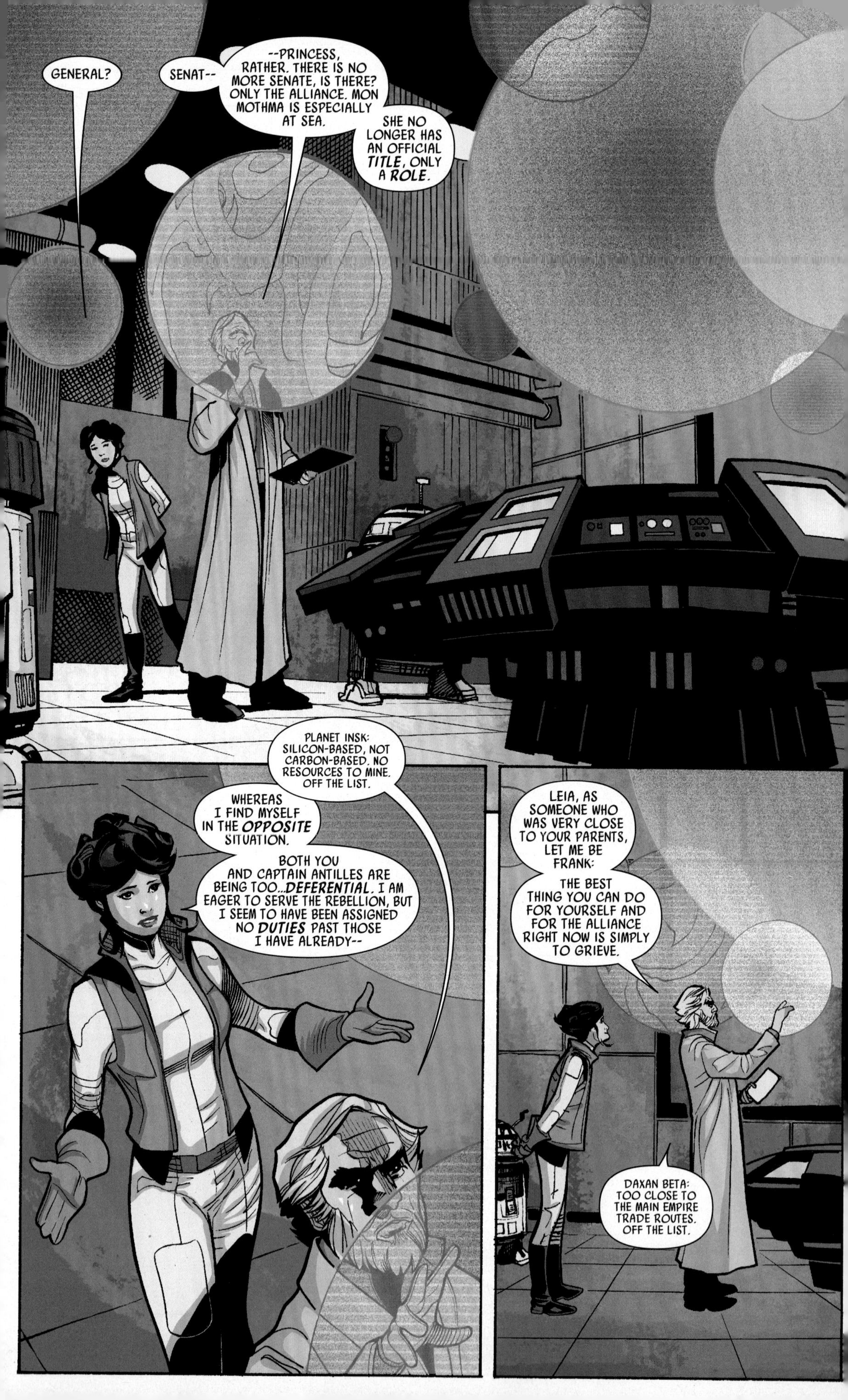
GENERAL?
SENAT--
--PRINCESS, RATHER. THERE IS NO MORE SENATE, IS THERE? ONLY THE ALLIANCE. MON MOTHMA IS ESPECIALLY AT SEA.
SHE NO LONGER HAS AN OFFICIAL TITLE, ONLY A ROLE.
PLANET INSK: SILICON-BASED, NOT CARBON-BASED. NO RESOURCES TO MINE. OFF THE LIST.
WHEREAS I FIND MYSELF IN THE OPPOSITE SITUATION.
BOTH YOU AND CAPTAIN ANTILLES ARE BEING TOO...DEFERENTIAL. I AM EAGER TO SERVE THE REBELLION, BUT I SEEM TO HAVE BEEN ASSIGNED NO DUTIES PAST THOSE I HAVE ALREADY--
LEIA, AS SOMEONE WHO WAS VERY CLOSE TO YOUR PARENTS, LET ME BE FRANK:
THE BEST THING YOU CAN DO FOR YOURSELF AND FOR THE ALLIANCE RIGHT NOW IS SIMPLY TO GRIEVE.
DAXAN BETA: TOO CLOSE TO THE MAIN EMPIRE TRADE ROUTES. OFF THE LIST.

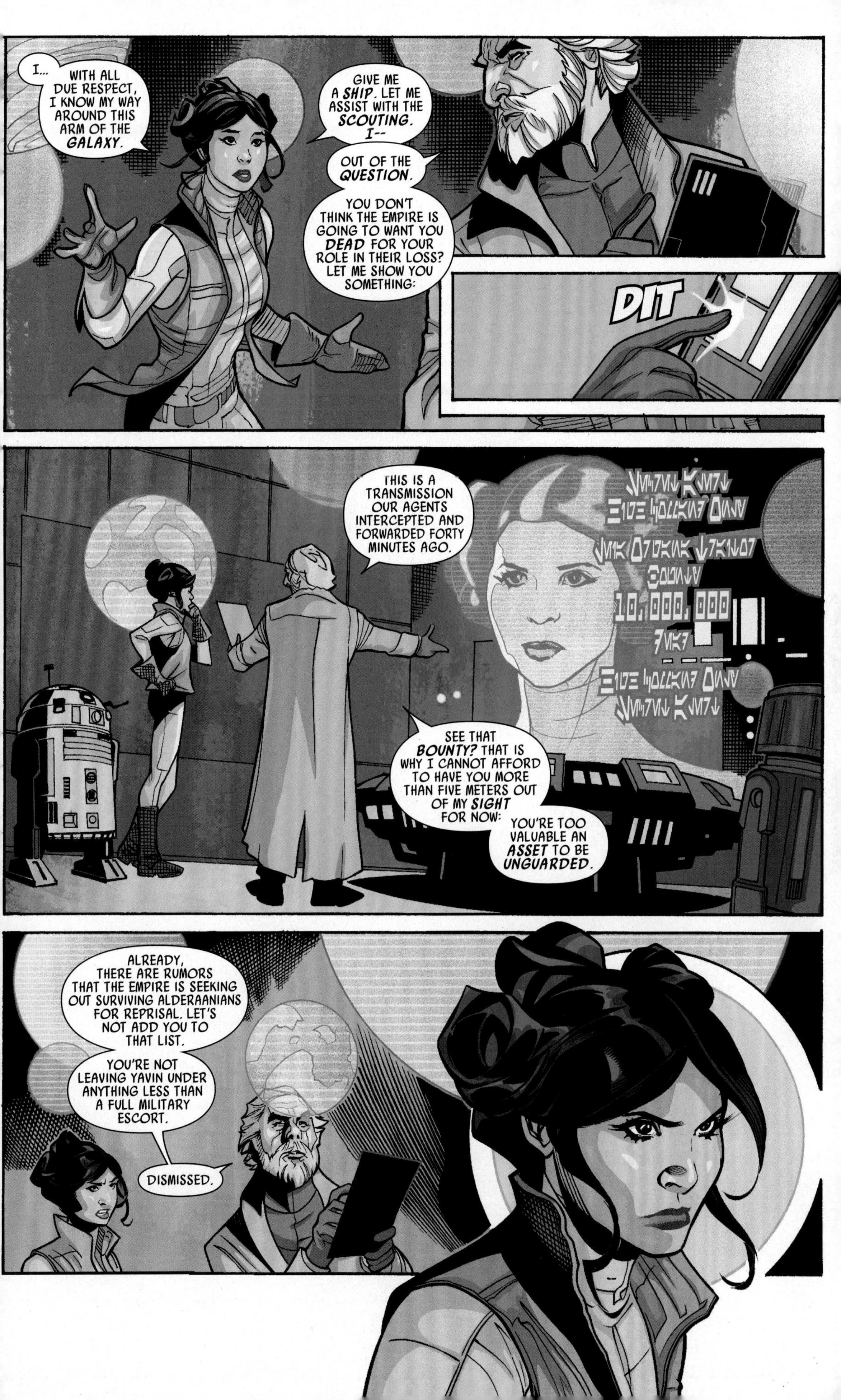

I...
WITH ALL DUE RESPECT, I KNOW MY WAY AROUND THIS ARM OF THE GALAXY.
GIVE ME A SHIP. LET ME ASSIST WITH THE SCOUTING. I--
OUT OF THE QUESTION.
YOU DON'T THINK THE EMPIRE IS GOING TO WANT YOU DEAD FOR YOUR ROLE IN THEIR LOSS? LET ME SHOW YOU SOMETHING:
DIT
THIS IS A TRANSMISSION OUR AGENTS INTERCEPTED AND FORWARDED FORTY MINUTES AGO.
10,000,000
SEE THAT BOUNTY? THAT IS WHY I CANNOT AFFORD TO HAVE YOU MORE THAN FIVE METERS OUT OF MY SIGHT FOR NOW:
YOU'RE TOO VALUABLE AN ASSET TO BE UNGUARDED.
ALREADY, THERE ARE RUMORS THAT THE EMPIRE IS SEEKING OUT SURVIVING ALDERAANIANS FOR REPRISAL. LET'S NOT ADD YOU TO THAT LIST.
YOU'RE NOT LEAVING YAVIN UNDER ANYTHING LESS THAN A FULL MILITARY ESCORT.
DISMISSED.

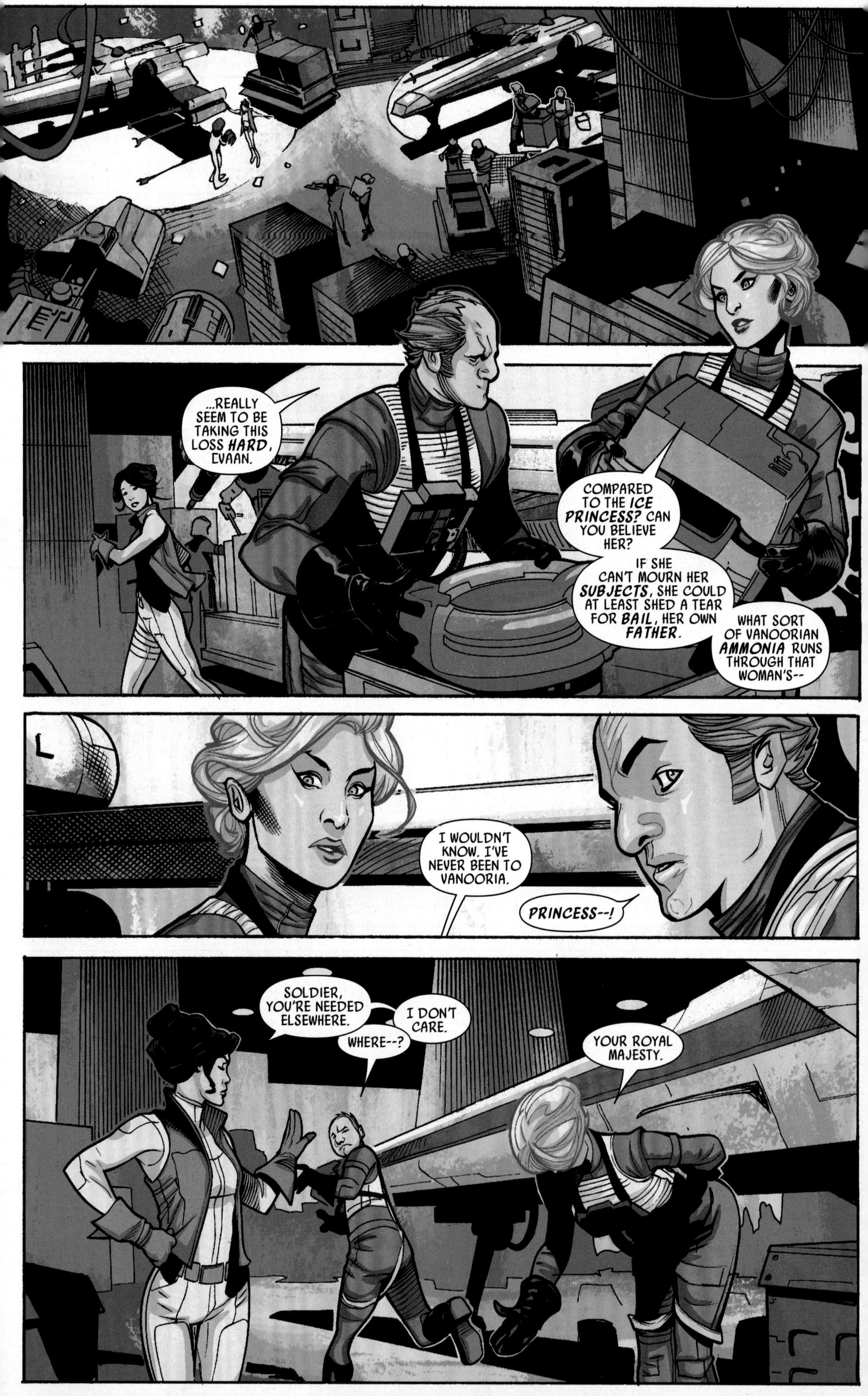

...REALLY SEEM TO BE TAKING THIS LOSS HARD, EVAAN.
COMPARED TO THE ICE PRINCESS? CAN YOU BELIEVE HER?
IF SHE CAN'T MOURN HER SUBJECTS, SHE COULD AT LEAST SHED A TEAR FOR BAIL, HER OWN FATHER.
WHAT SORT OF VANOORIAN AMMONIA RUNS THROUGH THAT WOMAN'S--
I WOULDN'T KNOW. I'VE NEVER BEEN TO VANOORIA.
PRINCESS--!
SOLDIER, YOU'RE NEEDED ELSEWHERE.
WHERE--?
I DON'T CARE.
YOUR ROYAL MAJESTY.

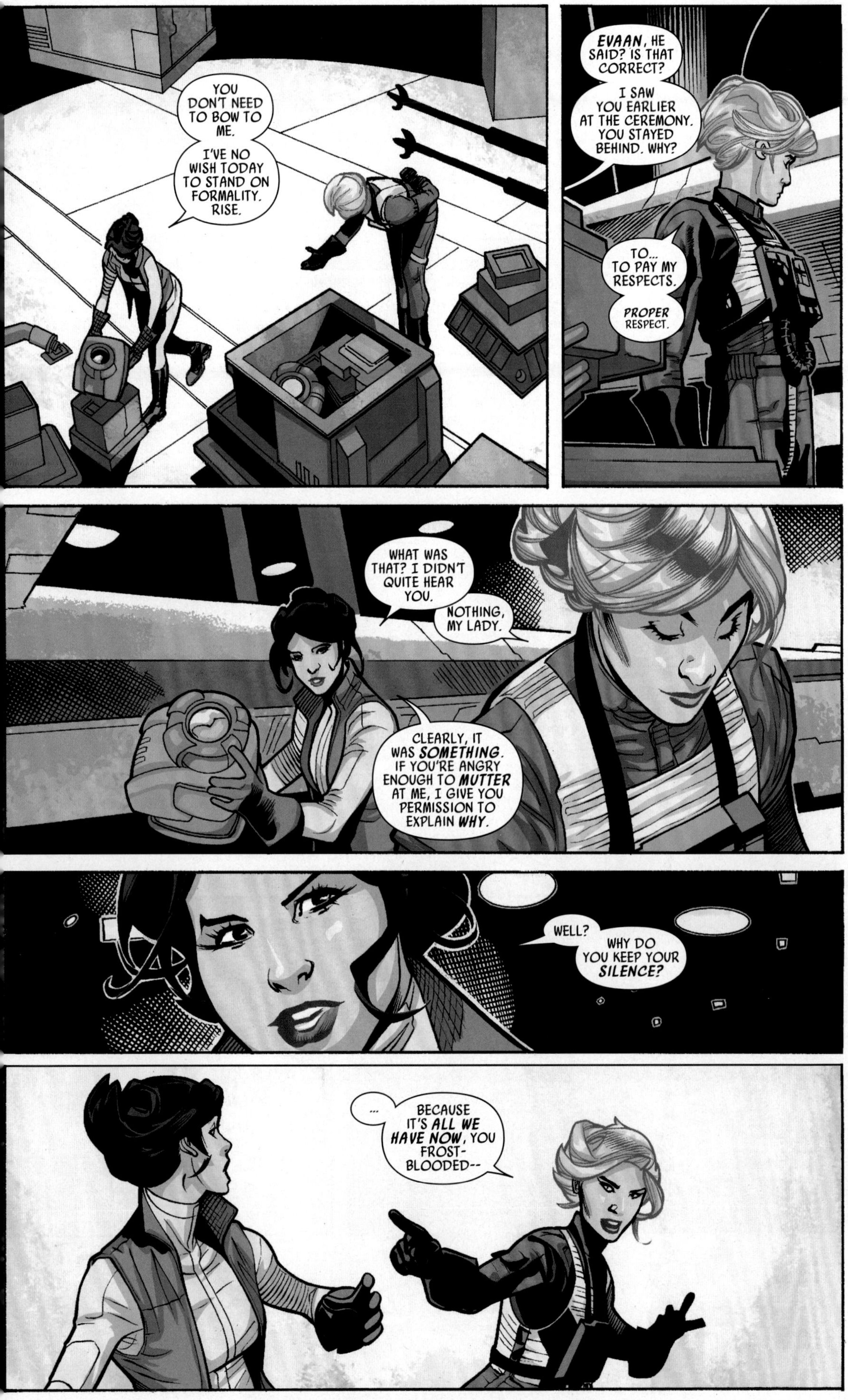

YOU DON'T NEED TO BOW TO ME.
I'VE NO WISH TODAY TO STAND ON FORMALITY. RISE.
EVAAN, HE SAID? IS THAT CORRECT?
I SAW YOU EARLIER AT THE CEREMONY. YOU STAYED BEHIND. WHY?
TO... TO PAY MY RESPECTS.
PROPER RESPECT.
WHAT WAS THAT? I DIDN'T QUITE HEAR YOU.
NOTHING, MY LADY.
CLEARLY, IT WAS SOMETHING. IF YOU'RE ANGRY ENOUGH TO MUTTER AT ME, I GIVE YOU PERMISSION TO EXPLAIN WHY.
WELL?
WHY DO YOU KEEP YOUR SILENCE?
...
BECAUSE IT'S ALL WE HAVE NOW, YOU FROST-BLOODED--

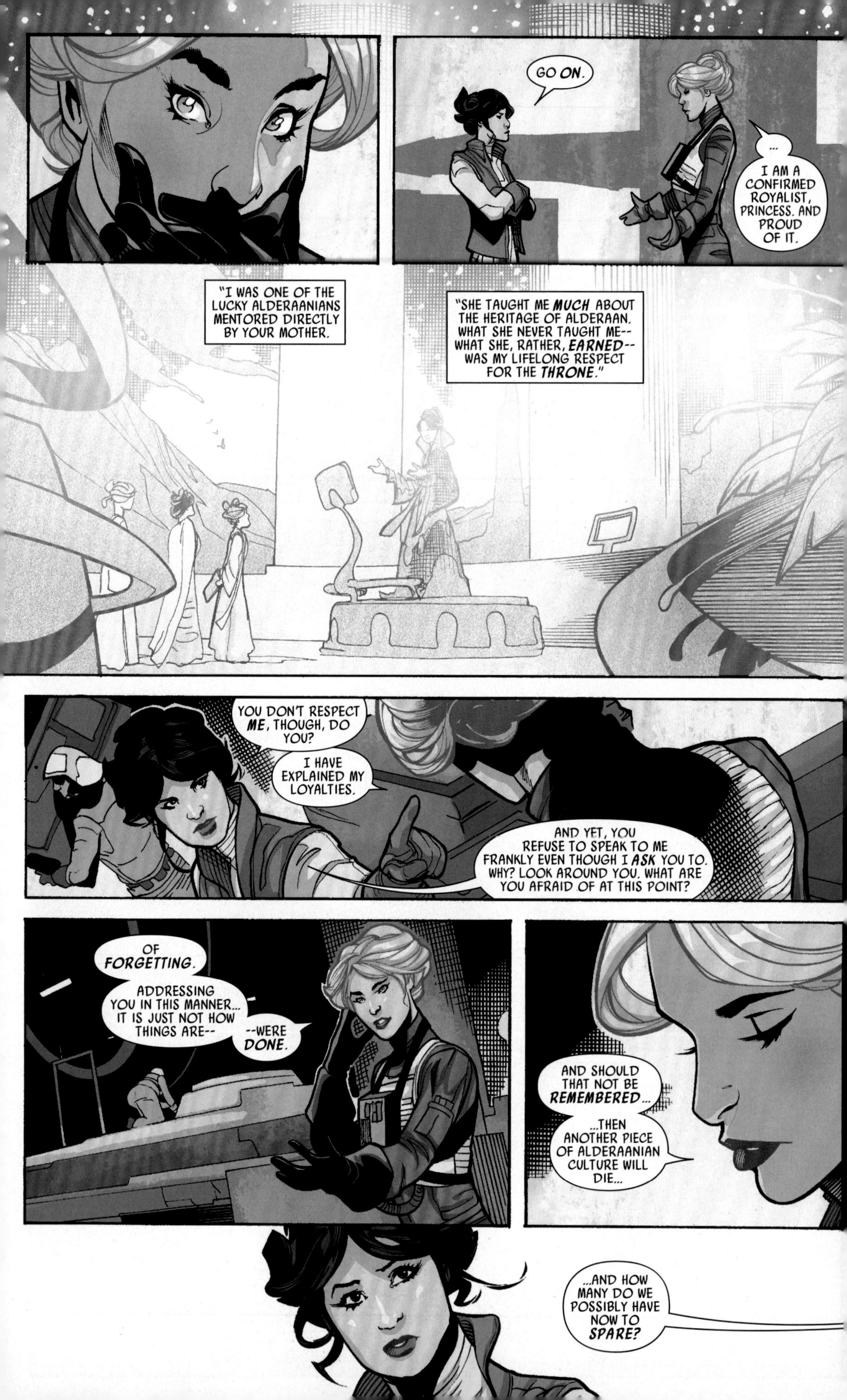
GO ON.
...
I AM A CONFIRMED ROYALIST, PRINCESS. AND PROUD OF IT.
"I WAS ONE OF THE LUCKY ALDERAANIANS MENTORED DIRECTLY BY YOUR MOTHER.
"SHE TAUGHT ME MUCH ABOUT THE HERITAGE OF ALDERAAN. WHAT SHE NEVER TAUGHT ME-- WHAT SHE, RATHER, EARNED-- WAS MY LIFELONG RESPECT FOR THE THRONE."
YOU DON'T RESPECT ME, THOUGH, DO YOU?
I HAVE EXPLAINED MY LOYALTIES.
AND YET, YOU REFUSE TO SPEAK TO ME FRANKLY EVEN THOUGH I ASK YOU TO. WHY? LOOK AROUND YOU. WHAT ARE YOU AFRAID OF AT THIS POINT?
OF FORGETTING.
ADDRESSING YOU IN THIS MANNER... IT IS JUST NOT HOW THINGS ARE--
--WERE DONE.
AND SHOULD THAT NOT BE REMEMBERED...
...THEN ANOTHER PIECE OF ALDERAANIAN CULTURE WILL DIE...
...AND HOW MANY DO WE POSSIBLY HAVE NOW TO SPARE?

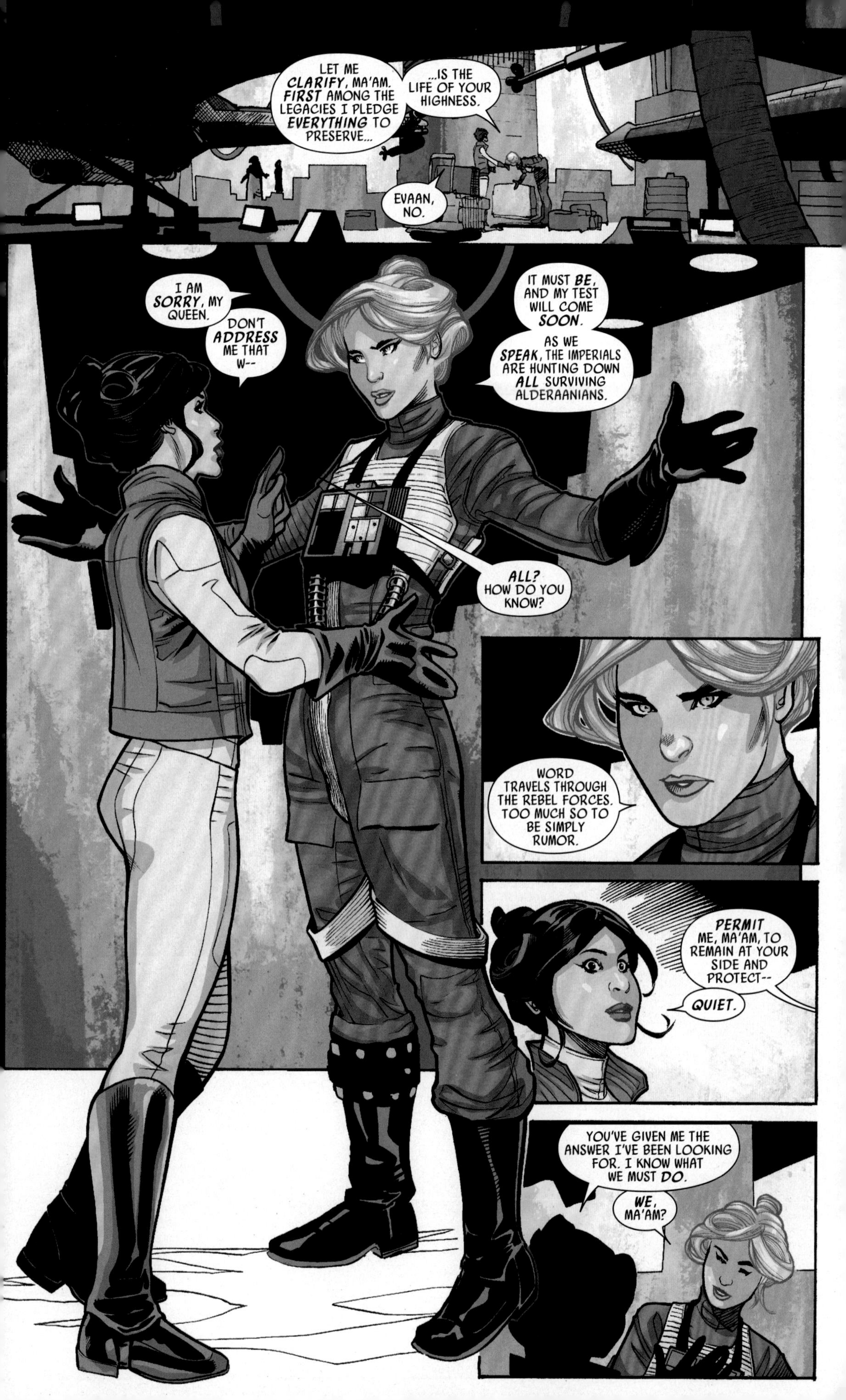
LET ME CLARIFY, MA'AM. FIRST AMONG THE LEGACIES I PLEDGE EVERYTHING TO PRESERVE...
...IS THE LIFE OF YOUR HIGHNESS.
EVAAN, NO.
I AM SORRY, MY QUEEN.
DON'T ADDRESS ME THAT W--
IT MUST BE, AND MY TEST WILL COME SOON.
AS WE SPEAK, THE IMPERIALS ARE HUNTING DOWN ALL SURVIVING ALDERAANIANS.
ALL? HOW DO YOU KNOW?
WORD TRAVELS THROUGH THE REBEL FORCES. TOO MUCH SO TO BE SIMPLY RUMOR.
PERMIT ME, MA'AM, TO REMAIN AT YOUR SIDE AND PROTECT--
QUIET.
YOU'VE GIVEN ME THE ANSWER I'VE BEEN LOOKING FOR. I KNOW WHAT WE MUST DO.
WE, MA'AM?

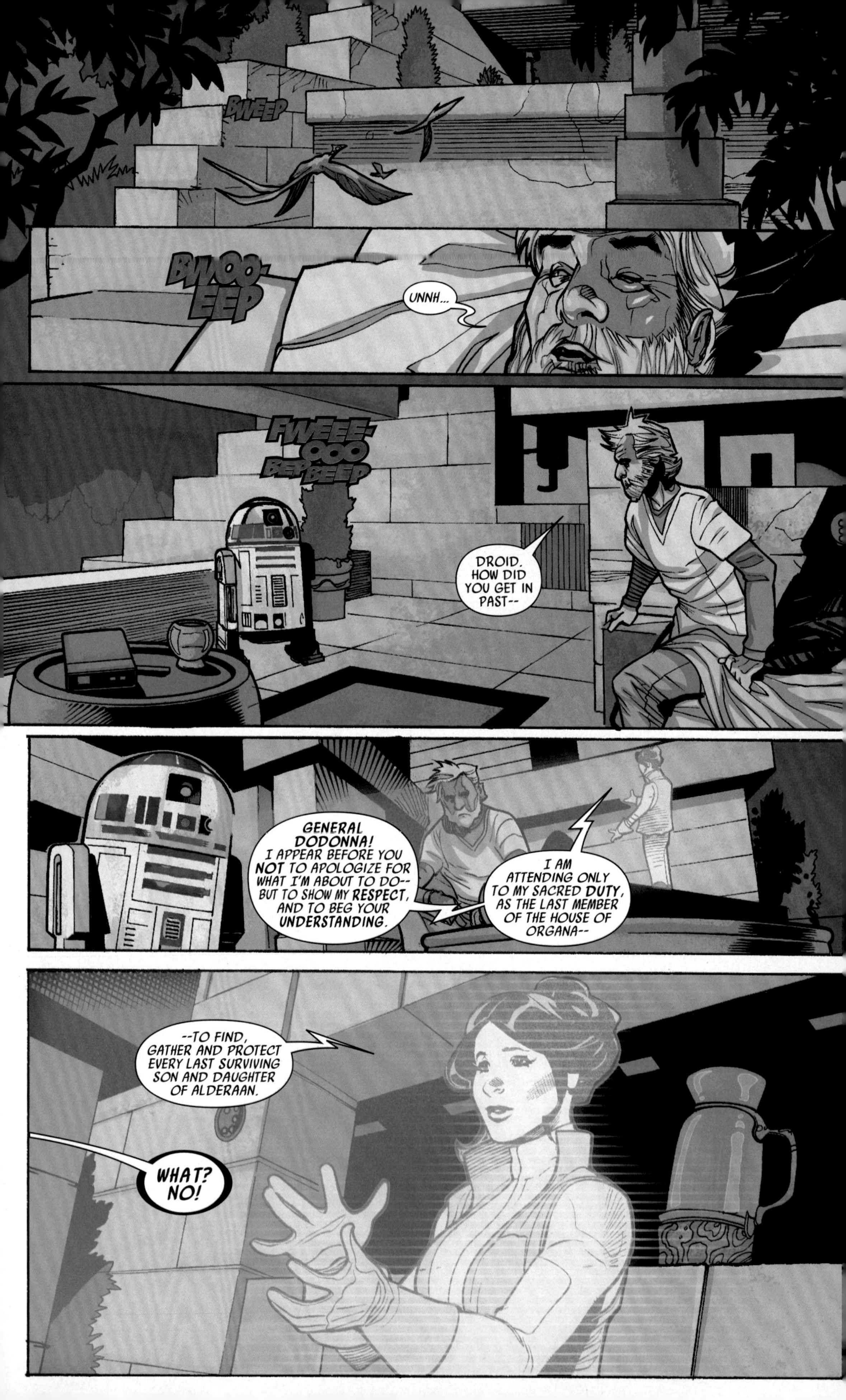
BWEEP
BWOO-EEP
UNNH...
FWEEE-OOO BEP BEEP
DROID. HOW DID YOU GET IN PAST--
GENERAL DODONNA! I APPEAR BEFORE YOU NOT TO APOLOGIZE FOR WHAT I'M ABOUT TO DO-- BUT TO SHOW MY RESPECT, AND TO BEG YOUR UNDERSTANDING.
I AM ATTENDING ONLY TO MY SACRED DUTY, AS THE LAST MEMBER OF THE HOUSE OF ORGANA--
--TO FIND, GATHER AND PROTECT EVERY LAST SURVIVING SON AND DAUGHTER OF ALDERAAN.
WHAT? NO!

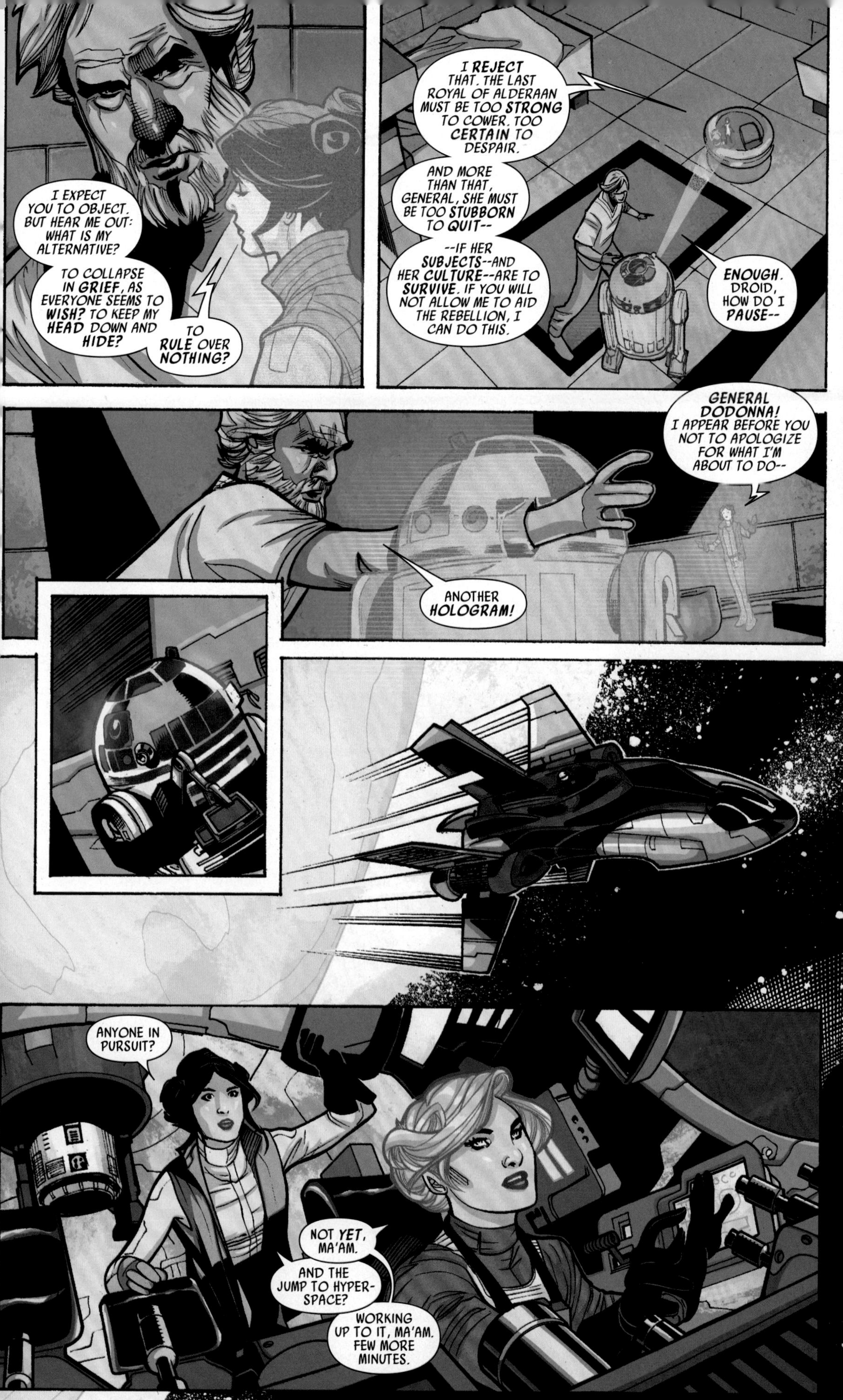
I EXPECT YOU TO OBJECT. BUT HEAR ME OUT: WHAT IS MY ALTERNATIVE?
TO COLLAPSE IN GRIEF, AS EVERYONE SEEMS TO WISH? TO KEEP MY HEAD DOWN AND HIDE?
TO RULE OVER NOTHING?
I REJECT THAT. THE LAST ROYAL OF ALDERAAN MUST BE TOO STRONG TO COWER. TOO CERTAIN TO DESPAIR.
AND MORE THAN THAT, GENERAL, SHE MUST BE TOO STUBBORN TO QUIT--
--IF HER SUBJECTS--AND HER CULTURE--ARE TO SURVIVE. IF YOU WILL NOT ALLOW ME TO AID THE REBELLION, I CAN DO THIS.
ENOUGH. DROID, HOW DO I PAUSE--
GENERAL DODONNA! I APPEAR BEFORE YOU NOT TO APOLOGIZE FOR WHAT I'M ABOUT TO DO--
ANOTHER HOLOGRAM!
ANYONE IN PURSUIT?
NOT YET, MA'AM.
AND THE JUMP TO HYPER-SPACE?
WORKING UP TO IT, MA'AM. FEW MORE MINUTES.

YOU'RE DOING WELL, EVAAN, BUT I MUST *INSIST* ON--

ANYTHING, HIGHNESS. WHATEVER YOU WISH.

--THE *TRUTH.*

FROM *YOU.* AT ALL TIMES. AND IF I FAIL TO *ASK,* I'LL EXPECT YOU TO *VOLUNTEER* IT.

RIGHT NOW, WE ARE ALDERAAN'S CHILDREN, EVAAN. YOU AND I. LET'S NOT DISHONOR THAT BY SPEAKING *FALSELY*-- OR BY NOT COMMUNICATING AT ALL.

IN THAT CASE, MA'AM--

GO ON.

--THIS IS A *BAD IDEA.* NOW THAT *DODONNA* KNOWS YOU'VE GONE, HE WILL PUT VALUABLE SHIPS AND PILOTS IN *HARM'S* WAY TO *RECOVER* YOU.

AND YOUR WHOLE *AMBITION* REEKS OF *IMPULSE.* SURELY A GRAND PLAN REQUIRES *SOME* THOUGHT.

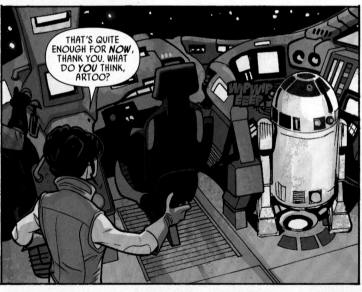

THAT'S QUITE ENOUGH FOR *NOW,* THANK YOU. WHAT DO *YOU* THINK, ARTOO?

WIPWIP EEER

MA'AM!

BWEOO FWEE

WE'RE BEING *PURSUED.*

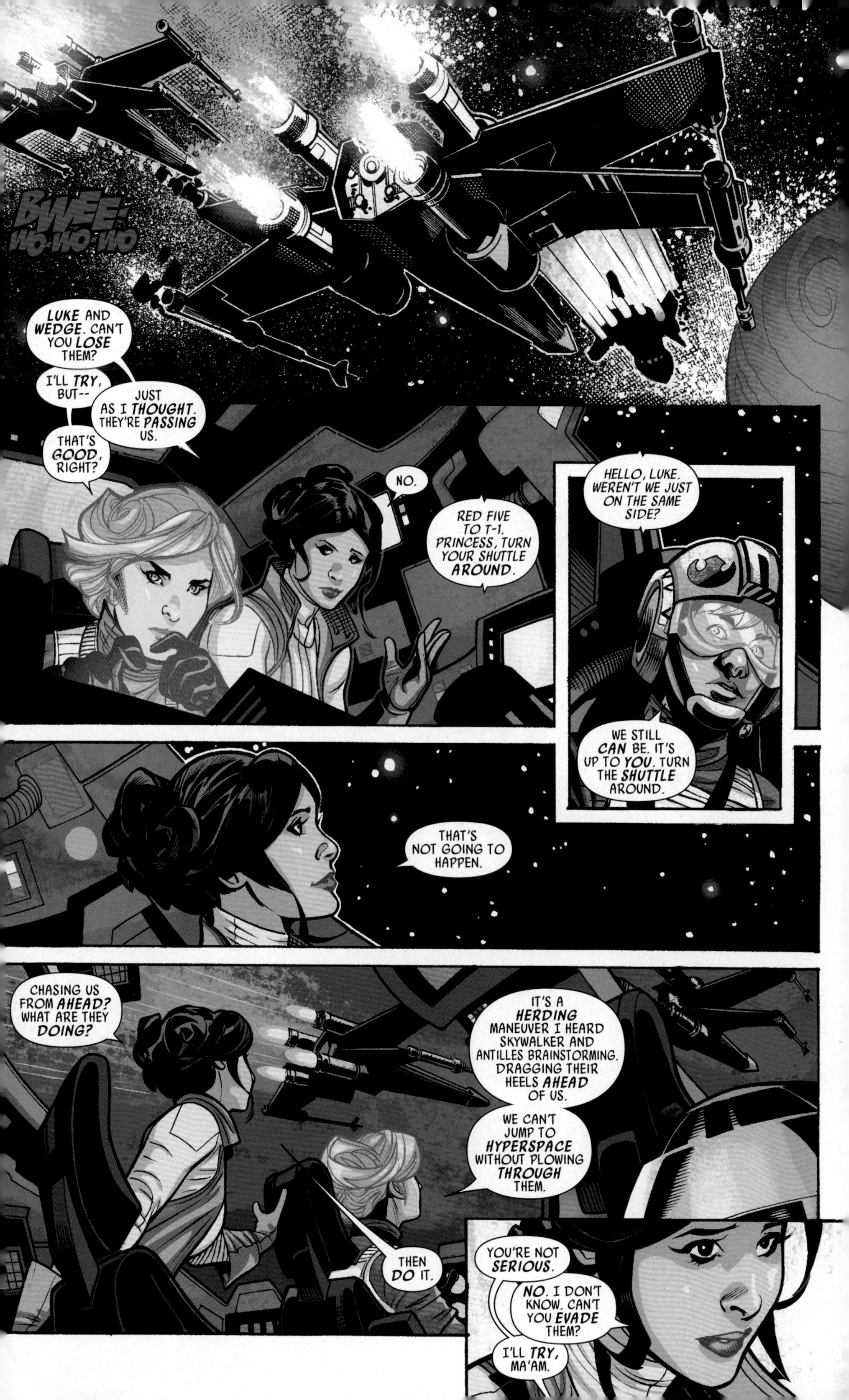
BWEE-WO-WO-WO
LUKE AND WEDGE. CAN'T YOU LOSE THEM?
I'LL TRY, BUT--
JUST AS I THOUGHT. THEY'RE PASSING US.
THAT'S GOOD, RIGHT?
NO.
RED FIVE TO T-1. PRINCESS, TURN YOUR SHUTTLE AROUND.
HELLO, LUKE. WEREN'T WE JUST ON THE SAME SIDE?
WE STILL CAN BE. IT'S UP TO YOU. TURN THE SHUTTLE AROUND.
THAT'S NOT GOING TO HAPPEN.
CHASING US FROM AHEAD? WHAT ARE THEY DOING?
IT'S A HERDING MANEUVER I HEARD SKYWALKER AND ANTILLES BRAINSTORMING. DRAGGING THEIR HEELS AHEAD OF US.
WE CAN'T JUMP TO HYPERSPACE WITHOUT PLOWING THROUGH THEM.
THEN DO IT.
YOU'RE NOT SERIOUS.
NO. I DON'T KNOW. CAN'T YOU EVADE THEM?
I'LL TRY, MA'AM.

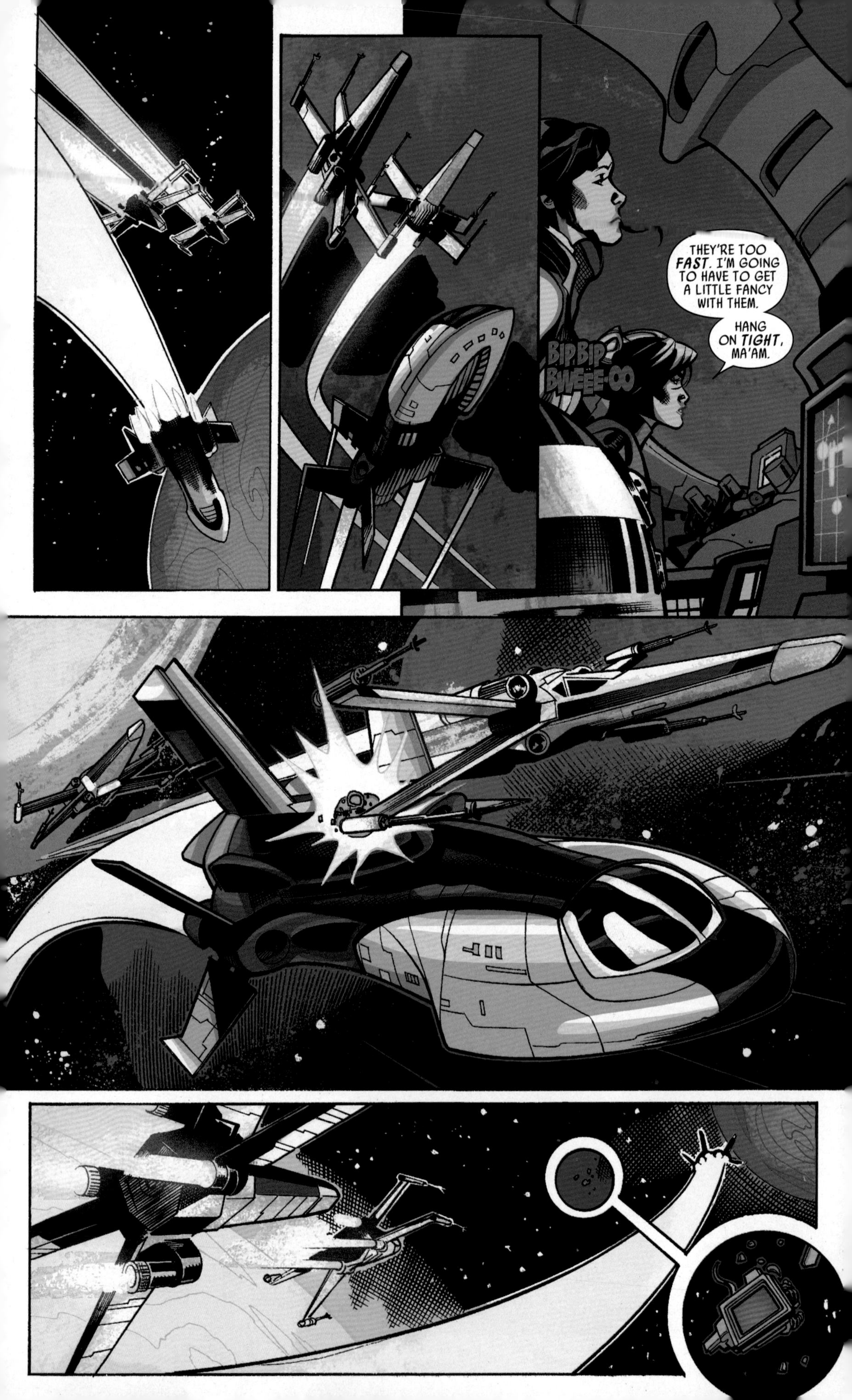
THEY'RE TOO FAST. I'M GOING TO HAVE TO GET A LITTLE FANCY WITH THEM.
HANG ON TIGHT, MA'AM.
BIP BIP BWEEE-OO

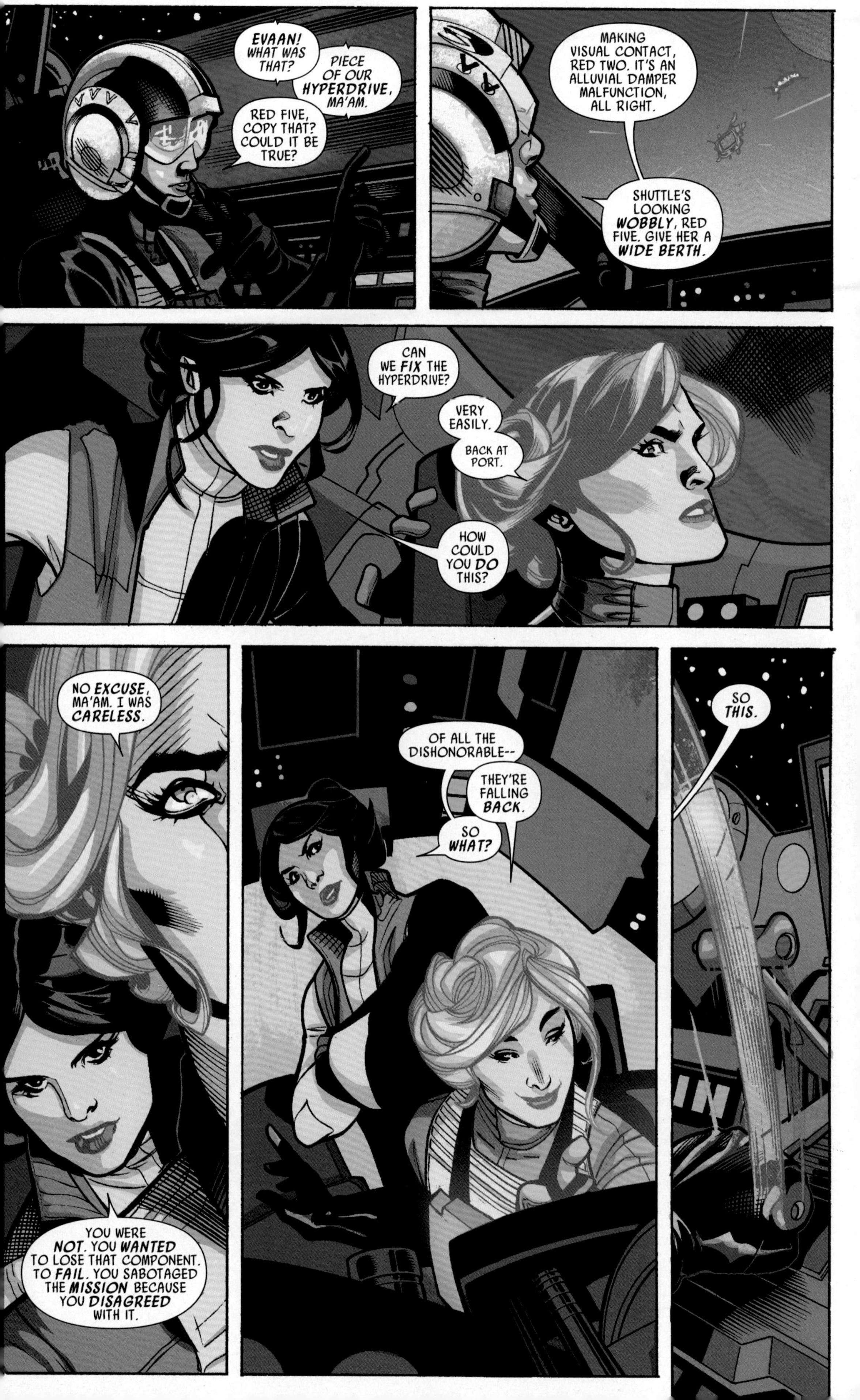
EVAAN! WHAT WAS THAT?
PIECE OF OUR HYPERDRIVE, MA'AM.
RED FIVE, COPY THAT? COULD IT BE TRUE?
MAKING VISUAL CONTACT, RED TWO. IT'S AN ALLUVIAL DAMPER MALFUNCTION, ALL RIGHT.
SHUTTLE'S LOOKING WOBBLY, RED FIVE. GIVE HER A WIDE BERTH.
CAN WE FIX THE HYPERDRIVE?
VERY EASILY.
BACK AT PORT.
HOW COULD YOU DO THIS?
NO EXCUSE, MA'AM. I WAS CARELESS.
YOU WERE NOT. YOU WANTED TO LOSE THAT COMPONENT. TO FAIL. YOU SABOTAGED THE MISSION BECAUSE YOU DISAGREED WITH IT.
OF ALL THE DISHONORABLE--
THEY'RE FALLING BACK.
SO WHAT?
SO THIS.

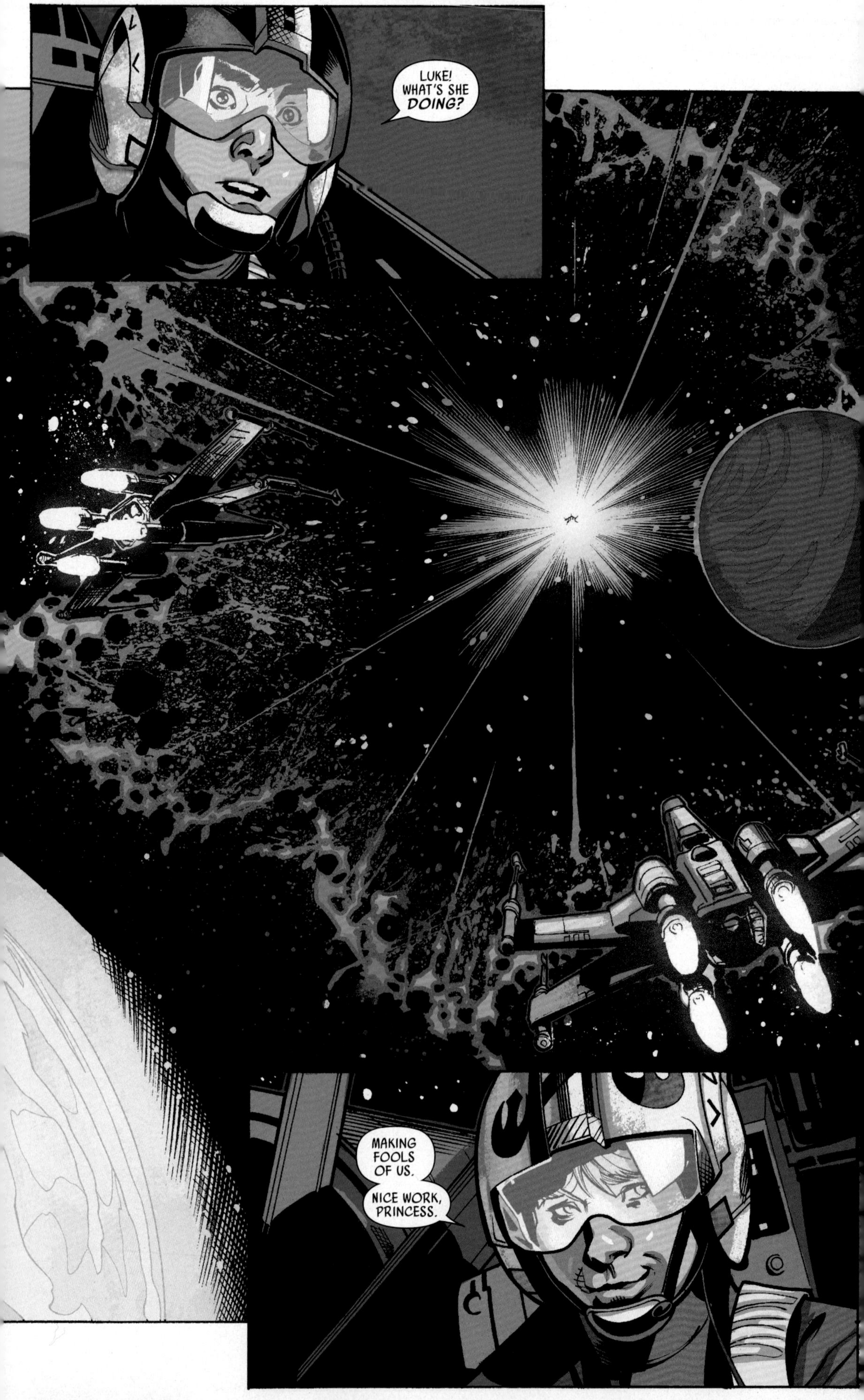
LUKE! WHAT'S SHE DOING?
MAKING FOOLS OF US.
NICE WORK, PRINCESS.

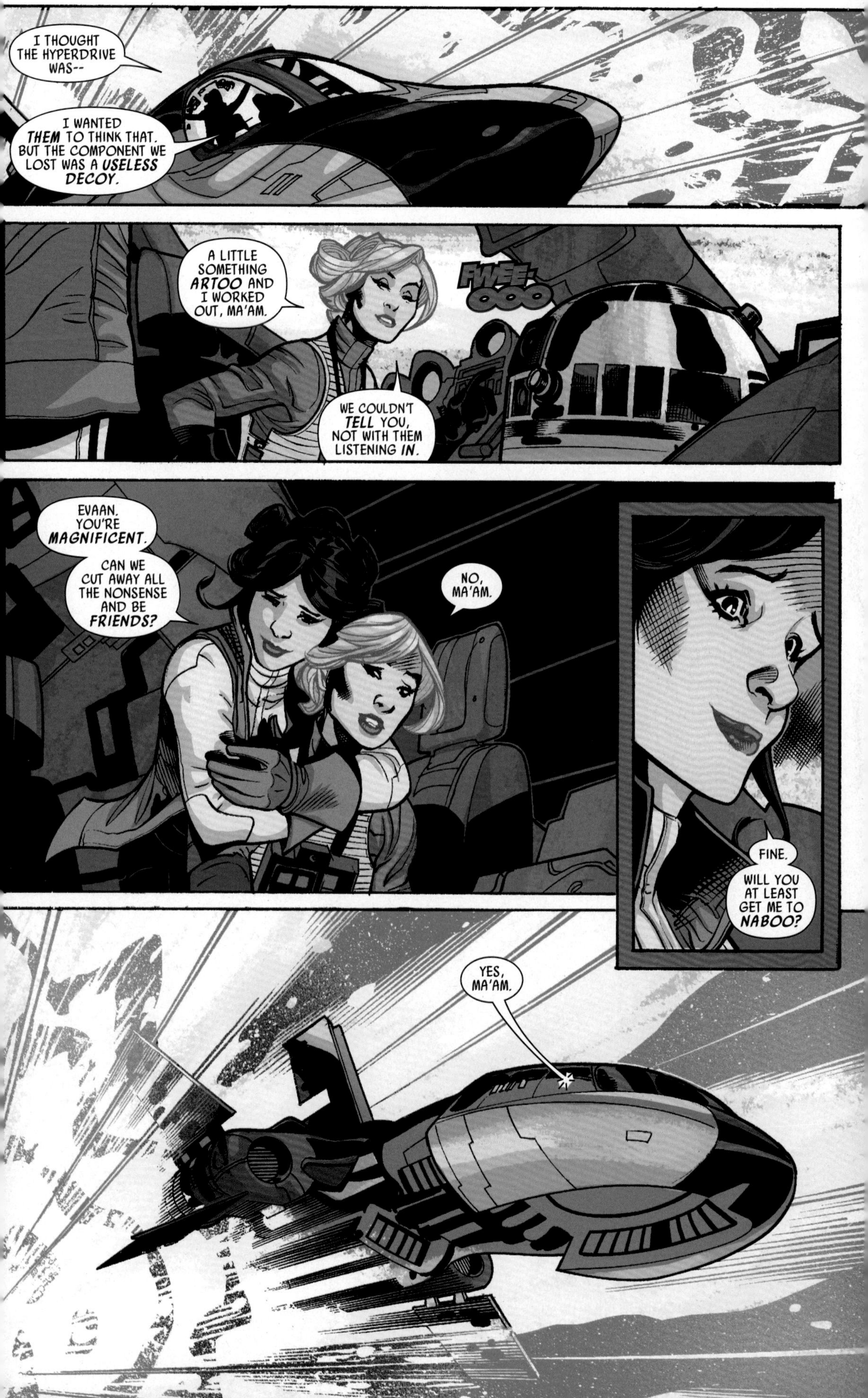
I THOUGHT THE HYPERDRIVE WAS--
I WANTED THEM TO THINK THAT. BUT THE COMPONENT WE LOST WAS A USELESS DECOY.
A LITTLE SOMETHING ARTOO AND I WORKED OUT, MA'AM.
FWEE-OOO
WE COULDN'T TELL YOU, NOT WITH THEM LISTENING IN.
EVAAN. YOU'RE MAGNIFICENT.
CAN WE CUT AWAY ALL THE NONSENSE AND BE FRIENDS?
NO, MA'AM.
FINE.
WILL YOU AT LEAST GET ME TO NABOO?
YES, MA'AM.

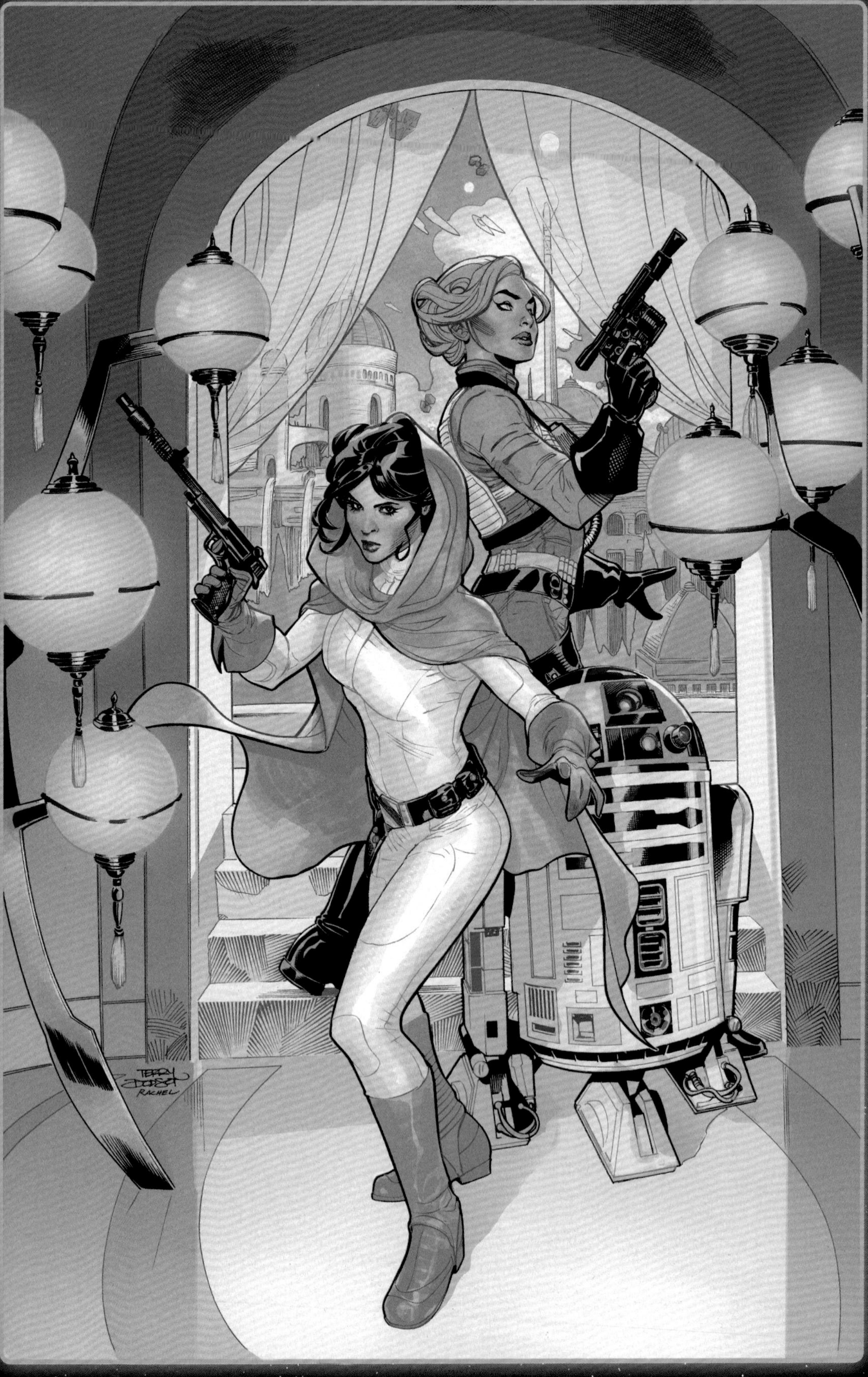
TERRY DODSON
RACHEL

2

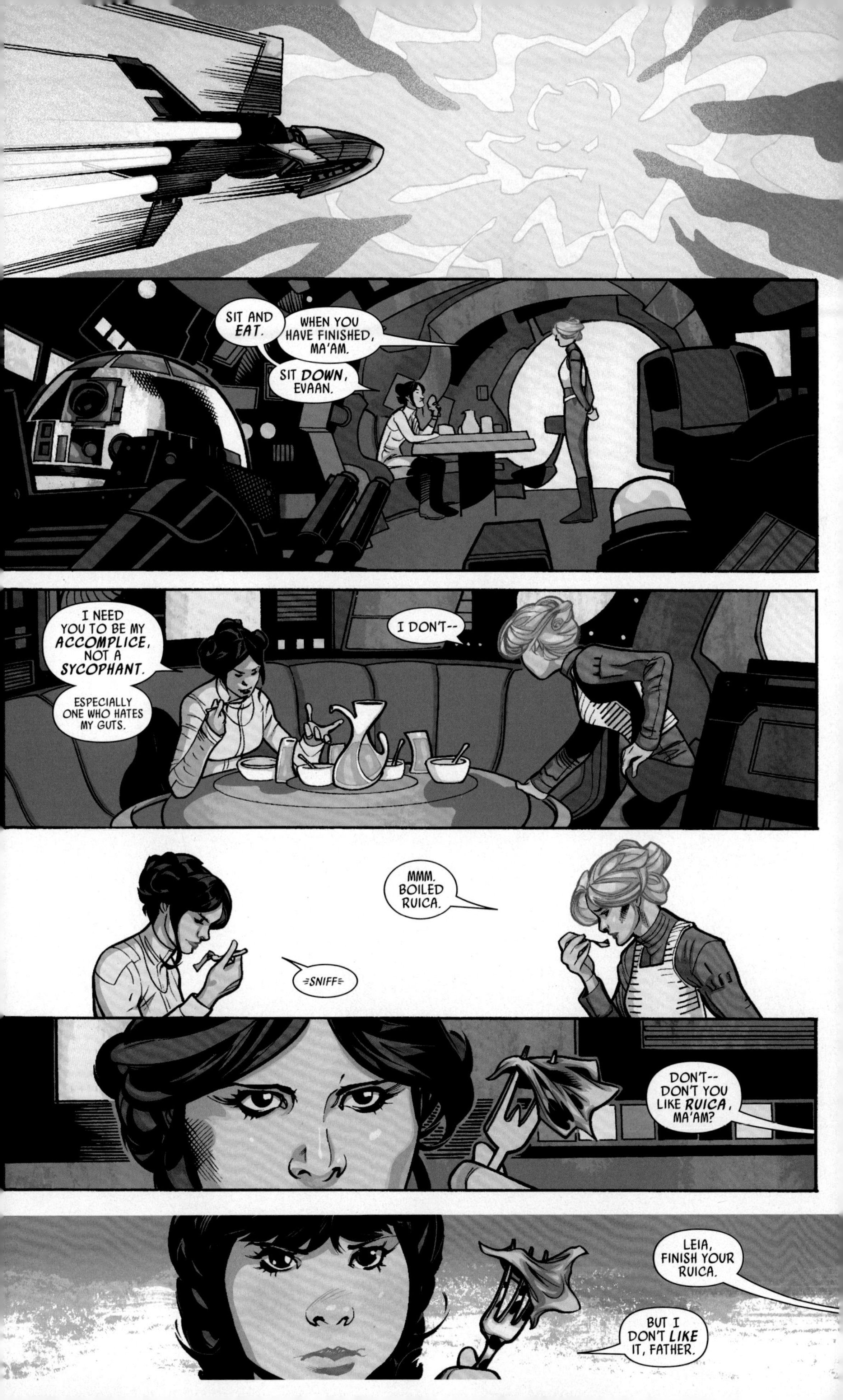

SIT AND EAT.
WHEN YOU HAVE FINISHED, MA'AM.
SIT DOWN, EVAAN.
I NEED YOU TO BE MY ACCOMPLICE, NOT A SYCOPHANT.
ESPECIALLY ONE WHO HATES MY GUTS.
I DON'T--
MMM. BOILED RUICA.
=SNIFF=
DON'T-- DON'T YOU LIKE RUICA, MA'AM?
LEIA, FINISH YOUR RUICA.
BUT I DON'T LIKE IT, FATHER.

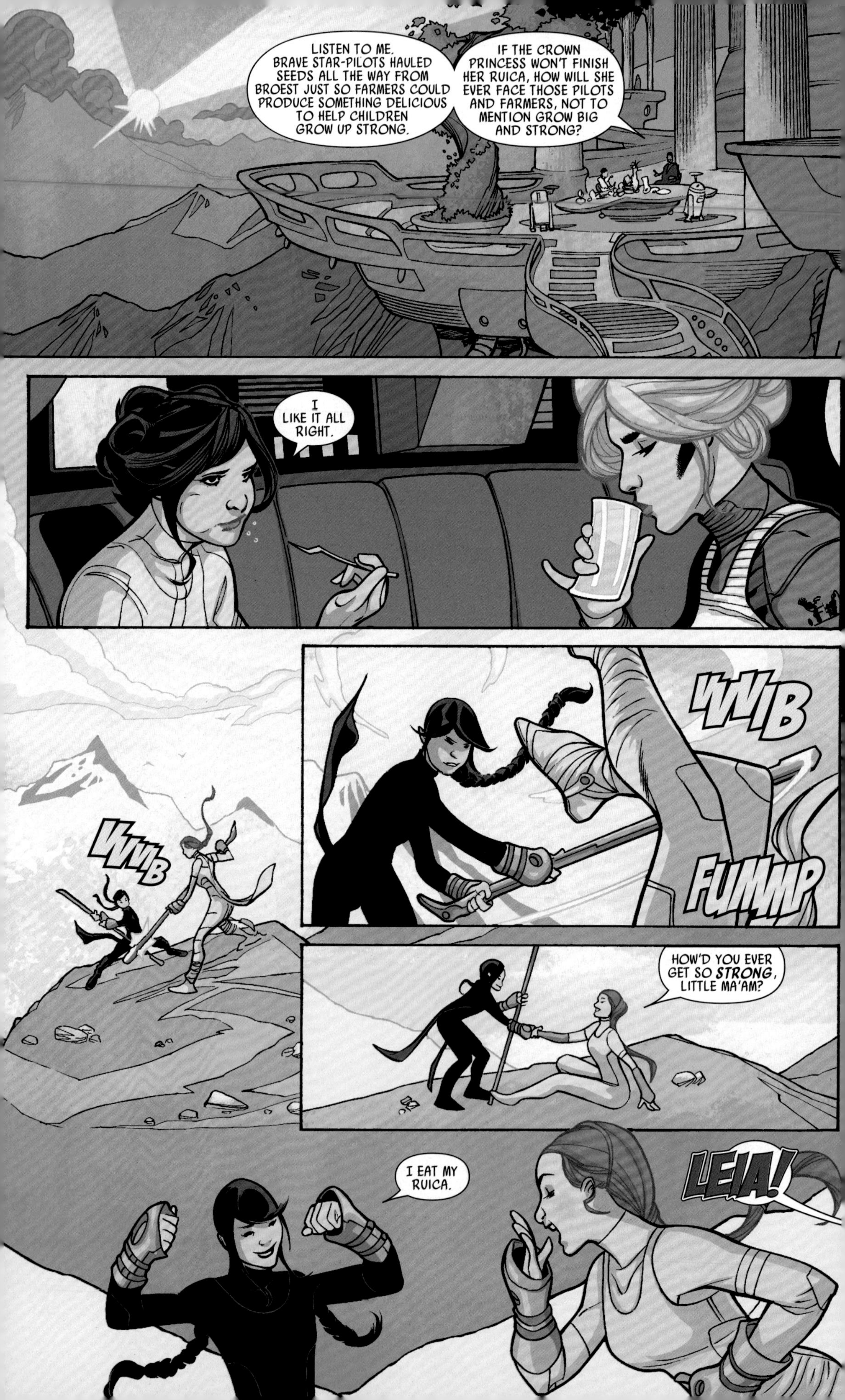
LISTEN TO ME. BRAVE STAR-PILOTS HAULED SEEDS ALL THE WAY FROM BROEST JUST SO FARMERS COULD PRODUCE SOMETHING DELICIOUS TO HELP CHILDREN GROW UP STRONG.
IF THE CROWN PRINCESS WON'T FINISH HER RUICA, HOW WILL SHE EVER FACE THOSE PILOTS AND FARMERS, NOT TO MENTION GROW BIG AND STRONG?
I LIKE IT ALL RIGHT.
WVIB
WVIB
FUMMP
HOW'D YOU EVER GET SO STRONG, LITTLE MA'AM?
I EAT MY RUICA.
LEIA!

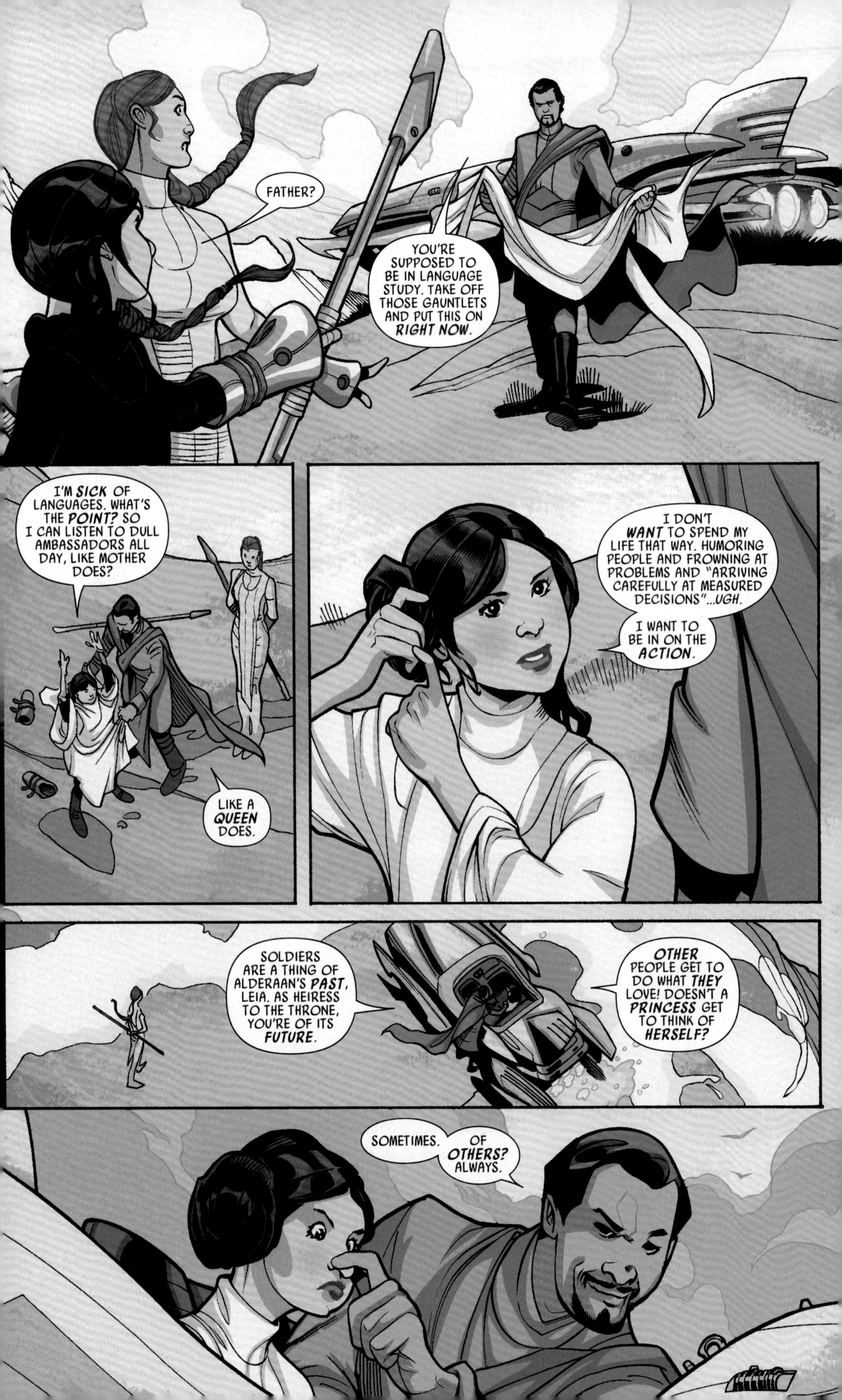
FATHER?
YOU'RE SUPPOSED TO BE IN LANGUAGE STUDY. TAKE OFF THOSE GAUNTLETS AND PUT THIS ON RIGHT NOW.
I'M SICK OF LANGUAGES. WHAT'S THE POINT? SO I CAN LISTEN TO DULL AMBASSADORS ALL DAY, LIKE MOTHER DOES?
LIKE A QUEEN DOES.
I DON'T WANT TO SPEND MY LIFE THAT WAY. HUMORING PEOPLE AND FROWNING AT PROBLEMS AND "ARRIVING CAREFULLY AT MEASURED DECISIONS"...UGH.
I WANT TO BE IN ON THE ACTION.
SOLDIERS ARE A THING OF ALDERAAN'S PAST, LEIA. AS HEIRESS TO THE THRONE, YOU'RE OF ITS FUTURE.
OTHER PEOPLE GET TO DO WHAT THEY LOVE! DOESN'T A PRINCESS GET TO THINK OF HERSELF?
SOMETIMES.
OF OTHERS? ALWAYS.

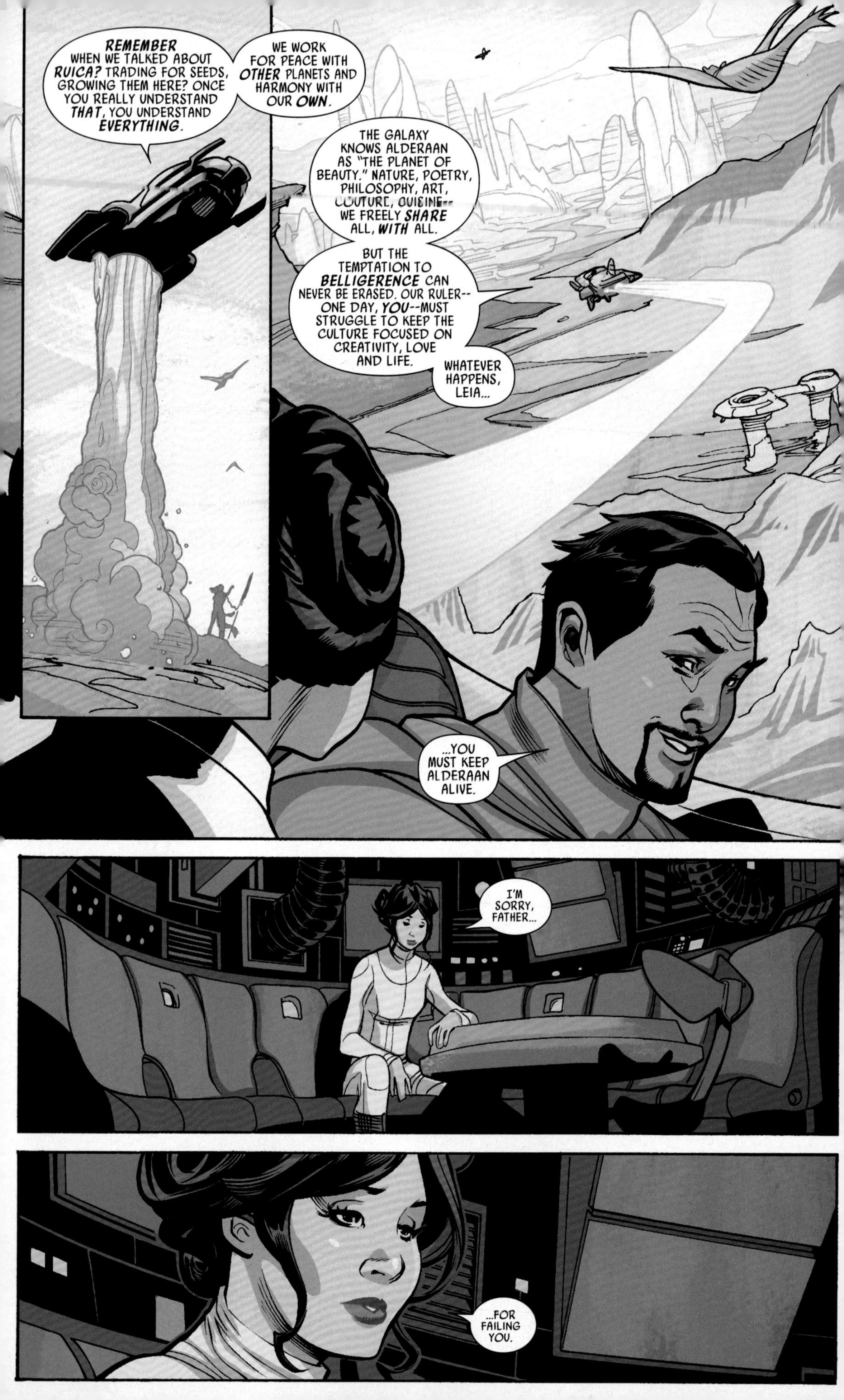
REMEMBER WHEN WE TALKED ABOUT RUICA? TRADING FOR SEEDS, GROWING THEM HERE? ONCE YOU REALLY UNDERSTAND THAT, YOU UNDERSTAND EVERYTHING.
WE WORK FOR PEACE WITH OTHER PLANETS AND HARMONY WITH OUR OWN.
THE GALAXY KNOWS ALDERAAN AS "THE PLANET OF BEAUTY." NATURE, POETRY, PHILOSOPHY, ART, COUTURE, CUISINE-- WE FREELY SHARE ALL, WITH ALL.
BUT THE TEMPTATION TO BELLIGERENCE CAN NEVER BE ERASED. OUR RULER-- ONE DAY, YOU--MUST STRUGGLE TO KEEP THE CULTURE FOCUSED ON CREATIVITY, LOVE AND LIFE.
WHATEVER HAPPENS, LEIA...
...YOU MUST KEEP ALDERAAN ALIVE.
I'M SORRY, FATHER...
...FOR FAILING YOU.

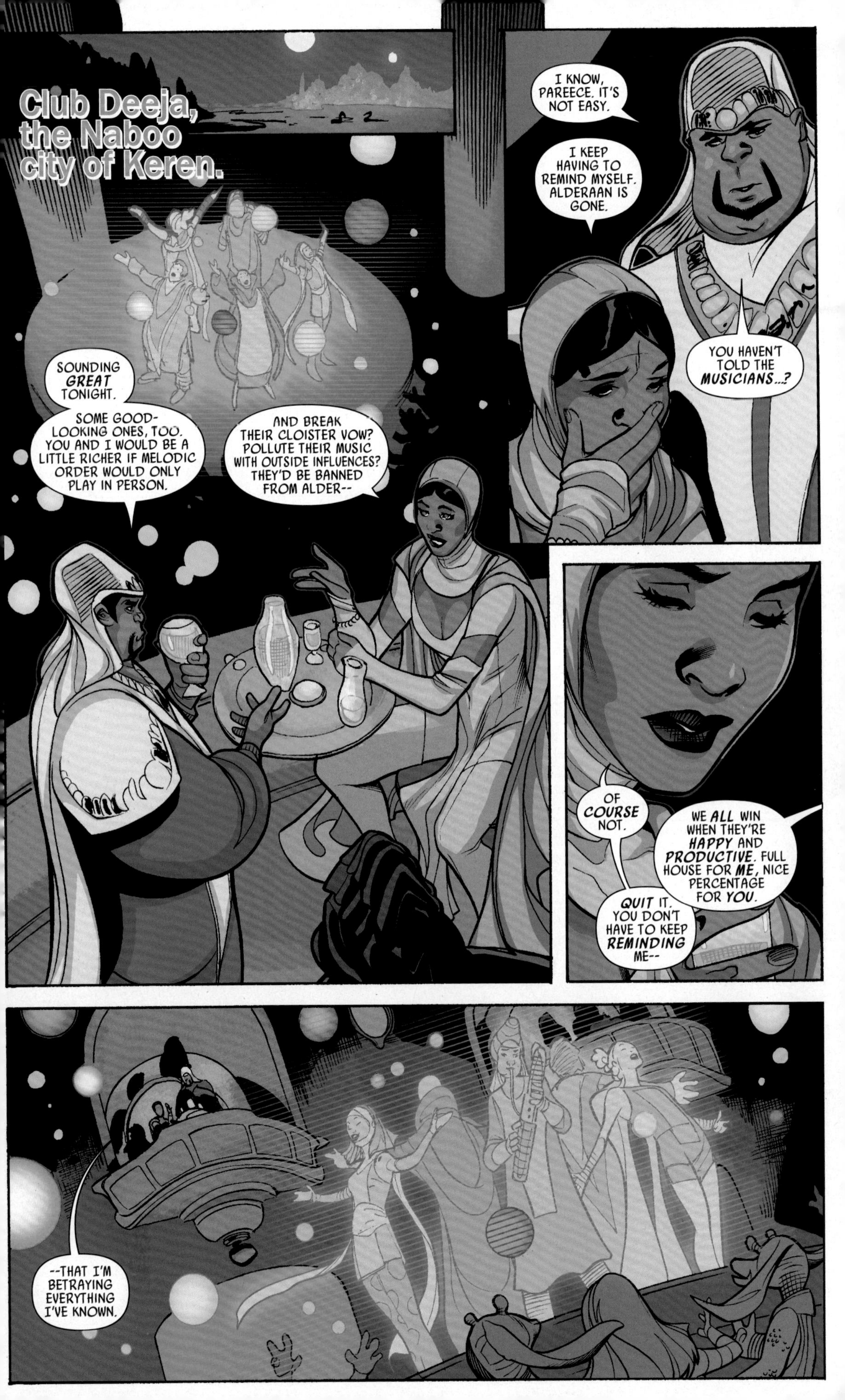
Club Deeja, the Naboo city of Keren.
SOUNDING GREAT TONIGHT.
SOME GOOD-LOOKING ONES, TOO. YOU AND I WOULD BE A LITTLE RICHER IF MELODIC ORDER WOULD ONLY PLAY IN PERSON.
AND BREAK THEIR CLOISTER VOW? POLLUTE THEIR MUSIC WITH OUTSIDE INFLUENCES? THEY'D BE BANNED FROM ALDER--
I KNOW, PAREECE. IT'S NOT EASY.
I KEEP HAVING TO REMIND MYSELF. ALDERAAN IS GONE.
YOU HAVEN'T TOLD THE MUSICIANS...?
OF COURSE NOT.
WE ALL WIN WHEN THEY'RE HAPPY AND PRODUCTIVE. FULL HOUSE FOR ME, NICE PERCENTAGE FOR YOU.
QUIT IT. YOU DON'T HAVE TO KEEP REMINDING ME--
--THAT I'M BETRAYING EVERYTHING I'VE KNOWN.

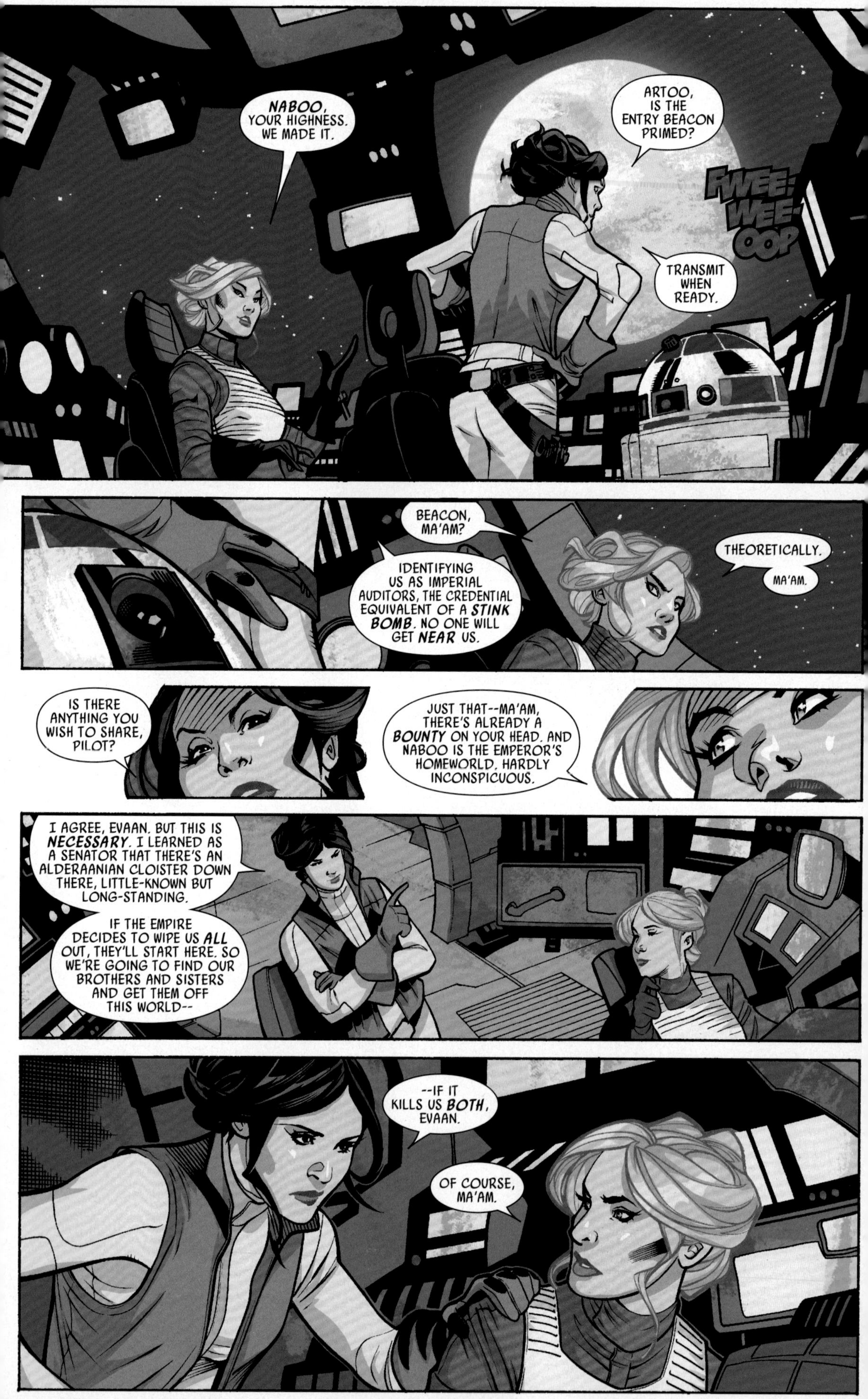
NABOO, YOUR HIGHNESS. WE MADE IT.
ARTOO, IS THE ENTRY BEACON PRIMED?
FWEE-WEE-OOP
TRANSMIT WHEN READY.
BEACON, MA'AM?
IDENTIFYING US AS IMPERIAL AUDITORS, THE CREDENTIAL EQUIVALENT OF A STINK BOMB. NO ONE WILL GET NEAR US.
THEORETICALLY.
MA'AM.
IS THERE ANYTHING YOU WISH TO SHARE, PILOT?
JUST THAT--MA'AM, THERE'S ALREADY A BOUNTY ON YOUR HEAD. AND NABOO IS THE EMPEROR'S HOMEWORLD. HARDLY INCONSPICUOUS.
I AGREE, EVAAN. BUT THIS IS NECESSARY. I LEARNED AS A SENATOR THAT THERE'S AN ALDERAANIAN CLOISTER DOWN THERE, LITTLE-KNOWN BUT LONG-STANDING.
IF THE EMPIRE DECIDES TO WIPE US ALL OUT, THEY'LL START HERE. SO WE'RE GOING TO FIND OUR BROTHERS AND SISTERS AND GET THEM OFF THIS WORLD--
--IF IT KILLS US BOTH, EVAAN.
OF COURSE, MA'AM.

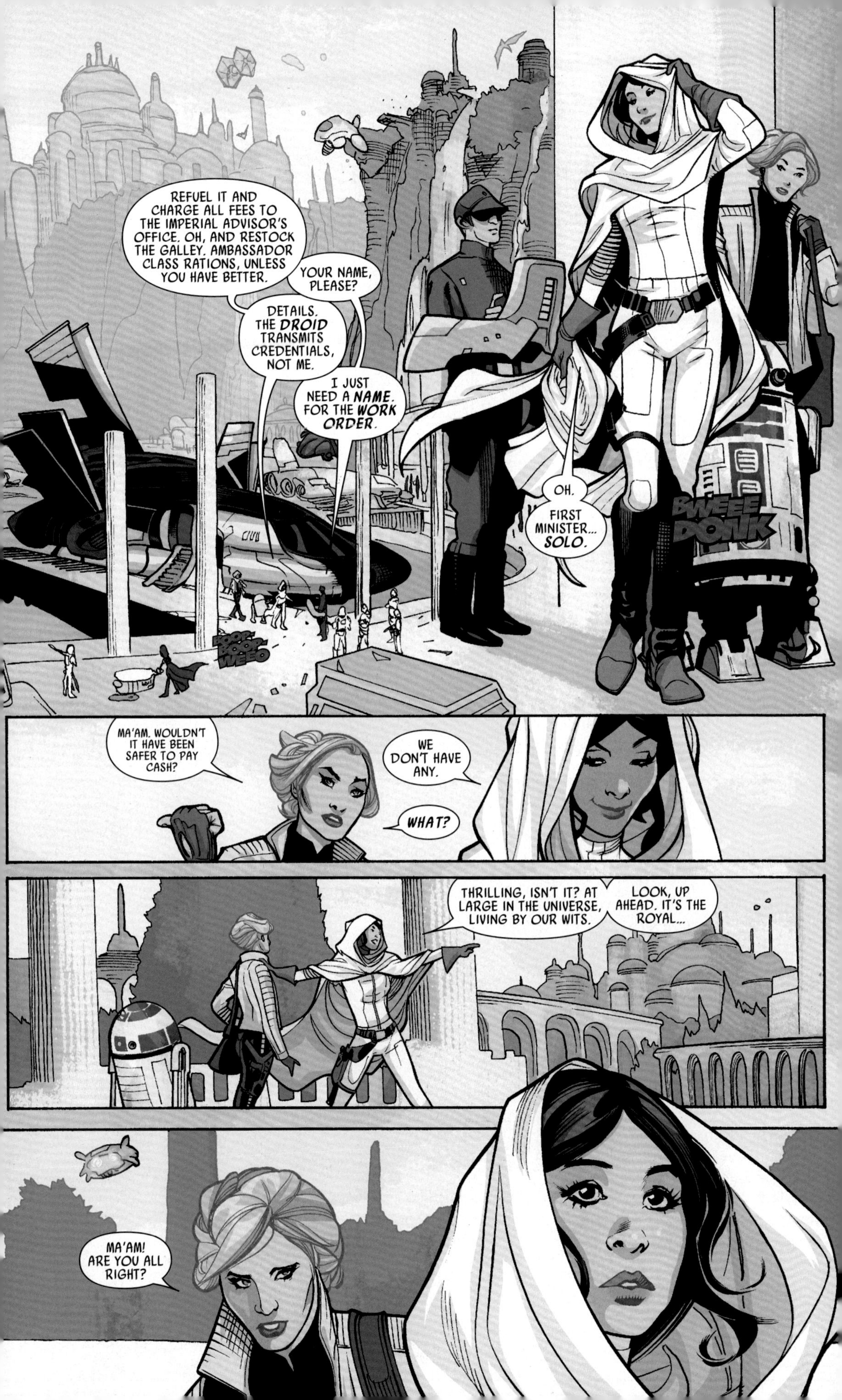
REFUEL IT AND CHARGE ALL FEES TO THE IMPERIAL ADVISOR'S OFFICE. OH, AND RESTOCK THE GALLEY. AMBASSADOR CLASS RATIONS, UNLESS YOU HAVE BETTER.
YOUR NAME, PLEASE?
DETAILS. THE DROID TRANSMITS CREDENTIALS, NOT ME.
I JUST NEED A NAME. FOR THE WORK ORDER.
OH. FIRST MINISTER... SOLO.
BWEEE DONK
BOOP-BOOP-WEEO
MA'AM. WOULDN'T IT HAVE BEEN SAFER TO PAY CASH?
WE DON'T HAVE ANY.
WHAT?
THRILLING, ISN'T IT? AT LARGE IN THE UNIVERSE, LIVING BY OUR WITS.
LOOK, UP AHEAD. IT'S THE ROYAL...
MA'AM! ARE YOU ALL RIGHT?

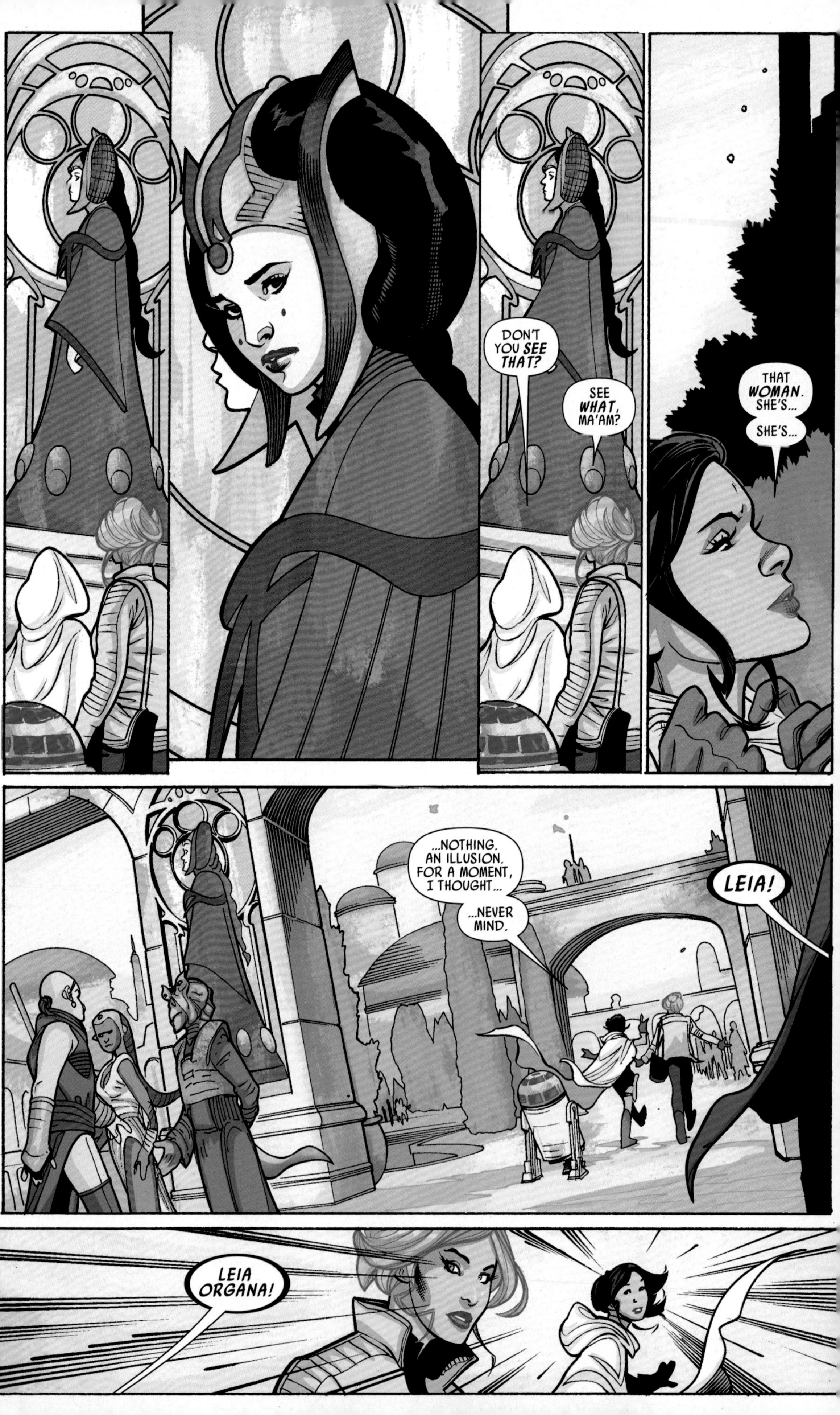
DON'T YOU SEE THAT?
SEE WHAT, MA'AM?
THAT WOMAN. SHE'S...
SHE'S...
...NOTHING. AN ILLUSION. FOR A MOMENT, I THOUGHT...
...NEVER MIND.
LEIA!
LEIA ORGANA!

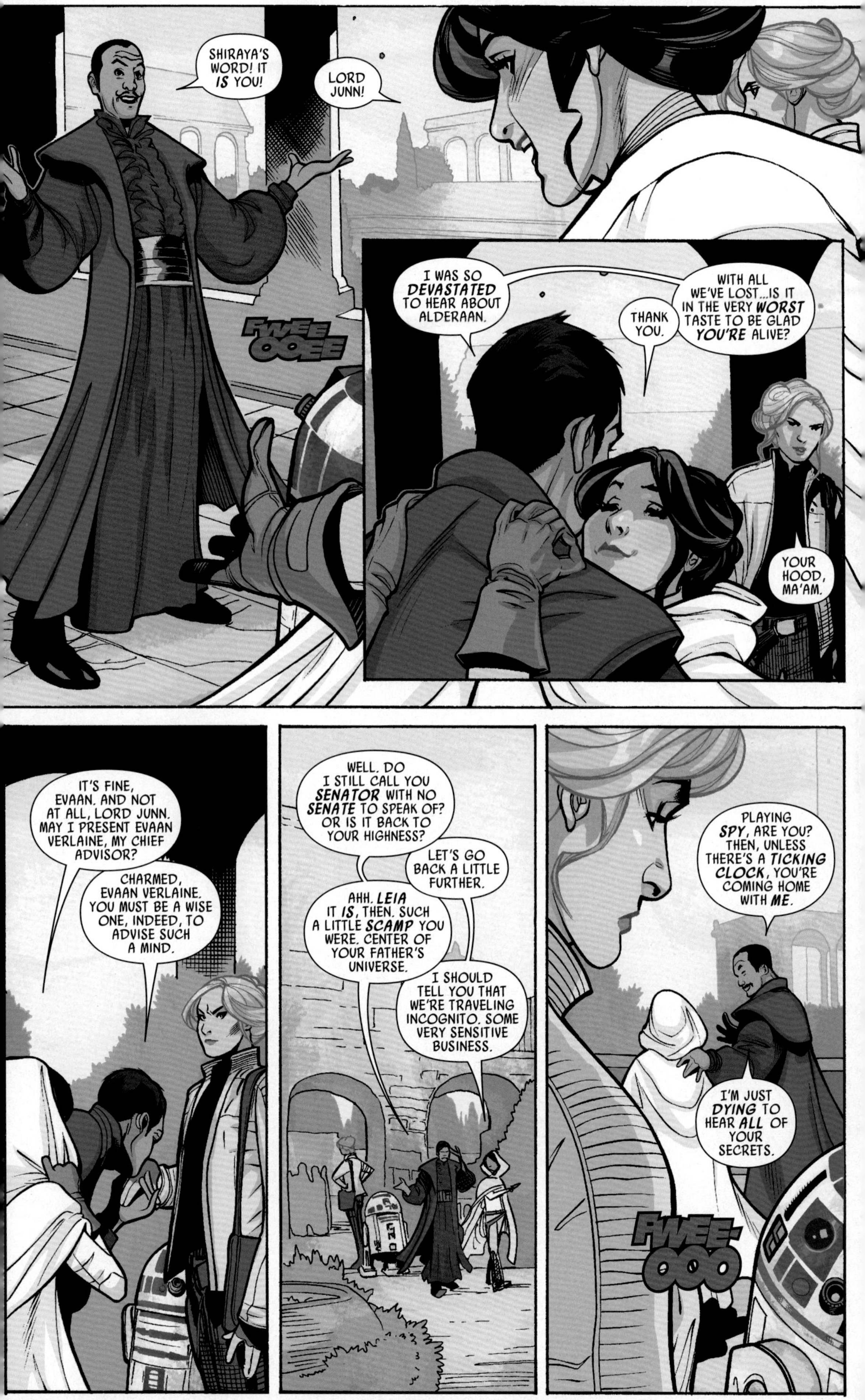
SHIRAYA'S WORD! IT IS YOU!
LORD JUNN!
FWEE OOEE
I WAS SO DEVASTATED TO HEAR ABOUT ALDERAAN.
THANK YOU.
WITH ALL WE'VE LOST...IS IT IN THE VERY WORST TASTE TO BE GLAD YOU'RE ALIVE?
YOUR HOOD, MA'AM.
IT'S FINE, EVAAN. AND NOT AT ALL, LORD JUNN. MAY I PRESENT EVAAN VERLAINE, MY CHIEF ADVISOR?
CHARMED, EVAAN VERLAINE. YOU MUST BE A WISE ONE, INDEED, TO ADVISE SUCH A MIND.
WELL. DO I STILL CALL YOU SENATOR WITH NO SENATE TO SPEAK OF? OR IS IT BACK TO YOUR HIGHNESS?
LET'S GO BACK A LITTLE FURTHER.
AHH. LEIA IT IS, THEN. SUCH A LITTLE SCAMP YOU WERE. CENTER OF YOUR FATHER'S UNIVERSE.
I SHOULD TELL YOU THAT WE'RE TRAVELING INCOGNITO. SOME VERY SENSITIVE BUSINESS.
PLAYING SPY, ARE YOU? THEN, UNLESS THERE'S A TICKING CLOCK, YOU'RE COMING HOME WITH ME.
I'M JUST DYING TO HEAR ALL OF YOUR SECRETS.
FWEE-OOO

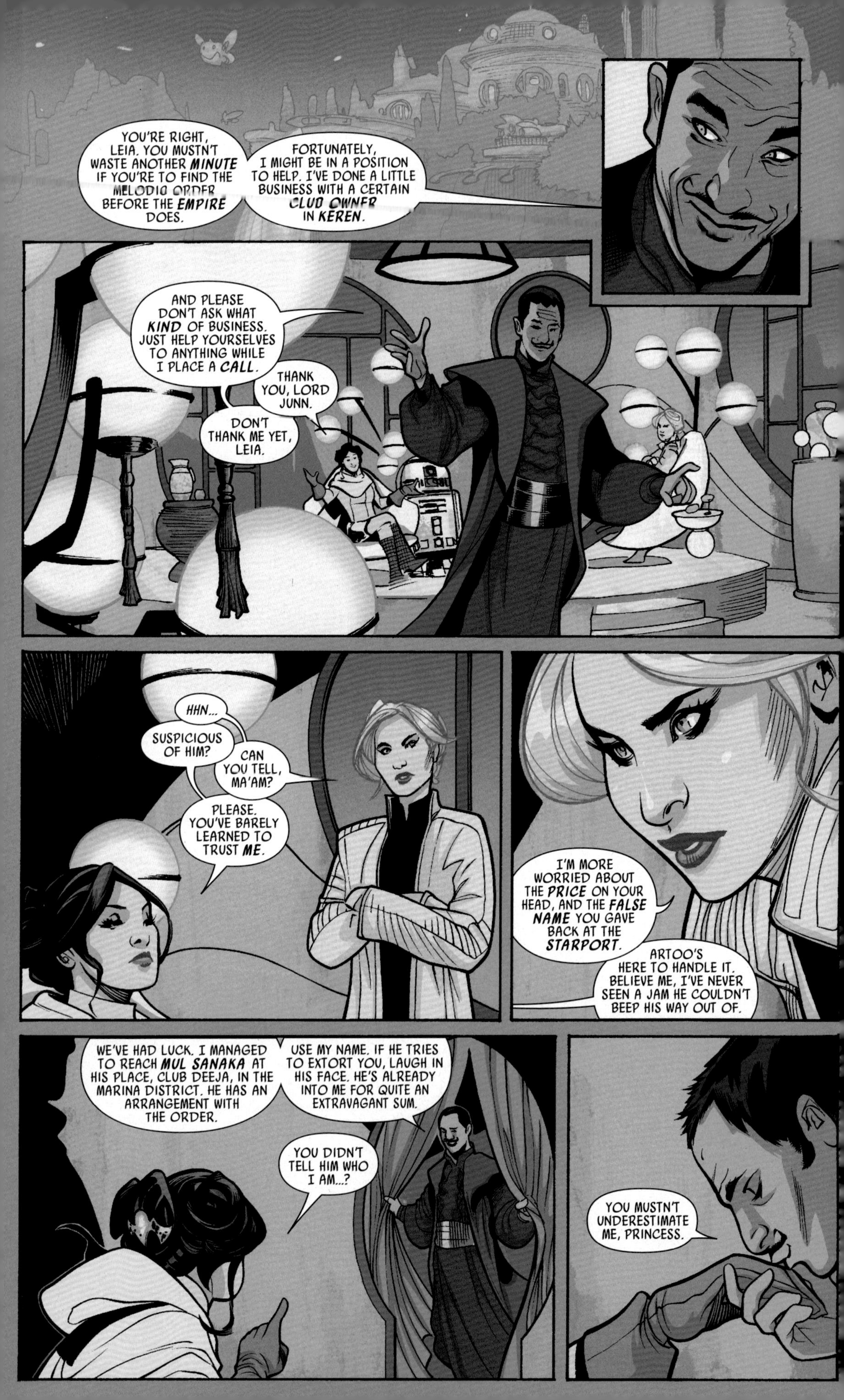
YOU'RE RIGHT, LEIA. YOU MUSTN'T WASTE ANOTHER MINUTE IF YOU'RE TO FIND THE MELODIO ORDER BEFORE THE EMPIRE DOES.
FORTUNATELY, I MIGHT BE IN A POSITION TO HELP. I'VE DONE A LITTLE BUSINESS WITH A CERTAIN CLUB OWNER IN KEREN.
AND PLEASE DON'T ASK WHAT KIND OF BUSINESS. JUST HELP YOURSELVES TO ANYTHING WHILE I PLACE A CALL.
THANK YOU, LORD JUNN.
DON'T THANK ME YET, LEIA.
HHN...
SUSPICIOUS OF HIM?
CAN YOU TELL, MA'AM?
PLEASE. YOU'VE BARELY LEARNED TO TRUST ME.
I'M MORE WORRIED ABOUT THE PRICE ON YOUR HEAD, AND THE FALSE NAME YOU GAVE BACK AT THE STARPORT.
ARTOO'S HERE TO HANDLE IT. BELIEVE ME, I'VE NEVER SEEN A JAM HE COULDN'T BEEP HIS WAY OUT OF.
WE'VE HAD LUCK. I MANAGED TO REACH MUL SANAKA AT HIS PLACE, CLUB DEEJA, IN THE MARINA DISTRICT. HE HAS AN ARRANGEMENT WITH THE ORDER.
USE MY NAME. IF HE TRIES TO EXTORT YOU, LAUGH IN HIS FACE. HE'S ALREADY INTO ME FOR QUITE AN EXTRAVAGANT SUM.
YOU DIDN'T TELL HIM WHO I AM...?
YOU MUSTN'T UNDERESTIMATE ME, PRINCESS.

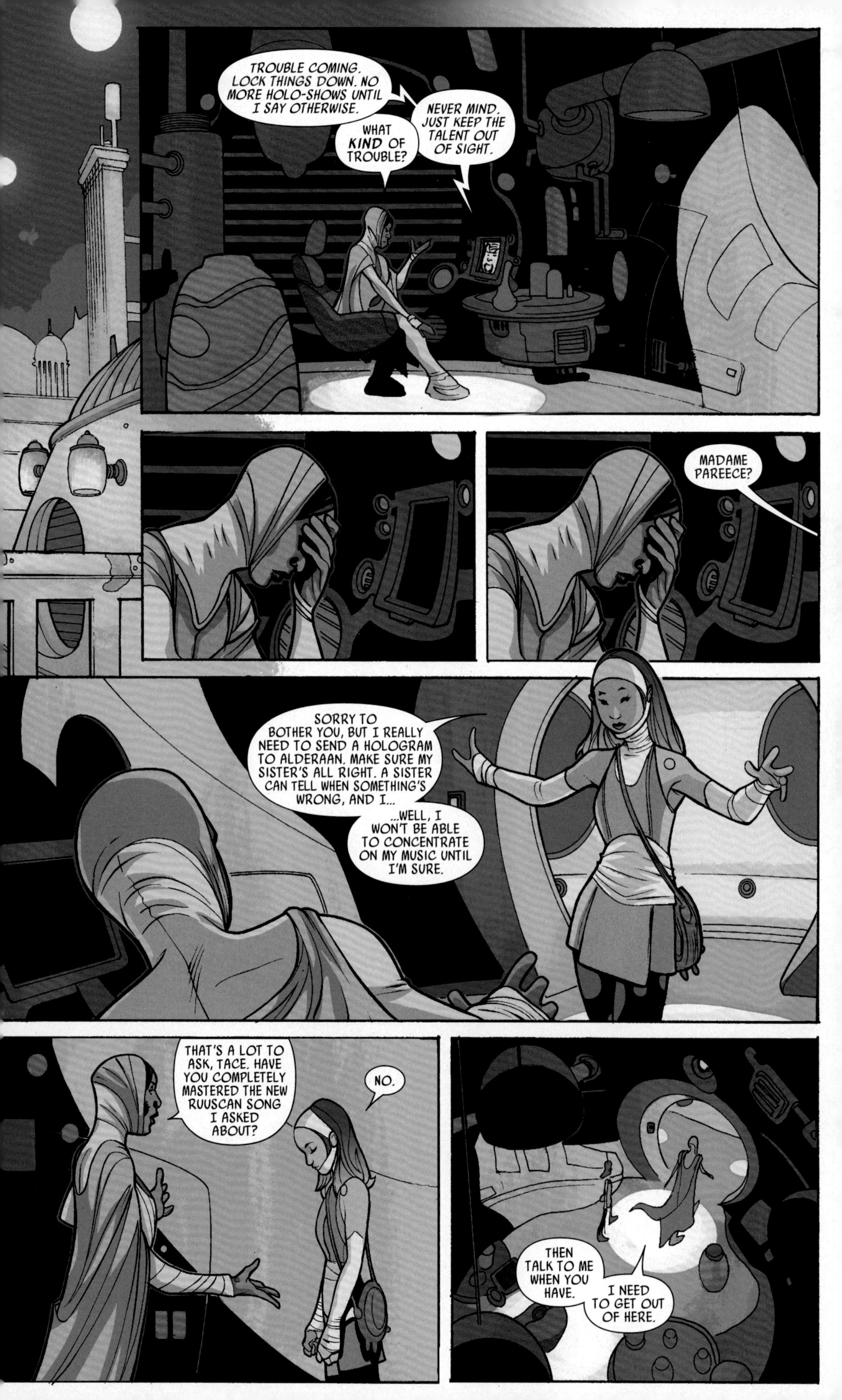
TROUBLE COMING. LOCK THINGS DOWN. NO MORE HOLO-SHOWS UNTIL I SAY OTHERWISE.
WHAT KIND OF TROUBLE?
NEVER MIND. JUST KEEP THE TALENT OUT OF SIGHT.
MADAME PAREECE?
SORRY TO BOTHER YOU, BUT I REALLY NEED TO SEND A HOLOGRAM TO ALDERAAN. MAKE SURE MY SISTER'S ALL RIGHT. A SISTER CAN TELL WHEN SOMETHING'S WRONG, AND I...
...WELL, I WON'T BE ABLE TO CONCENTRATE ON MY MUSIC UNTIL I'M SURE.
THAT'S A LOT TO ASK, TACE. HAVE YOU COMPLETELY MASTERED THE NEW RUUSCAN SONG I ASKED ABOUT?
NO.
THEN TALK TO ME WHEN YOU HAVE.
I NEED TO GET OUT OF HERE.

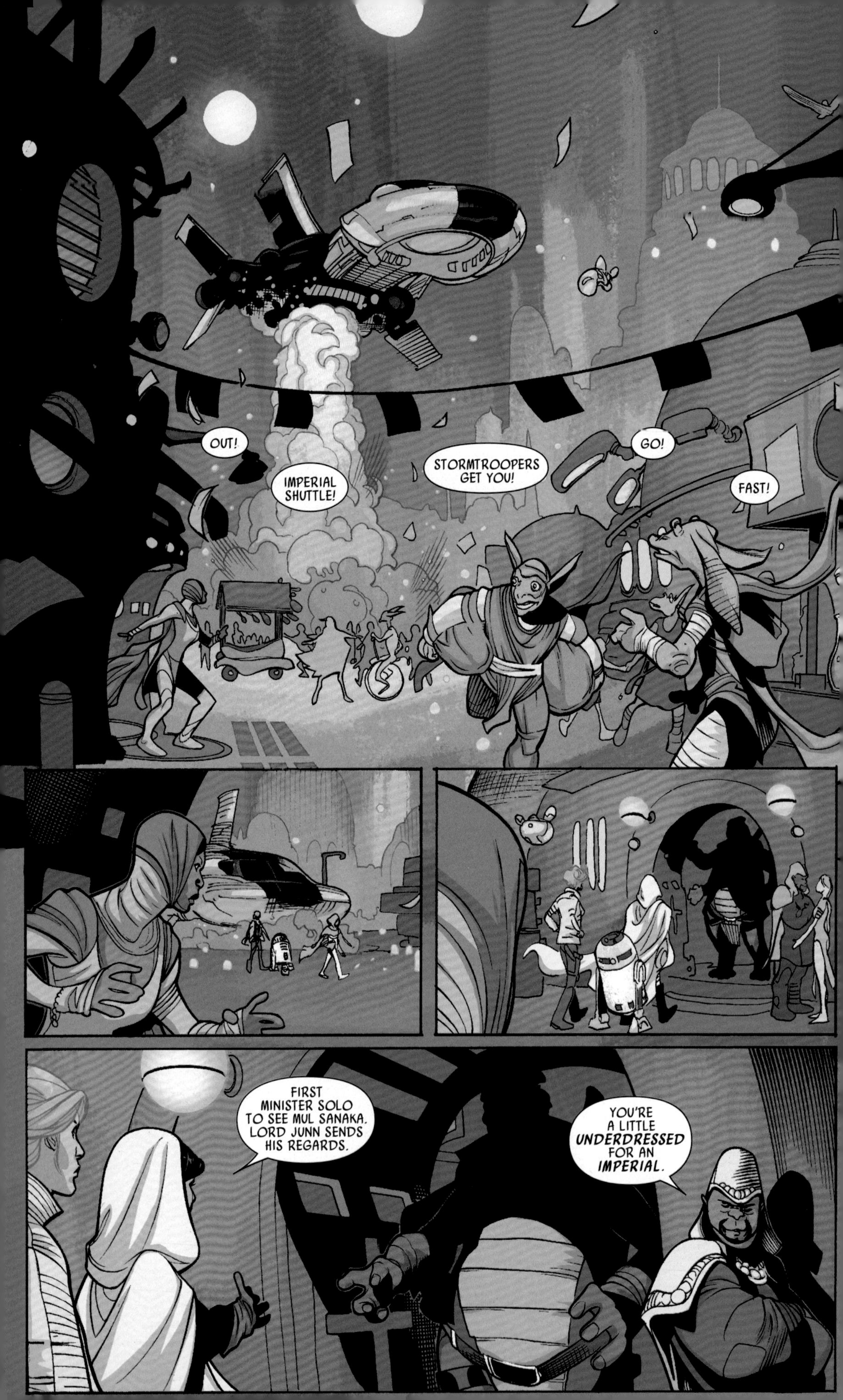
OUT!
IMPERIAL SHUTTLE!
STORMTROOPERS GET YOU!
GO!
FAST!
FIRST MINISTER SOLO TO SEE MUL SANAKA. LORD JUNN SENDS HIS REGARDS.
YOU'RE A LITTLE UNDERDRESSED FOR AN IMPERIAL.

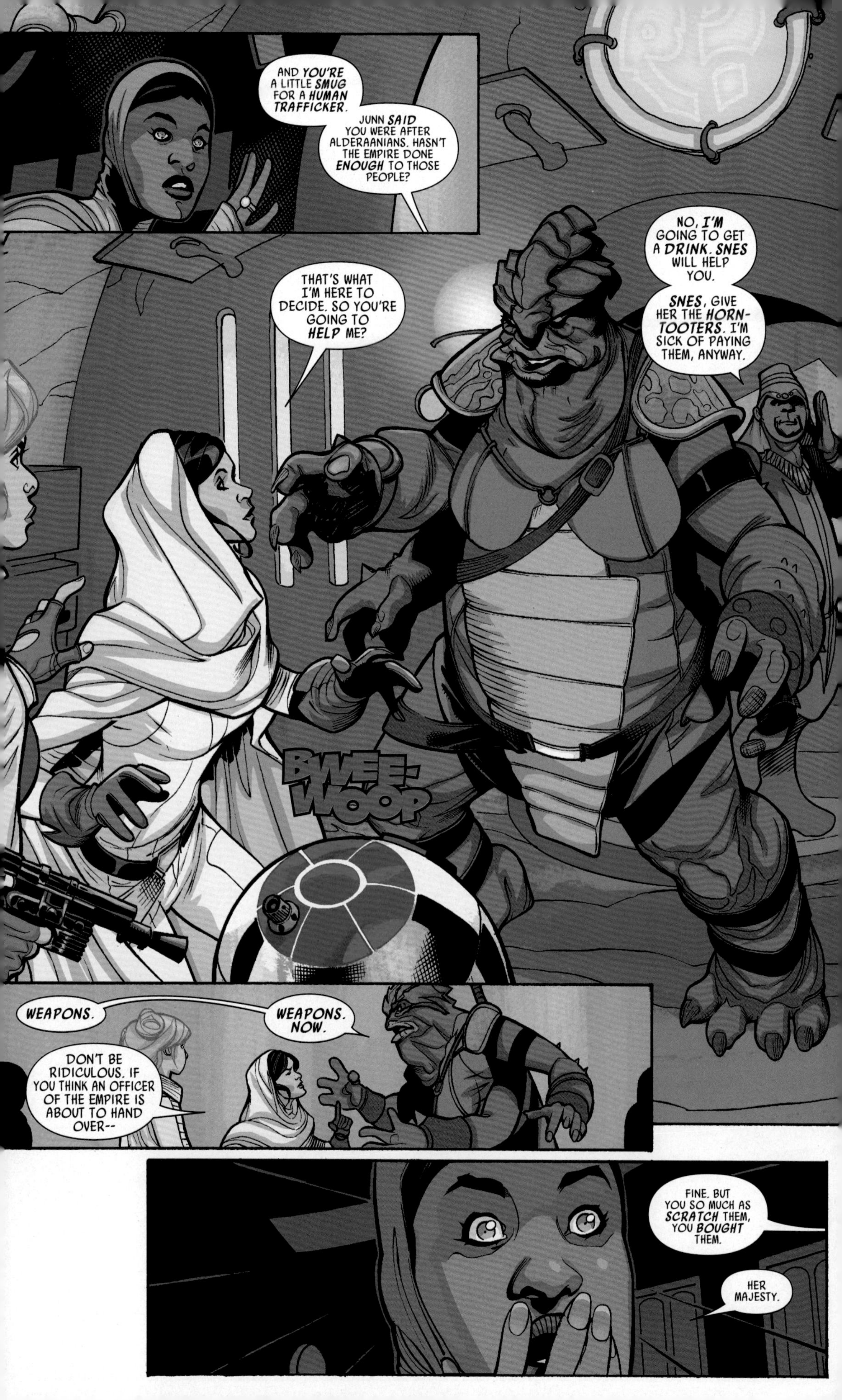

AND YOU'RE A LITTLE SMUG FOR A HUMAN TRAFFICKER.
JUNN SAID YOU WERE AFTER ALDERAANIANS. HASN'T THE EMPIRE DONE ENOUGH TO THOSE PEOPLE?
THAT'S WHAT I'M HERE TO DECIDE. SO YOU'RE GOING TO HELP ME?
NO, I'M GOING TO GET A DRINK. SNES WILL HELP YOU.
SNES, GIVE HER THE HORN-TOOTERS. I'M SICK OF PAYING THEM, ANYWAY.
BWEE-WOOP
WEAPONS.
WEAPONS. NOW.
DON'T BE RIDICULOUS. IF YOU THINK AN OFFICER OF THE EMPIRE IS ABOUT TO HAND OVER--
FINE. BUT YOU SO MUCH AS SCRATCH THEM, YOU BOUGHT THEM.
HER MAJESTY.

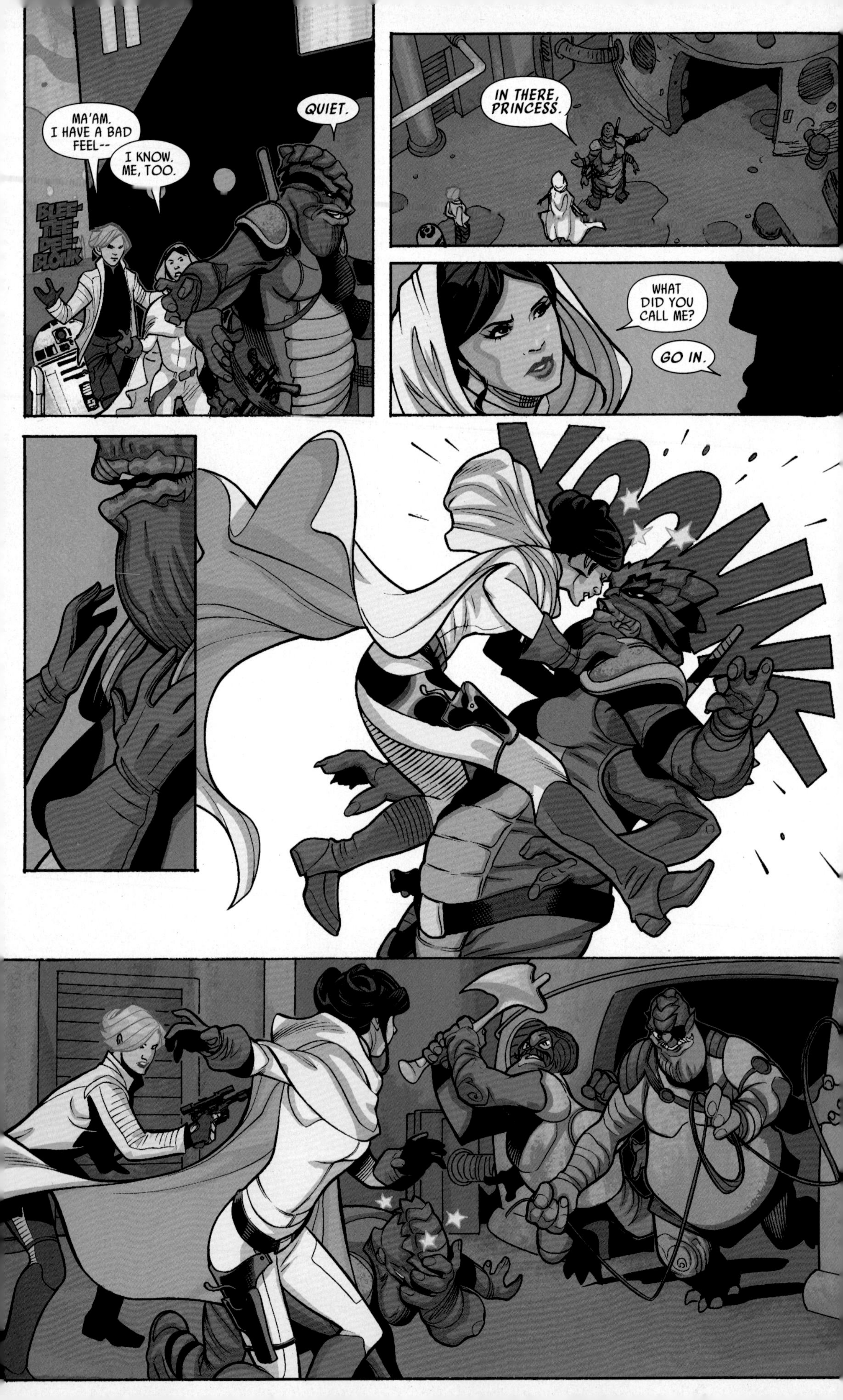
MA'AM. I HAVE A BAD FEEL--
I KNOW. ME, TOO.
BLEE-TEE-DEE-BLONK
QUIET.
IN THERE, PRINCESS.
WHAT DID YOU CALL ME?
GO IN.

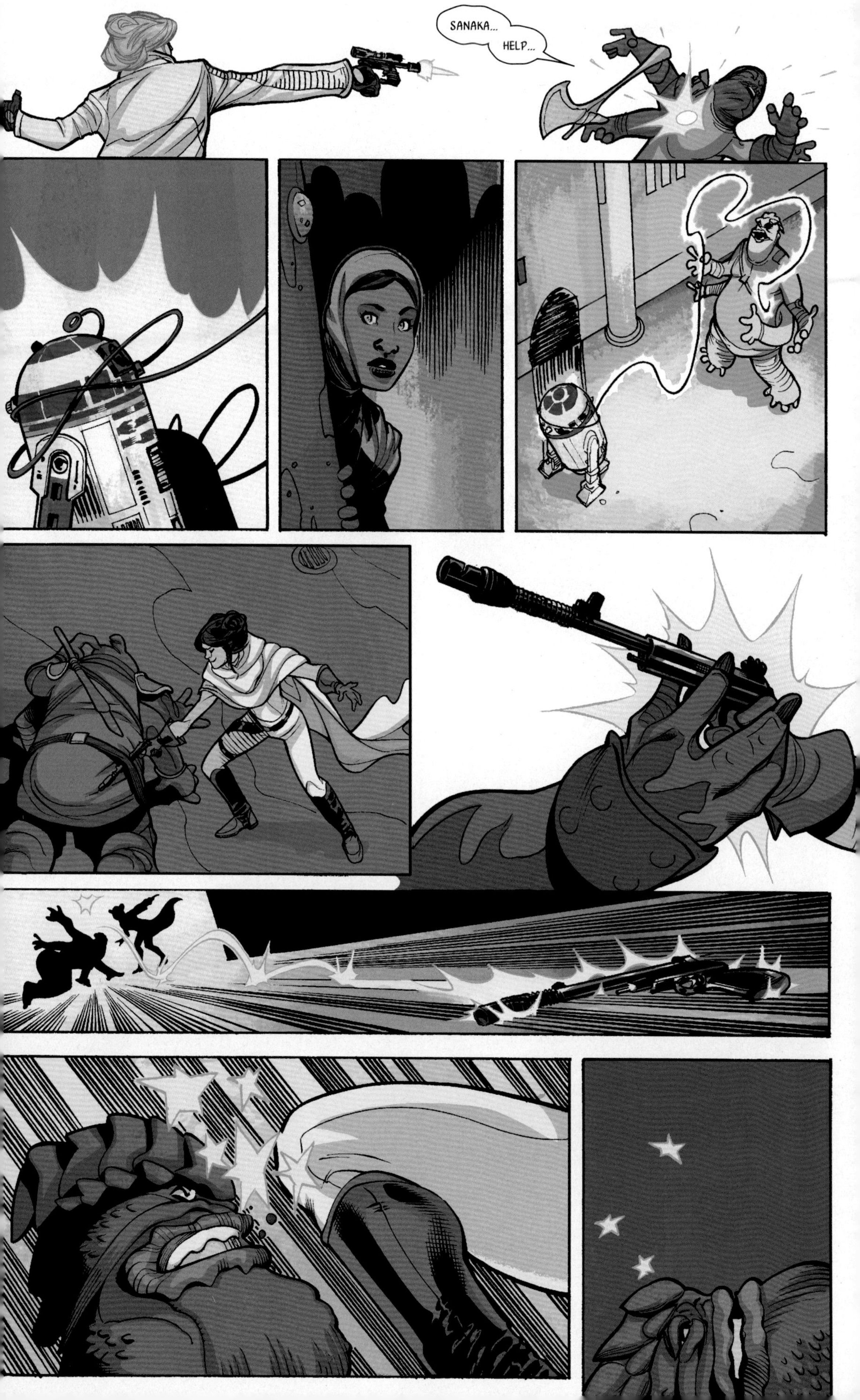
SANAKA...
HELP...

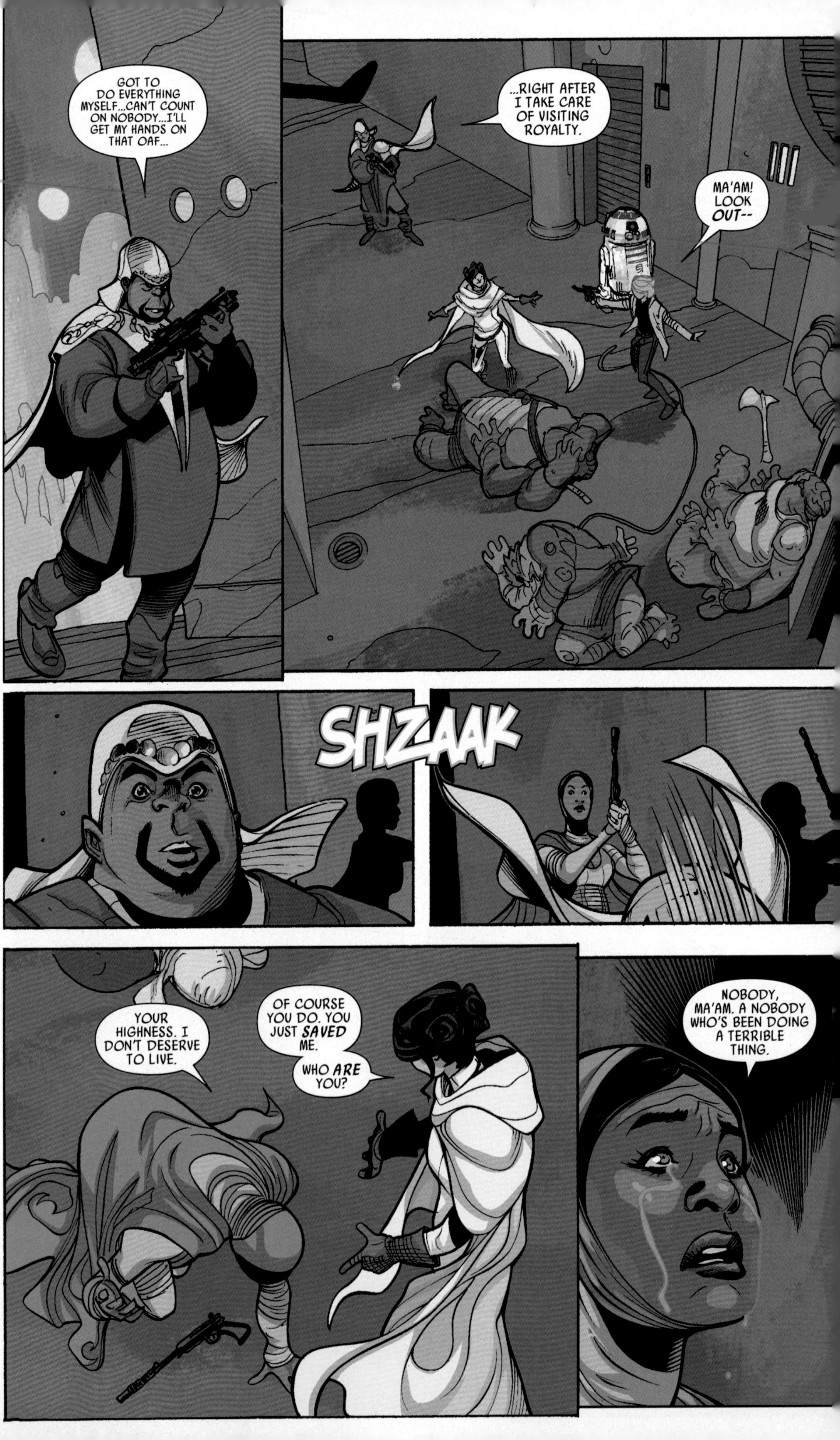
GOT TO DO EVERYTHING MYSELF...CAN'T COUNT ON NOBODY...I'LL GET MY HANDS ON THAT OAF...
...RIGHT AFTER I TAKE CARE OF VISITING ROYALTY.
MA'AM! LOOK OUT--
SHZAAK
YOUR HIGHNESS. I DON'T DESERVE TO LIVE.
OF COURSE YOU DO. YOU JUST SAVED ME.
WHO ARE YOU?
NOBODY, MA'AM. A NOBODY WHO'S BEEN DOING A TERRIBLE THING.

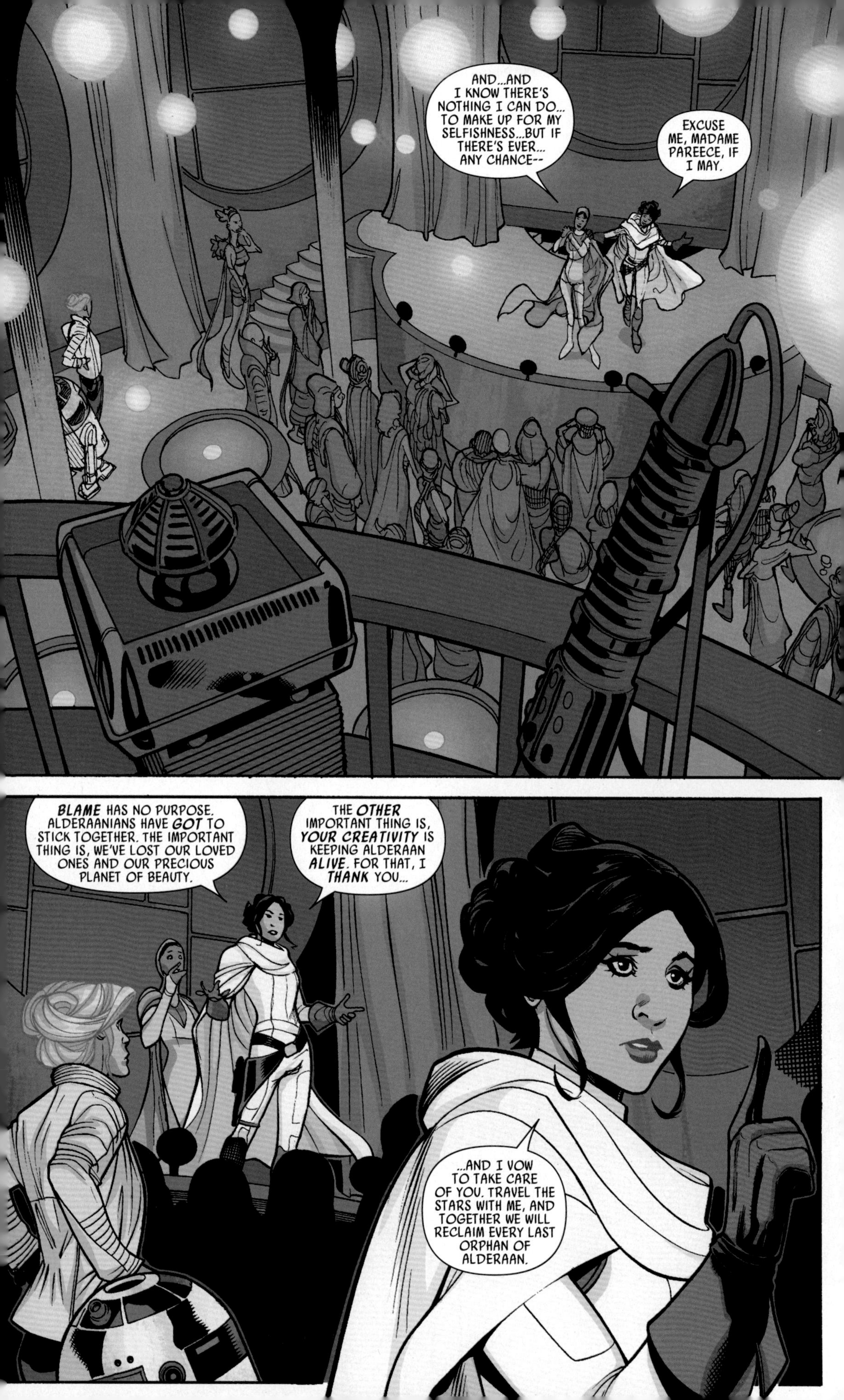
AND...AND I KNOW THERE'S NOTHING I CAN DO... TO MAKE UP FOR MY SELFISHNESS...BUT IF THERE'S EVER... ANY CHANCE--
EXCUSE ME, MADAME PAREECE, IF I MAY.
BLAME HAS NO PURPOSE. ALDERAANIANS HAVE GOT TO STICK TOGETHER. THE IMPORTANT THING IS, WE'VE LOST OUR LOVED ONES AND OUR PRECIOUS PLANET OF BEAUTY.
THE OTHER IMPORTANT THING IS, YOUR CREATIVITY IS KEEPING ALDERAAN ALIVE. FOR THAT, I THANK YOU...
...AND I VOW TO TAKE CARE OF YOU. TRAVEL THE STARS WITH ME, AND TOGETHER WE WILL RECLAIM EVERY LAST ORPHAN OF ALDERAAN.

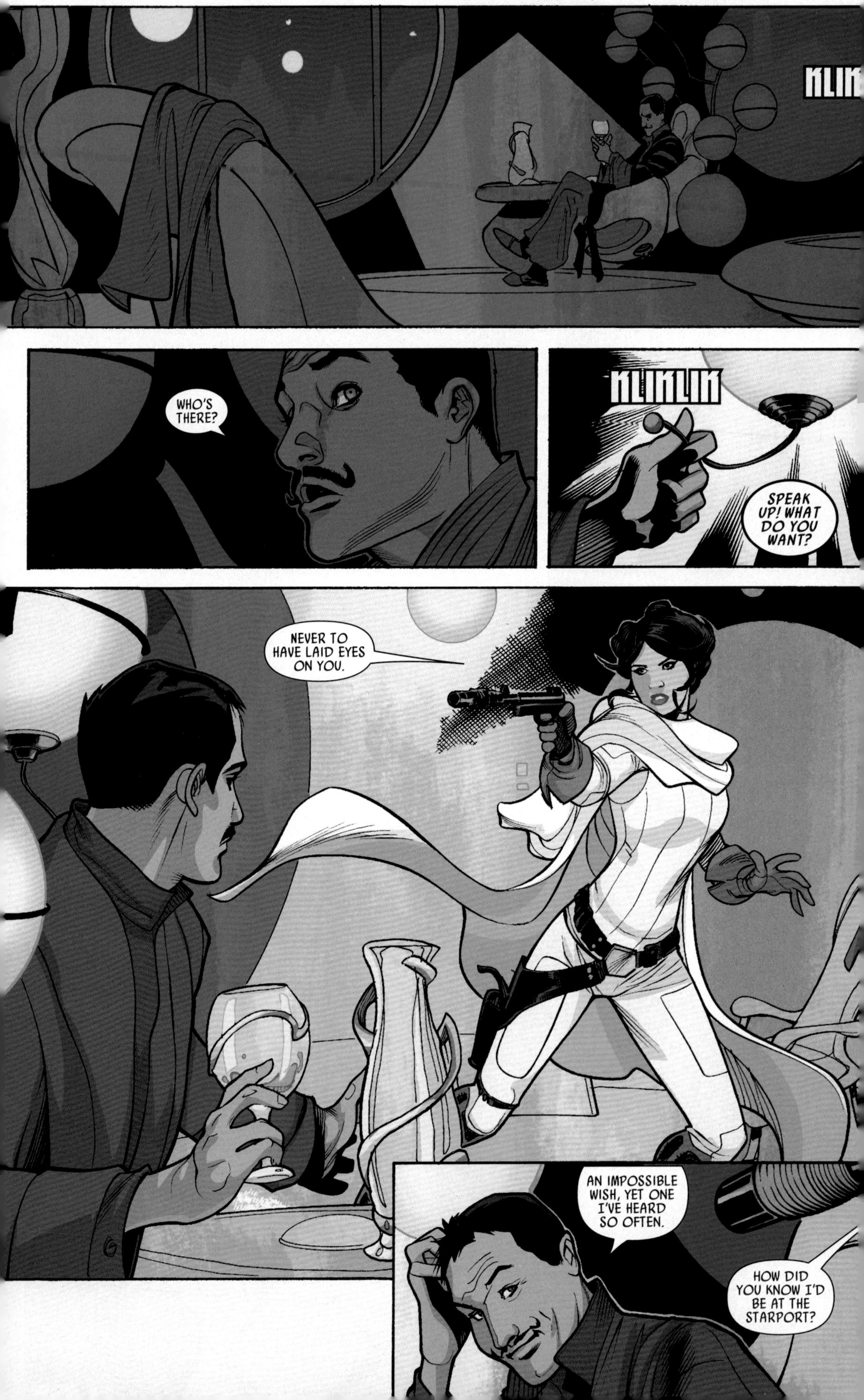
KLIK
WHO'S THERE?
KLIKLIK
SPEAK UP! WHAT DO YOU WANT?
NEVER TO HAVE LAID EYES ON YOU.
AN IMPOSSIBLE WISH, YET ONE I'VE HEARD SO OFTEN.
HOW DID YOU KNOW I'D BE AT THE STARPORT?

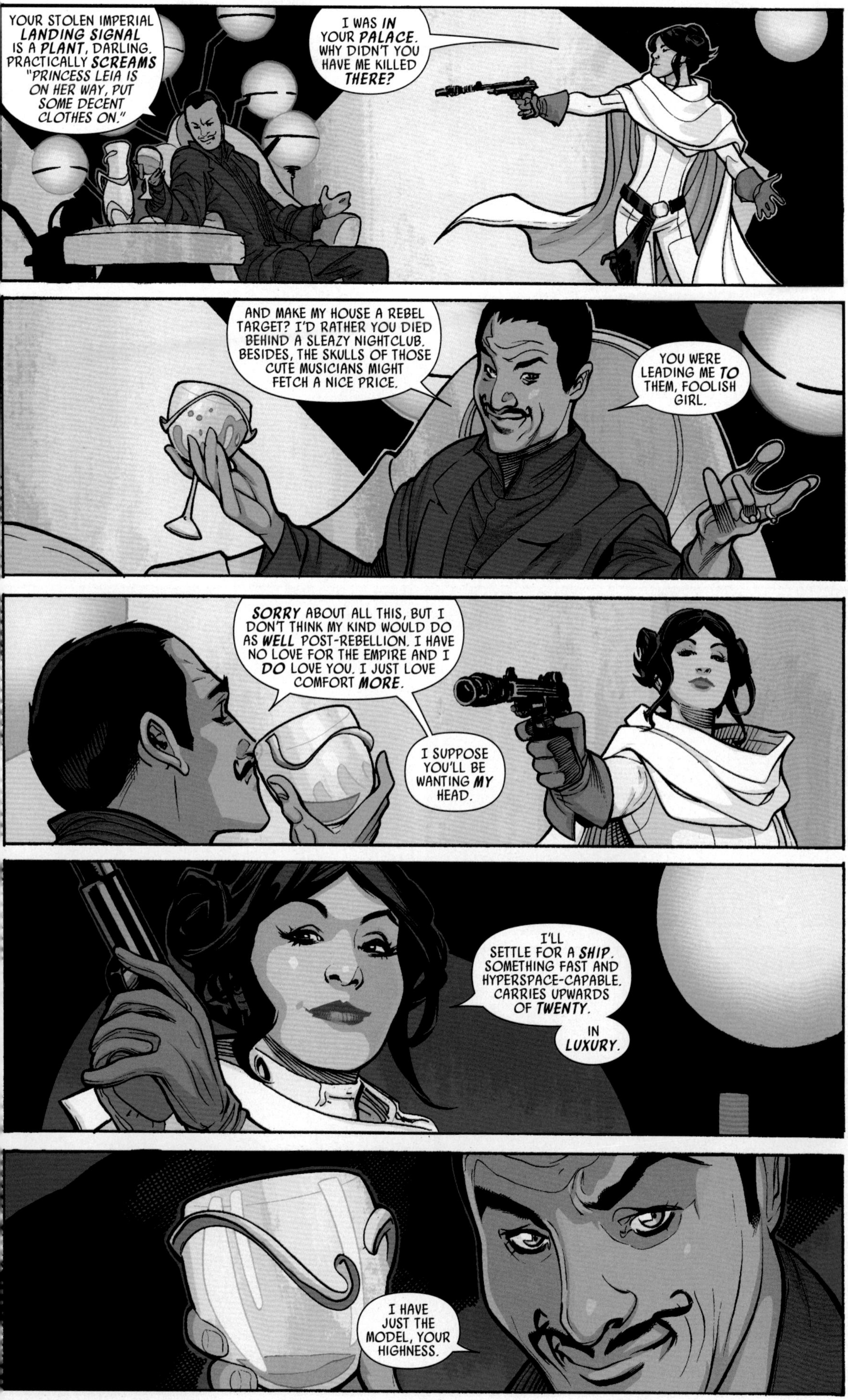
YOUR STOLEN IMPERIAL LANDING SIGNAL IS A PLANT, DARLING. PRACTICALLY SCREAMS "PRINCESS LEIA IS ON HER WAY, PUT SOME DECENT CLOTHES ON."
I WAS IN YOUR PALACE. WHY DIDN'T YOU HAVE ME KILLED THERE?
AND MAKE MY HOUSE A REBEL TARGET? I'D RATHER YOU DIED BEHIND A SLEAZY NIGHTCLUB. BESIDES, THE SKULLS OF THOSE CUTE MUSICIANS MIGHT FETCH A NICE PRICE.
YOU WERE LEADING ME TO THEM, FOOLISH GIRL.
SORRY ABOUT ALL THIS, BUT I DON'T THINK MY KIND WOULD DO AS WELL POST-REBELLION. I HAVE NO LOVE FOR THE EMPIRE AND I DO LOVE YOU. I JUST LOVE COMFORT MORE.
I SUPPOSE YOU'LL BE WANTING MY HEAD.
I'LL SETTLE FOR A SHIP. SOMETHING FAST AND HYPERSPACE-CAPABLE. CARRIES UPWARDS OF TWENTY.
IN LUXURY.
I HAVE JUST THE MODEL, YOUR HIGHNESS.

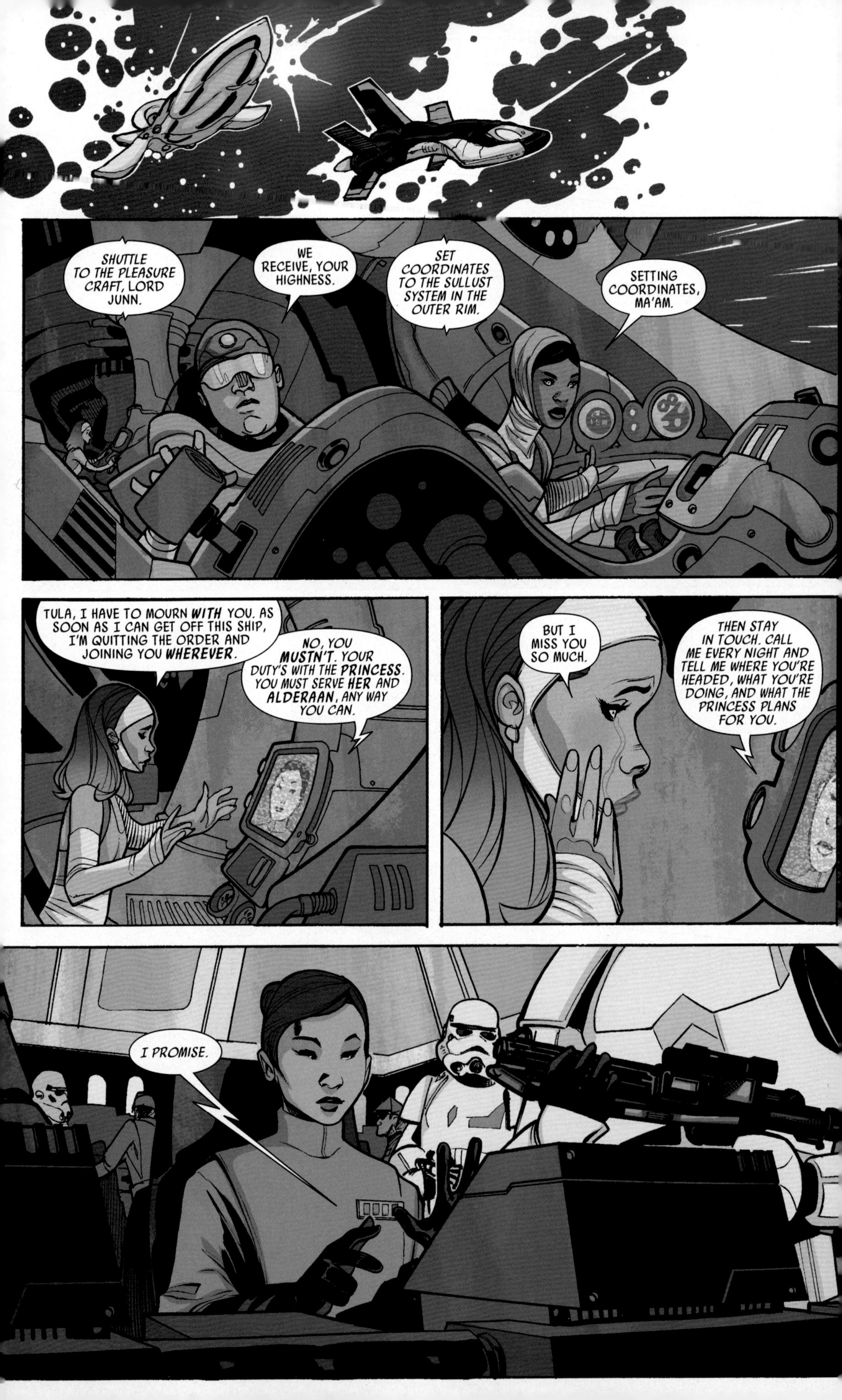
SHUTTLE TO THE PLEASURE CRAFT, LORD JUNN.
WE RECEIVE, YOUR HIGHNESS.
SET COORDINATES TO THE SULLUST SYSTEM IN THE OUTER RIM.
SETTING COORDINATES, MA'AM.
TULA, I HAVE TO MOURN WITH YOU. AS SOON AS I CAN GET OFF THIS SHIP, I'M QUITTING THE ORDER AND JOINING YOU WHEREVER.
NO, YOU MUSTN'T. YOUR DUTY'S WITH THE PRINCESS. YOU MUST SERVE HER AND ALDERAAN, ANY WAY YOU CAN.
BUT I MISS YOU SO MUCH.
THEN STAY IN TOUCH. CALL ME EVERY NIGHT AND TELL ME WHERE YOU'RE HEADED, WHAT YOU'RE DOING, AND WHAT THE PRINCESS PLANS FOR YOU.
I PROMISE.

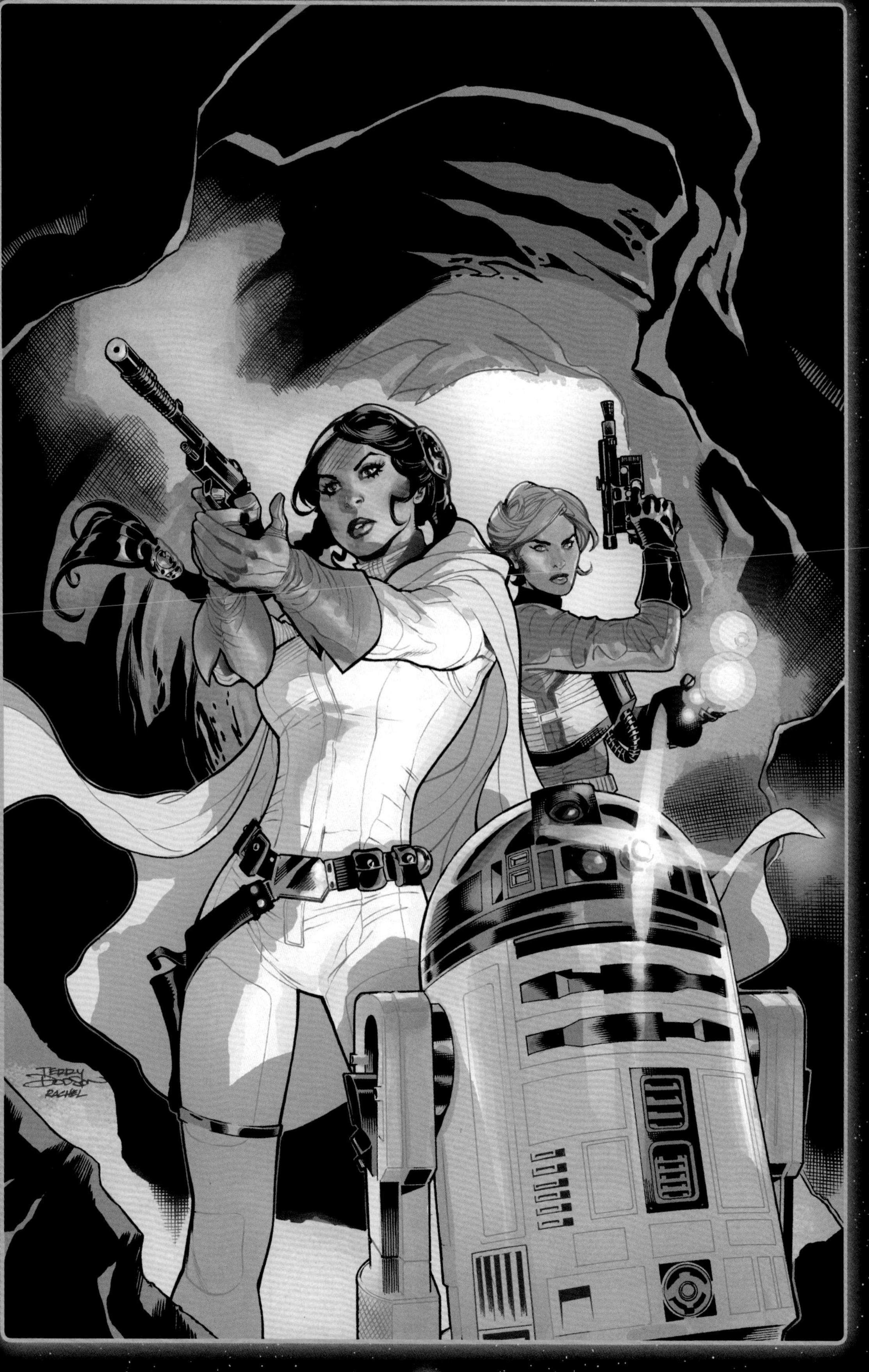
TERRY DODSON
RACHEL

3

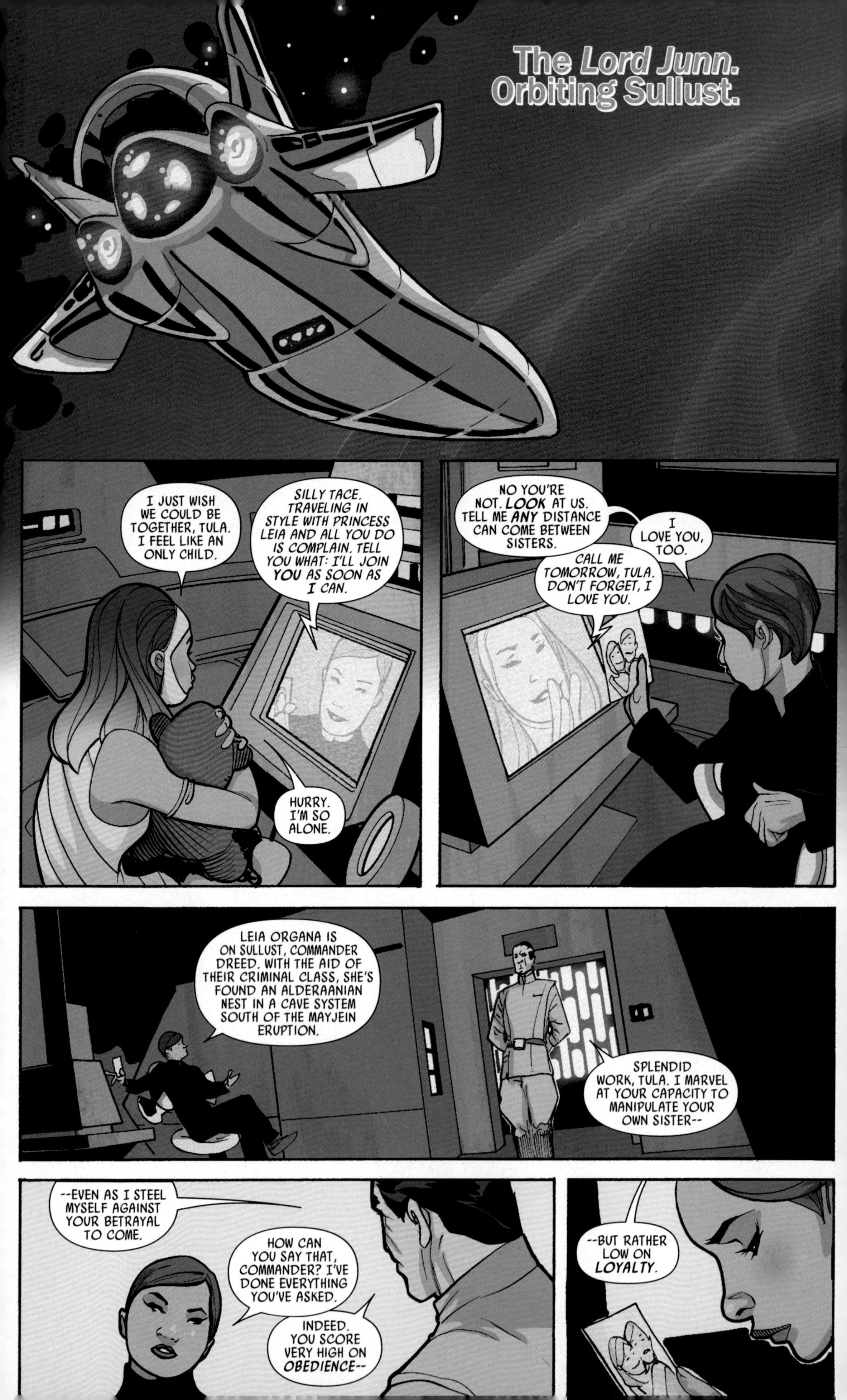
The Lord Junn. Orbiting Sullust.
I JUST WISH WE COULD BE TOGETHER, TULA. I FEEL LIKE AN ONLY CHILD.
SILLY TACE. TRAVELING IN STYLE WITH PRINCESS LEIA AND ALL YOU DO IS COMPLAIN. TELL YOU WHAT: I'LL JOIN YOU AS SOON AS I CAN.
HURRY. I'M SO ALONE.
NO YOU'RE NOT. LOOK AT US. TELL ME ANY DISTANCE CAN COME BETWEEN SISTERS.
I LOVE YOU, TOO.
CALL ME TOMORROW, TULA. DON'T FORGET, I LOVE YOU.
LEIA ORGANA IS ON SULLUST, COMMANDER DREED. WITH THE AID OF THEIR CRIMINAL CLASS, SHE'S FOUND AN ALDERAANIAN NEST IN A CAVE SYSTEM SOUTH OF THE MAYJEIN ERUPTION.
SPLENDID WORK, TULA. I MARVEL AT YOUR CAPACITY TO MANIPULATE YOUR OWN SISTER--
--EVEN AS I STEEL MYSELF AGAINST YOUR BETRAYAL TO COME.
HOW CAN YOU SAY THAT, COMMANDER? I'VE DONE EVERYTHING YOU'VE ASKED.
INDEED. YOU SCORE VERY HIGH ON OBEDIENCE--
--BUT RATHER LOW ON LOYALTY.

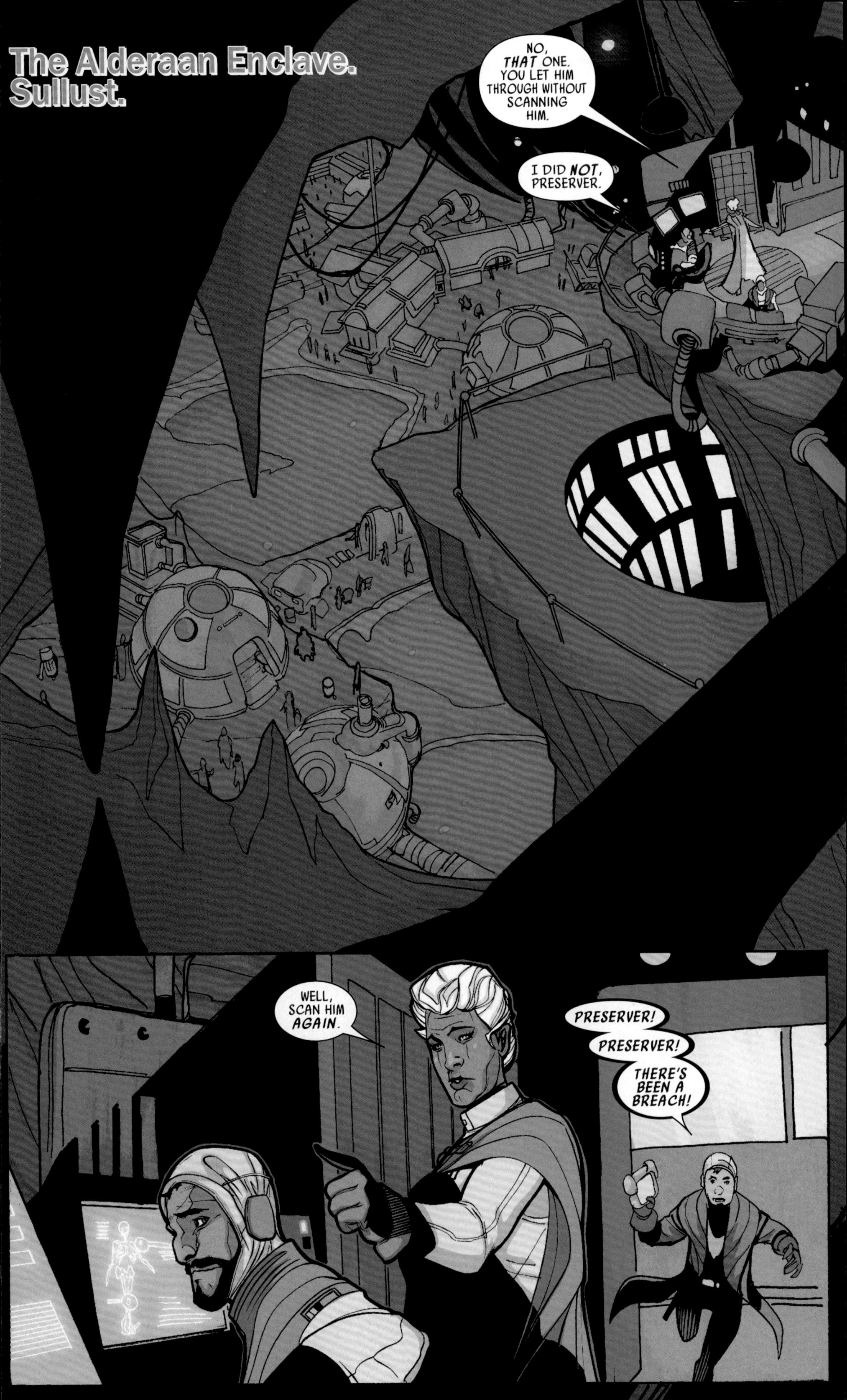

The Alderaan Enclave. Sullust.
NO, THAT ONE. YOU LET HIM THROUGH WITHOUT SCANNING HIM.
I DID NOT, PRESERVER.
WELL, SCAN HIM AGAIN.
PRESERVER!
PRESERVER!
THERE'S BEEN A BREACH!

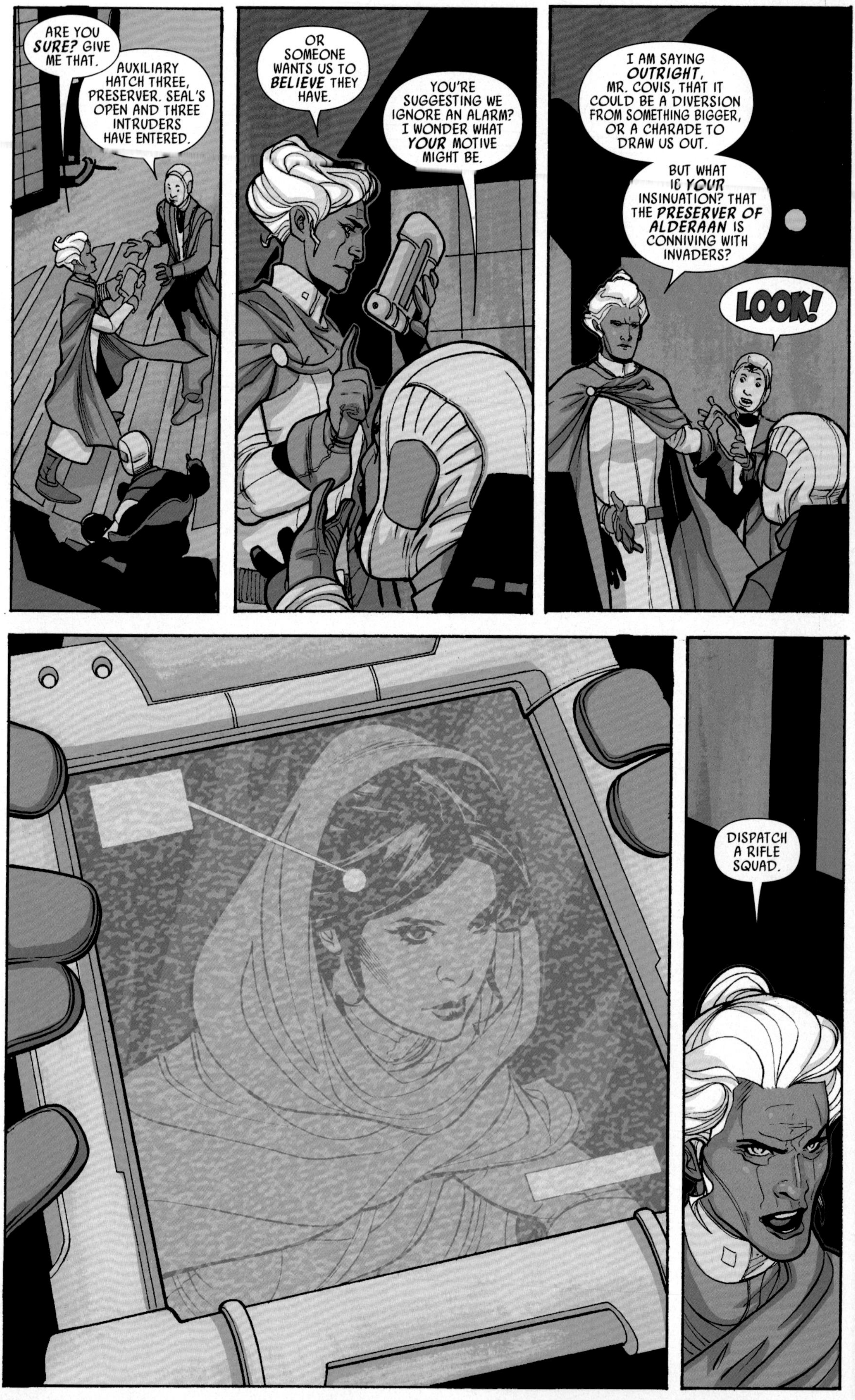
ARE YOU SURE? GIVE ME THAT.
AUXILIARY HATCH THREE, PRESERVER. SEAL'S OPEN AND THREE INTRUDERS HAVE ENTERED.
OR SOMEONE WANTS US TO BELIEVE THEY HAVE.
YOU'RE SUGGESTING WE IGNORE AN ALARM? I WONDER WHAT YOUR MOTIVE MIGHT BE.
I AM SAYING OUTRIGHT, MR. COVIS, THAT IT COULD BE A DIVERSION FROM SOMETHING BIGGER, OR A CHARADE TO DRAW US OUT.
BUT WHAT IS YOUR INSINUATION? THAT THE PRESERVER OF ALDERAAN IS CONNIVING WITH INVADERS?
LOOK!
DISPATCH A RIFLE SQUAD.

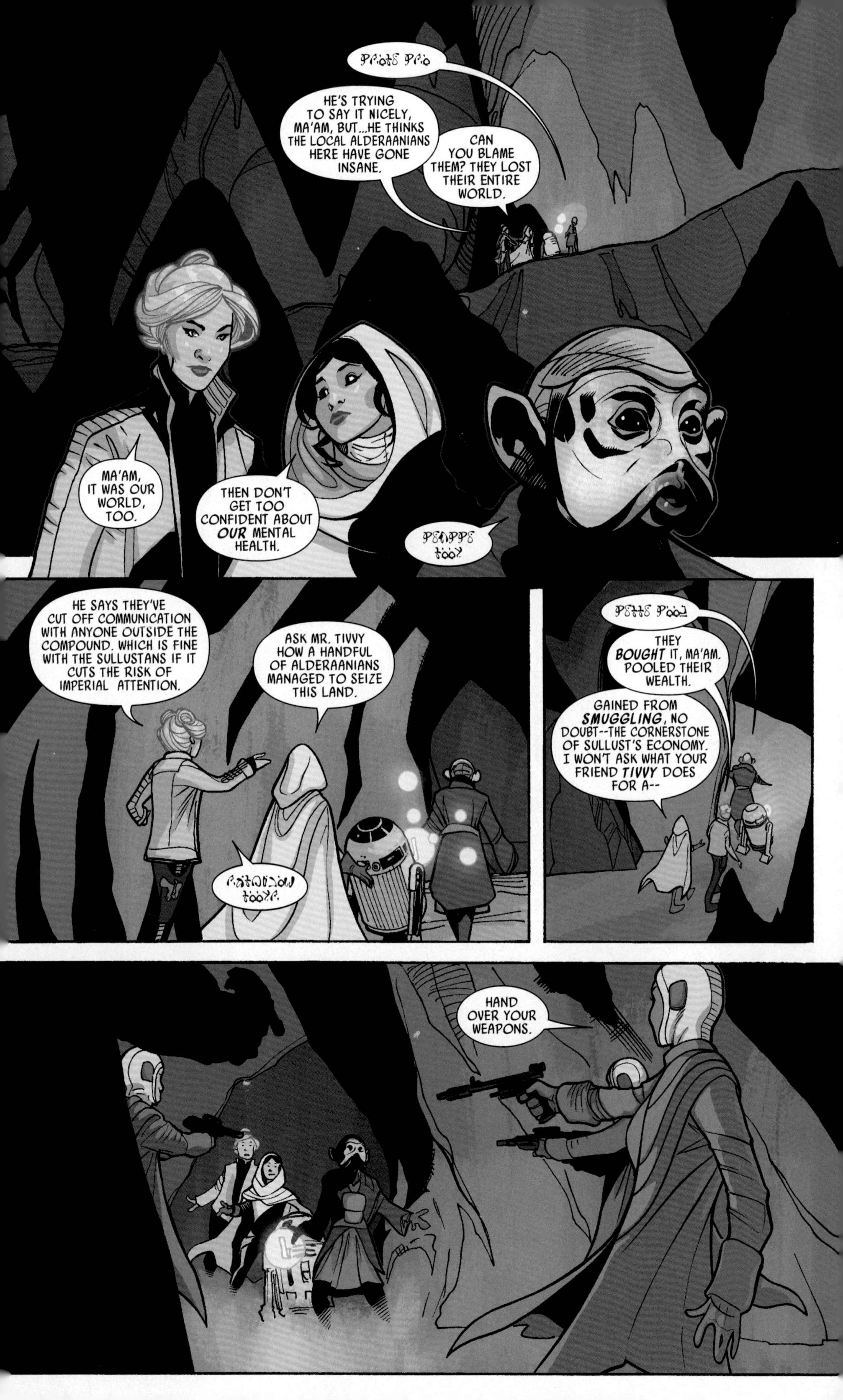
HE'S TRYING TO SAY IT NICELY, MA'AM, BUT...HE THINKS THE LOCAL ALDERAANIANS HERE HAVE GONE INSANE.
CAN YOU BLAME THEM? THEY LOST THEIR ENTIRE WORLD.
MA'AM, IT WAS OUR WORLD, TOO.
THEN DON'T GET TOO CONFIDENT ABOUT OUR MENTAL HEALTH.
HE SAYS THEY'VE CUT OFF COMMUNICATION WITH ANYONE OUTSIDE THE COMPOUND. WHICH IS FINE WITH THE SULLUSTANS IF IT CUTS THE RISK OF IMPERIAL ATTENTION.
ASK MR. TIVVY HOW A HANDFUL OF ALDERAANIANS MANAGED TO SEIZE THIS LAND.
THEY BOUGHT IT, MA'AM. POOLED THEIR WEALTH.
GAINED FROM SMUGGLING, NO DOUBT--THE CORNERSTONE OF SULLUST'S ECONOMY. I WON'T ASK WHAT YOUR FRIEND TIVVY DOES FOR A--
HAND OVER YOUR WEAPONS.

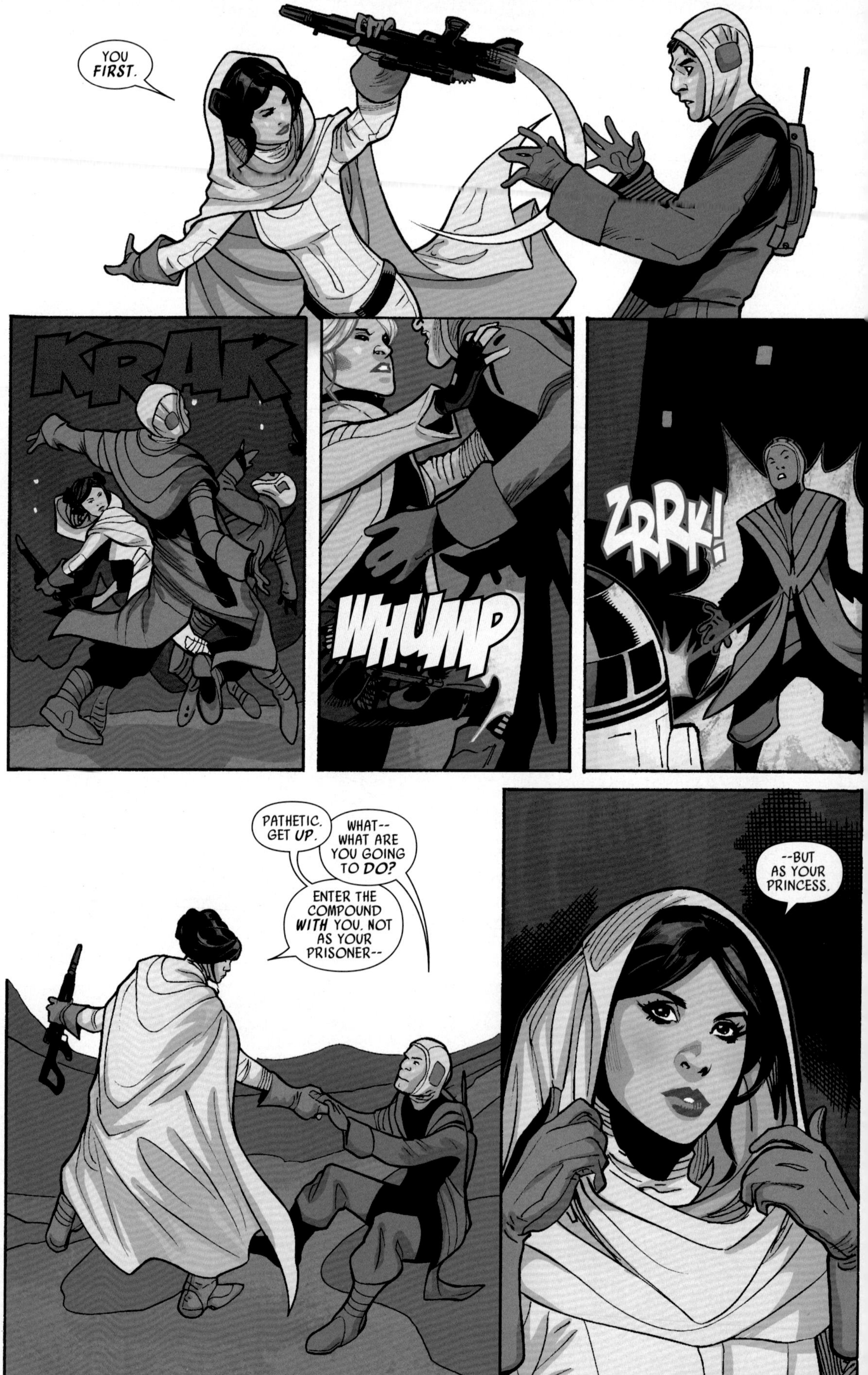
YOU FIRST.
KRAK
WHUMP
ZRRK!
PATHETIC. GET UP.
WHAT-- WHAT ARE YOU GOING TO DO?
ENTER THE COMPOUND WITH YOU. NOT AS YOUR PRISONER--
--BUT AS YOUR PRINCESS.

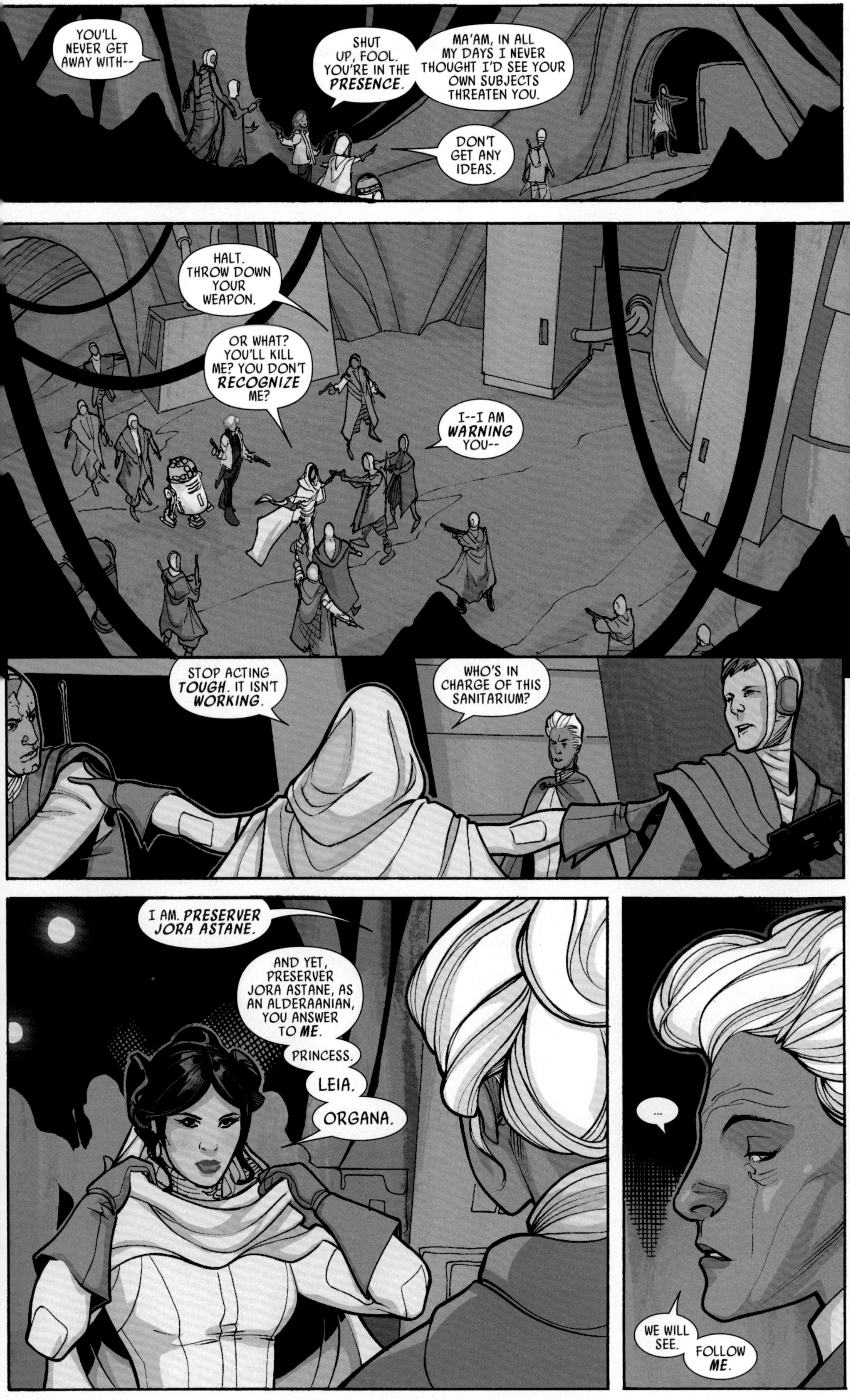
YOU'LL NEVER GET AWAY WITH--
SHUT UP, FOOL. YOU'RE IN THE PRESENCE.
MA'AM, IN ALL MY DAYS I NEVER THOUGHT I'D SEE YOUR OWN SUBJECTS THREATEN YOU.
DON'T GET ANY IDEAS.
HALT. THROW DOWN YOUR WEAPON.
OR WHAT? YOU'LL KILL ME? YOU DON'T RECOGNIZE ME?
I--I AM WARNING YOU--
STOP ACTING TOUGH. IT ISN'T WORKING.
WHO'S IN CHARGE OF THIS SANITARIUM?
I AM. PRESERVER JORA ASTANE.
AND YET, PRESERVER JORA ASTANE, AS AN ALDERAANIAN, YOU ANSWER TO ME.
PRINCESS.
LEIA.
ORGANA.
...
WE WILL SEE.
FOLLOW ME.

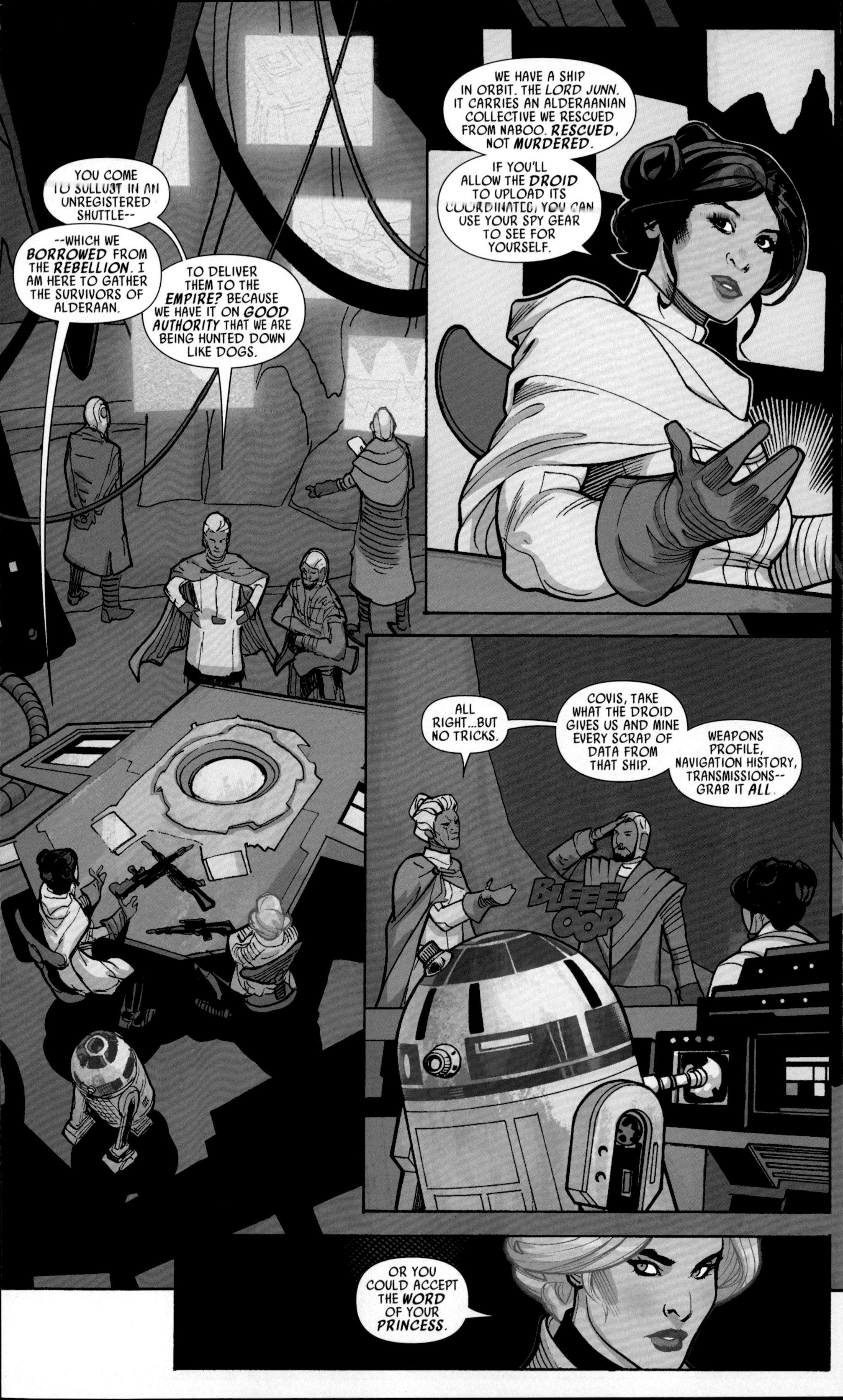

YOU COME TO SULLUST IN AN UNREGISTERED SHUTTLE--
--WHICH WE **BORROWED** FROM THE **REBELLION**. I AM HERE TO GATHER THE SURVIVORS OF ALDERAAN.
TO DELIVER THEM TO THE **EMPIRE?** BECAUSE WE HAVE IT ON **GOOD AUTHORITY** THAT WE ARE BEING HUNTED DOWN LIKE DOGS.
WE HAVE A SHIP IN ORBIT. THE *LORD JUNN*. IT CARRIES AN ALDERAANIAN COLLECTIVE WE RESCUED FROM NABOO. **RESCUED**, NOT **MURDERED**.
IF YOU'LL ALLOW THE **DROID** TO UPLOAD ITS COORDINATES, YOU CAN USE YOUR SPY GEAR TO SEE FOR YOURSELF.
ALL RIGHT...BUT NO TRICKS.
COVIS, TAKE WHAT THE DROID GIVES US AND MINE EVERY SCRAP OF DATA FROM THAT SHIP.
WEAPONS PROFILE, NAVIGATION HISTORY, TRANSMISSIONS-- GRAB IT **ALL**.
BLEEE-OOP
OR YOU COULD ACCEPT THE **WORD** OF YOUR **PRINCESS**.

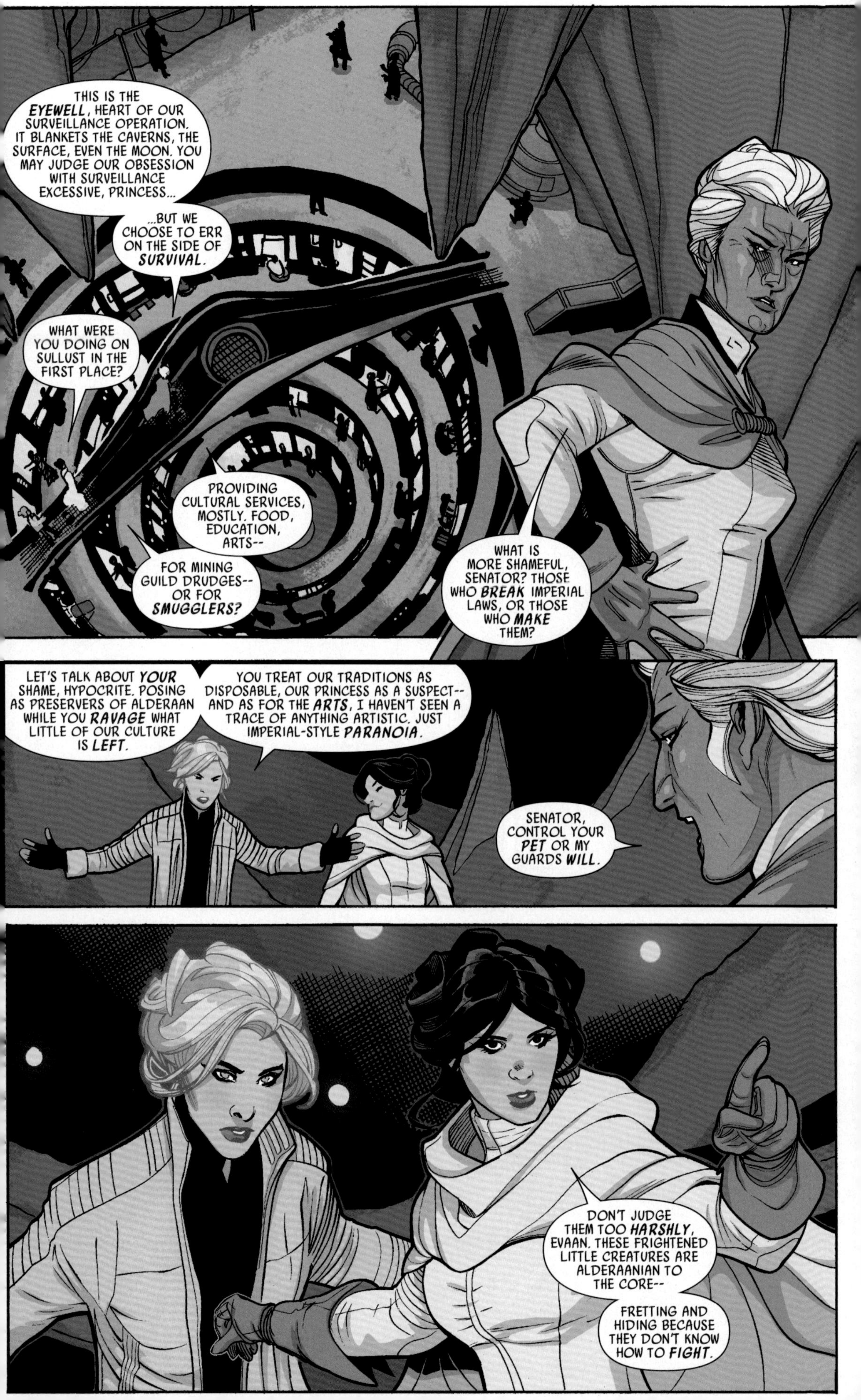
THIS IS THE EYEWELL, HEART OF OUR SURVEILLANCE OPERATION. IT BLANKETS THE CAVERNS, THE SURFACE, EVEN THE MOON. YOU MAY JUDGE OUR OBSESSION WITH SURVEILLANCE EXCESSIVE, PRINCESS...
...BUT WE CHOOSE TO ERR ON THE SIDE OF SURVIVAL.
WHAT WERE YOU DOING ON SULLUST IN THE FIRST PLACE?
PROVIDING CULTURAL SERVICES, MOSTLY. FOOD, EDUCATION, ARTS--
FOR MINING GUILD DRUDGES--OR FOR SMUGGLERS?
WHAT IS MORE SHAMEFUL, SENATOR? THOSE WHO BREAK IMPERIAL LAWS, OR THOSE WHO MAKE THEM?
LET'S TALK ABOUT YOUR SHAME, HYPOCRITE. POSING AS PRESERVERS OF ALDERAAN WHILE YOU RAVAGE WHAT LITTLE OF OUR CULTURE IS LEFT.
YOU TREAT OUR TRADITIONS AS DISPOSABLE, OUR PRINCESS AS A SUSPECT--AND AS FOR THE ARTS, I HAVEN'T SEEN A TRACE OF ANYTHING ARTISTIC. JUST IMPERIAL-STYLE PARANOIA.
SENATOR, CONTROL YOUR PET OR MY GUARDS WILL.
DON'T JUDGE THEM TOO HARSHLY, EVAAN. THESE FRIGHTENED LITTLE CREATURES ARE ALDERAANIAN TO THE CORE--
FRETTING AND HIDING BECAUSE THEY DON'T KNOW HOW TO FIGHT.

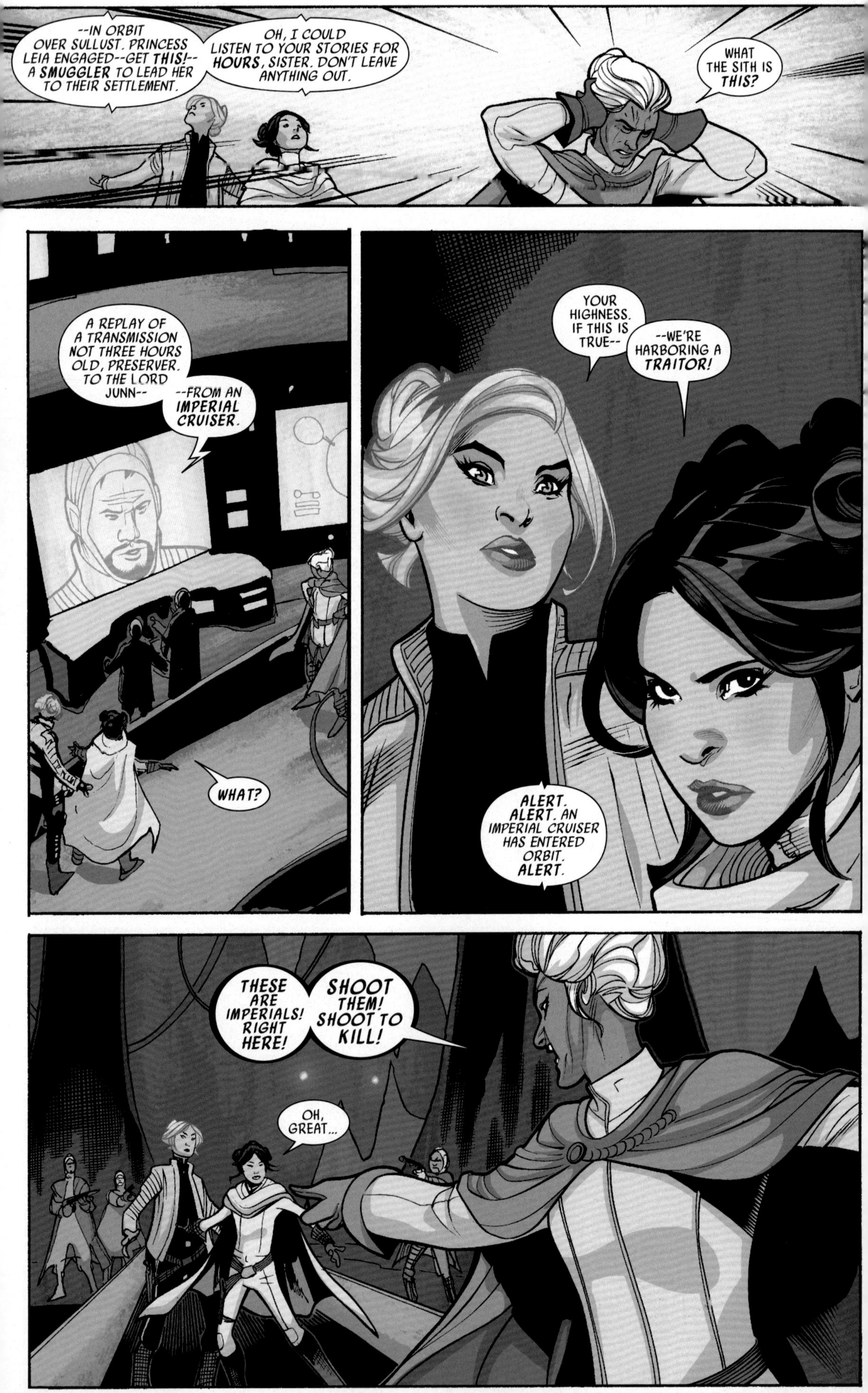

--IN ORBIT OVER SULLUST. PRINCESS LEIA ENGAGED--GET THIS!--A SMUGGLER TO LEAD HER TO THEIR SETTLEMENT.
OH, I COULD LISTEN TO YOUR STORIES FOR HOURS, SISTER. DON'T LEAVE ANYTHING OUT.
WHAT THE SITH IS THIS?
A REPLAY OF A TRANSMISSION NOT THREE HOURS OLD, PRESERVER. TO THE LORD JUNN--
--FROM AN IMPERIAL CRUISER.
WHAT?
YOUR HIGHNESS. IF THIS IS TRUE--
--WE'RE HARBORING A TRAITOR!
ALERT. ALERT. AN IMPERIAL CRUISER HAS ENTERED ORBIT. ALERT.
THESE ARE IMPERIALS! RIGHT HERE!
SHOOT THEM! SHOOT TO KILL!
OH, GREAT...

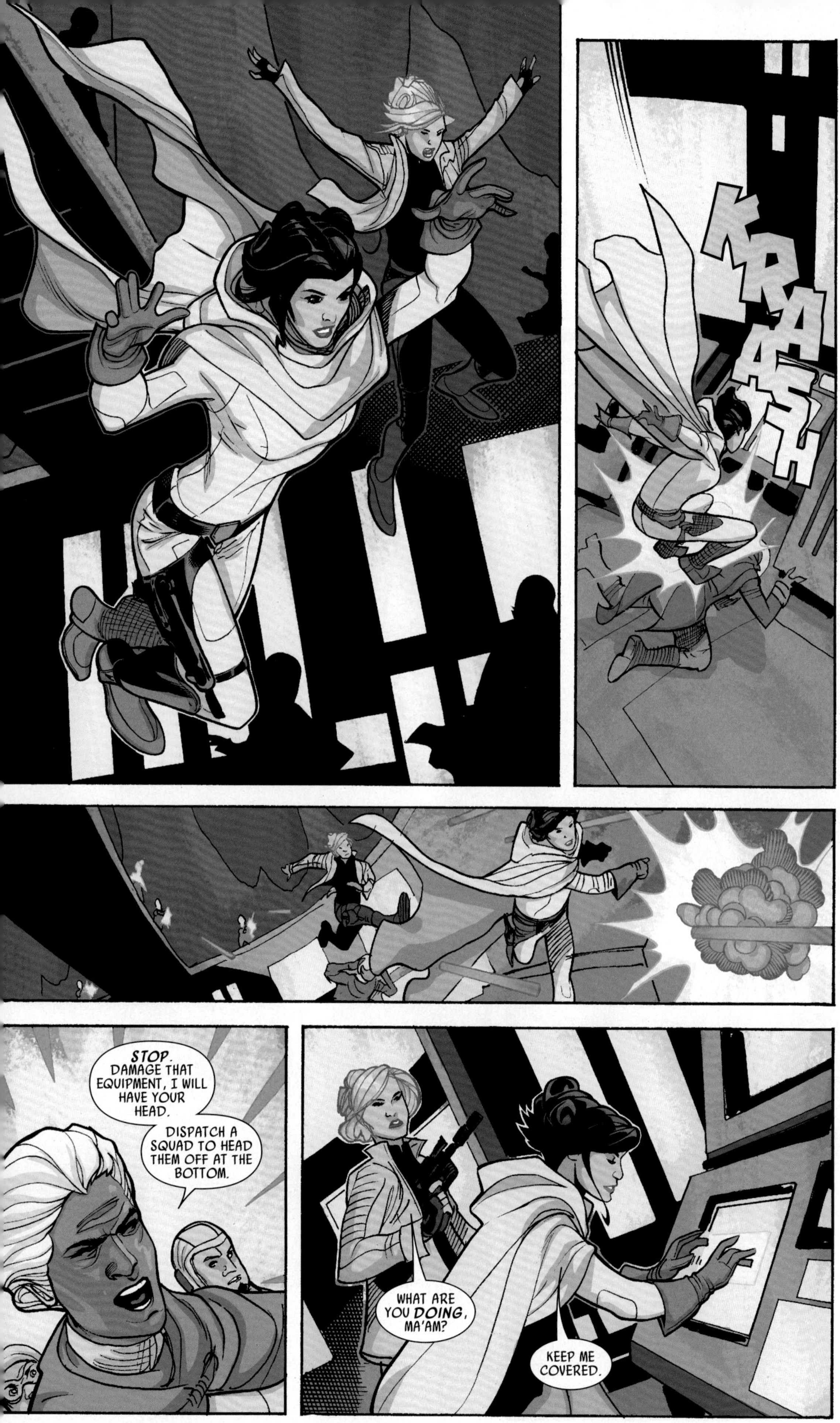
KRAKASH
STOP. DAMAGE THAT EQUIPMENT, I WILL HAVE YOUR HEAD.
DISPATCH A SQUAD TO HEAD THEM OFF AT THE BOTTOM.
WHAT ARE YOU DOING, MA'AM?
KEEP ME COVERED.

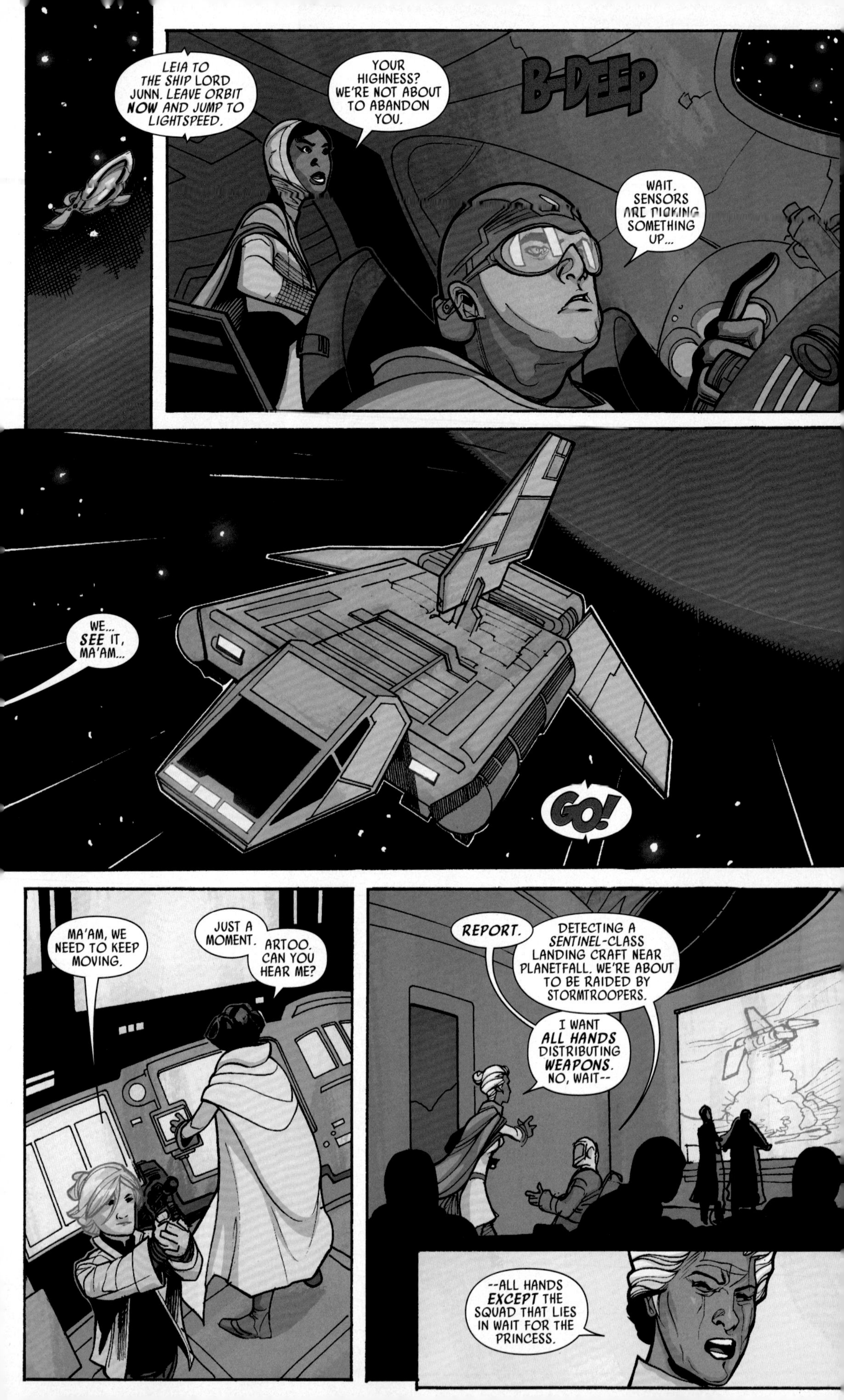
LEIA TO THE SHIP LORD JUNN. LEAVE ORBIT NOW AND JUMP TO LIGHTSPEED.
YOUR HIGHNESS? WE'RE NOT ABOUT TO ABANDON YOU.
B-DEEP
WAIT. SENSORS ARE PICKING SOMETHING UP...
WE... SEE IT, MA'AM...
GO!
MA'AM, WE NEED TO KEEP MOVING.
JUST A MOMENT.
ARTOO. CAN YOU HEAR ME?
REPORT.
DETECTING A SENTINEL-CLASS LANDING CRAFT NEAR PLANETFALL. WE'RE ABOUT TO BE RAIDED BY STORMTROOPERS.
I WANT ALL HANDS DISTRIBUTING WEAPONS. NO, WAIT--
--ALL HANDS EXCEPT THE SQUAD THAT LIES IN WAIT FOR THE PRINCESS.

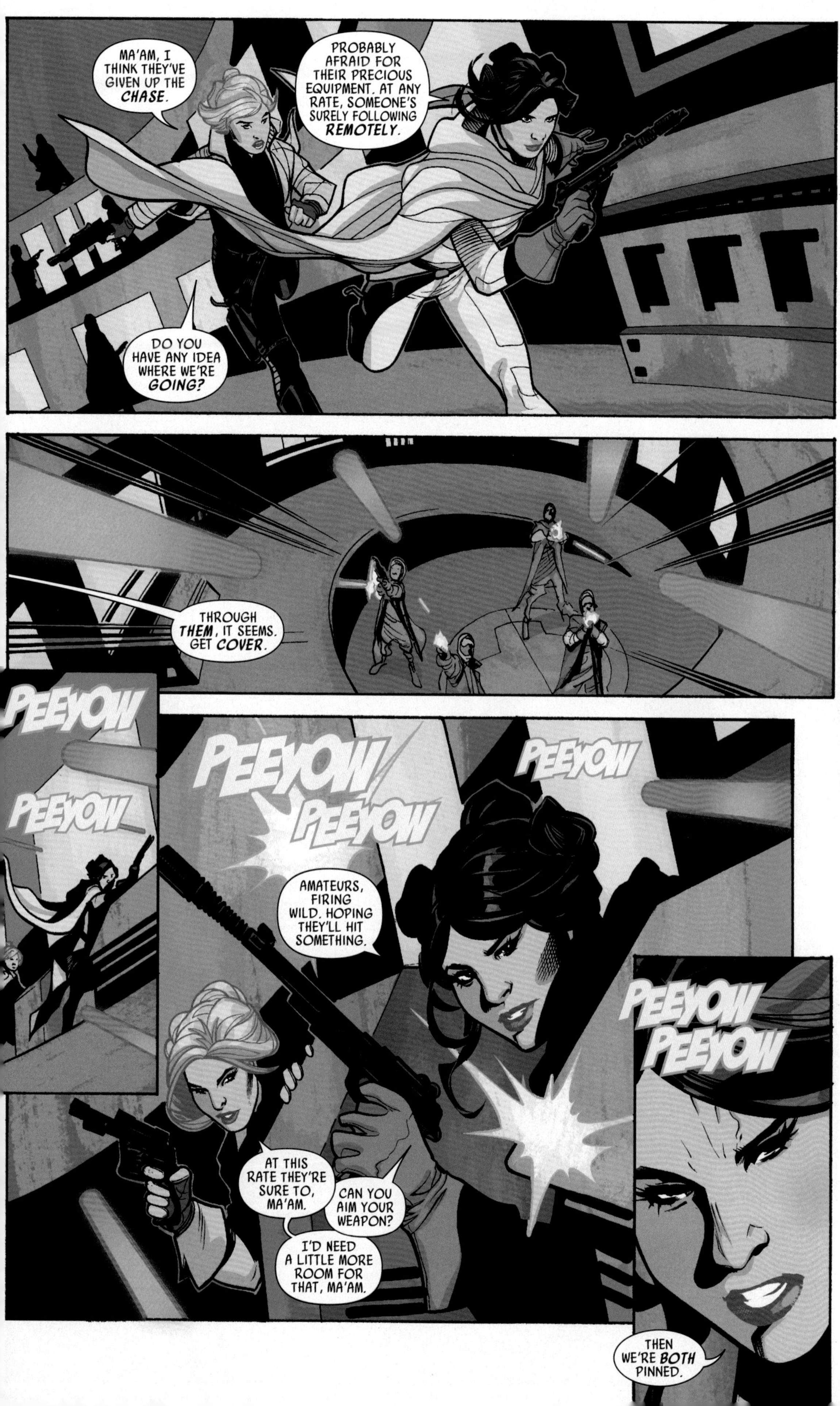
MA'AM, I THINK THEY'VE GIVEN UP THE CHASE.
PROBABLY AFRAID FOR THEIR PRECIOUS EQUIPMENT. AT ANY RATE, SOMEONE'S SURELY FOLLOWING REMOTELY.
DO YOU HAVE ANY IDEA WHERE WE'RE GOING?
THROUGH THEM, IT SEEMS. GET COVER.
PEEYOW
PEEYOW
PEEYOW
PEEYOW
PEEYOW
AMATEURS, FIRING WILD. HOPING THEY'LL HIT SOMETHING.
AT THIS RATE THEY'RE SURE TO, MA'AM.
CAN YOU AIM YOUR WEAPON?
I'D NEED A LITTLE MORE ROOM FOR THAT, MA'AM.
PEEYOW PEEYOW
THEN WE'RE BOTH PINNED.

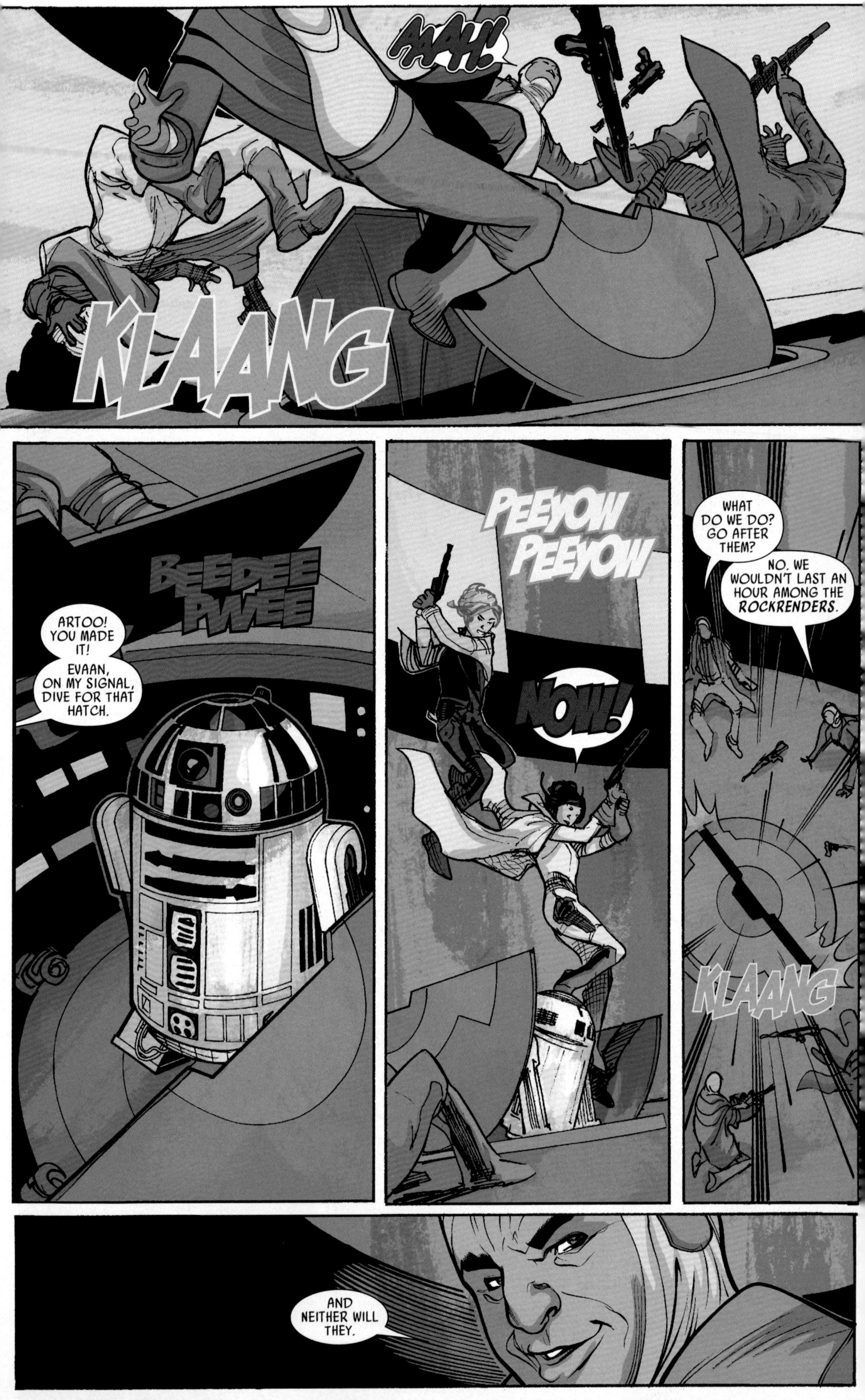
AAAH!
KLAANG
BEEDEE PWEE
ARTOO! YOU MADE IT!
EVAAN, ON MY SIGNAL, DIVE FOR THAT HATCH.
PEEYOW PEEYOW
NOW!
WHAT DO WE DO? GO AFTER THEM?
NO. WE WOULDN'T LAST AN HOUR AMONG THE ROCKRENDERS.
KLAANG
AND NEITHER WILL THEY.

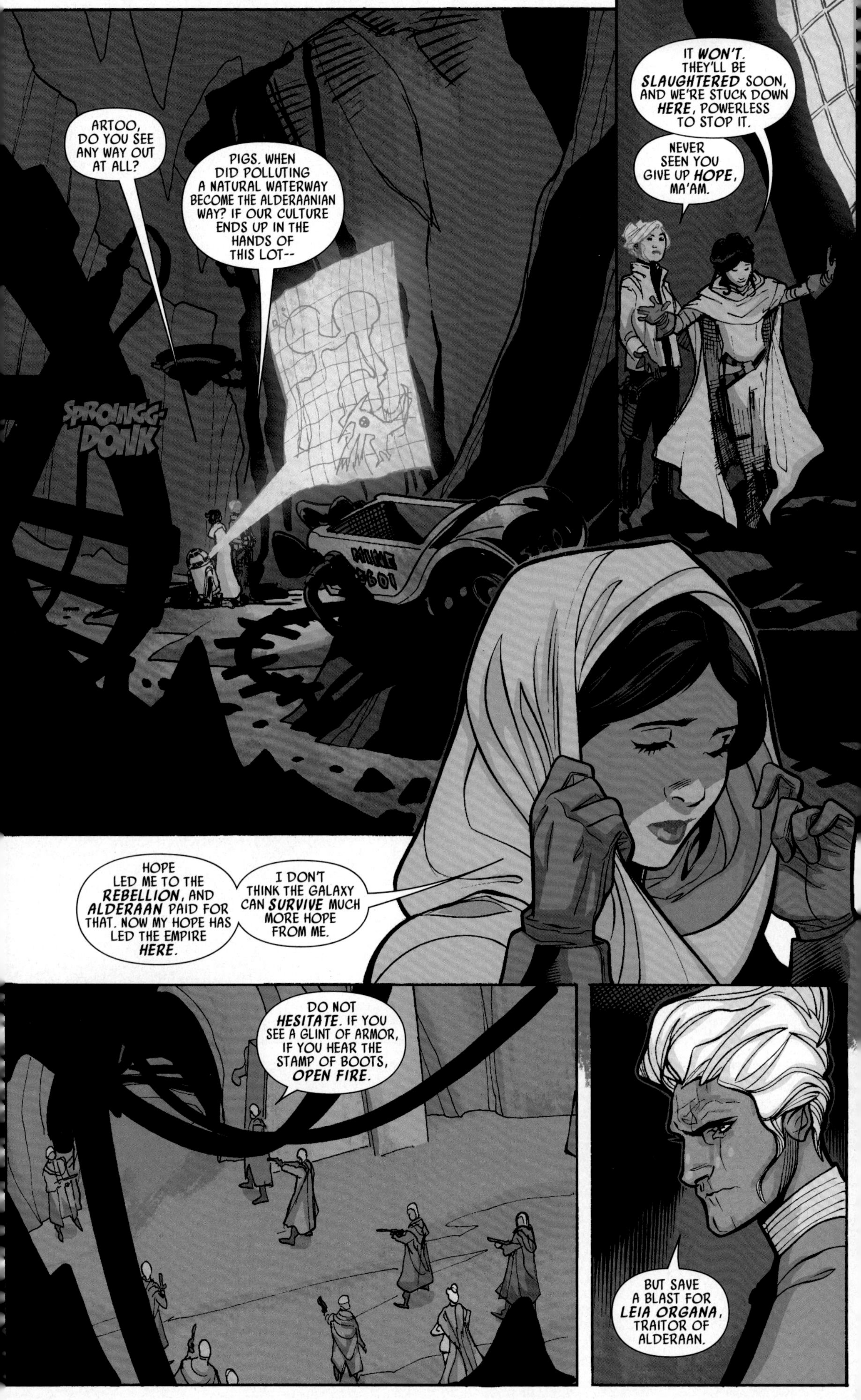
ARTOO, DO YOU SEE ANY WAY OUT AT ALL?
PIGS. WHEN DID POLLUTING A NATURAL WATERWAY BECOME THE ALDERAANIAN WAY? IF OUR CULTURE ENDS UP IN THE HANDS OF THIS LOT--
SPROINGG-DONK
IT WON'T. THEY'LL BE SLAUGHTERED SOON, AND WE'RE STUCK DOWN HERE, POWERLESS TO STOP IT.
NEVER SEEN YOU GIVE UP HOPE, MA'AM.
HOPE LED ME TO THE REBELLION, AND ALDERAAN PAID FOR THAT. NOW MY HOPE HAS LED THE EMPIRE HERE.
I DON'T THINK THE GALAXY CAN SURVIVE MUCH MORE HOPE FROM ME.
DO NOT HESITATE. IF YOU SEE A GLINT OF ARMOR, IF YOU HEAR THE STAMP OF BOOTS, OPEN FIRE.
BUT SAVE A BLAST FOR LEIA ORGANA, TRAITOR OF ALDERAAN.

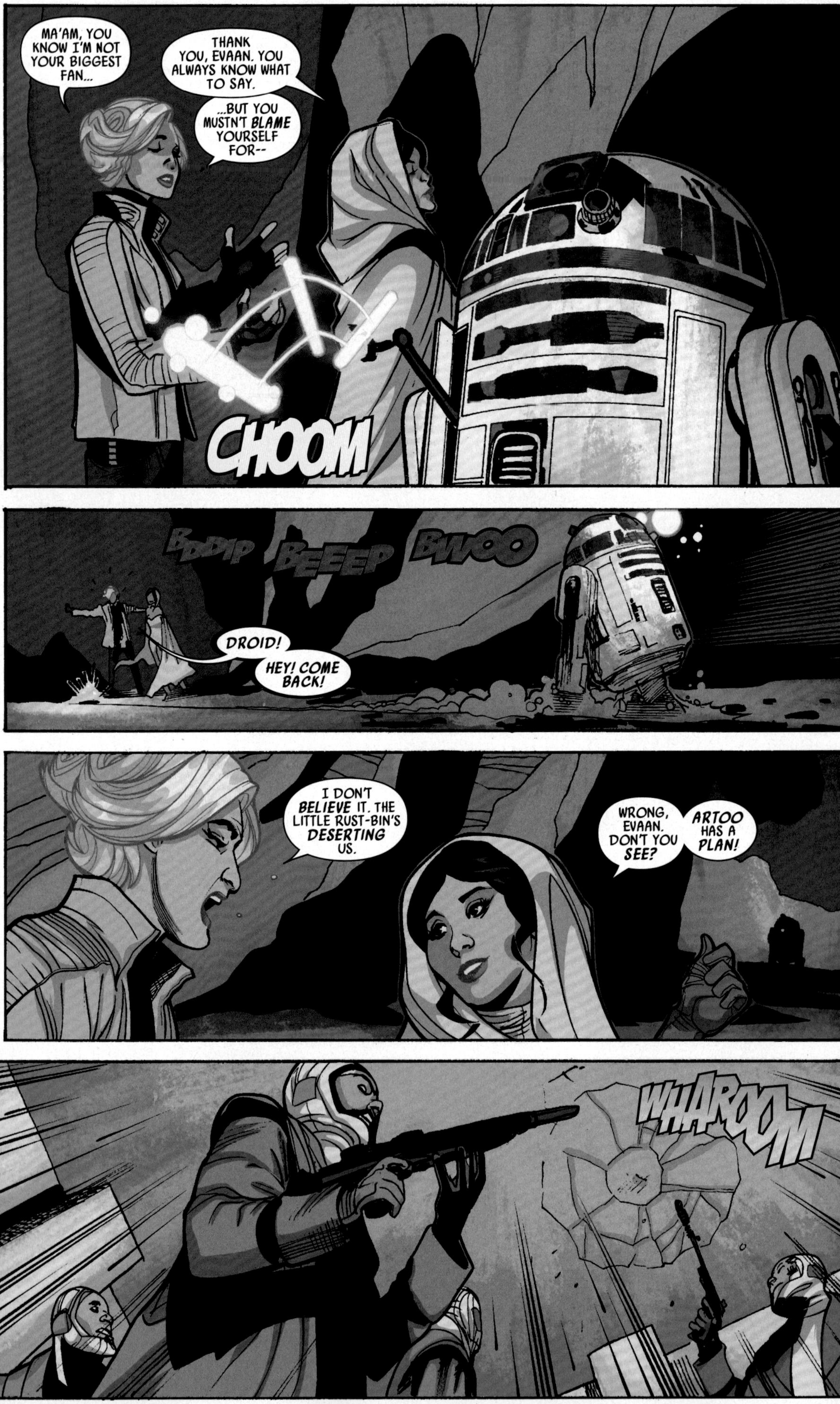
MA'AM, YOU KNOW I'M NOT YOUR BIGGEST FAN...
THANK YOU, EVAAN. YOU ALWAYS KNOW WHAT TO SAY.
...BUT YOU MUSTN'T BLAME YOURSELF FOR--
CHOOM
BDDIP BEEEEP BWOO
DROID!
HEY! COME BACK!
I DON'T BELIEVE IT. THE LITTLE RUST-BIN'S DESERTING US.
WRONG, EVAAN. DON'T YOU SEE?
ARTOO HAS A PLAN!
WHAROOM

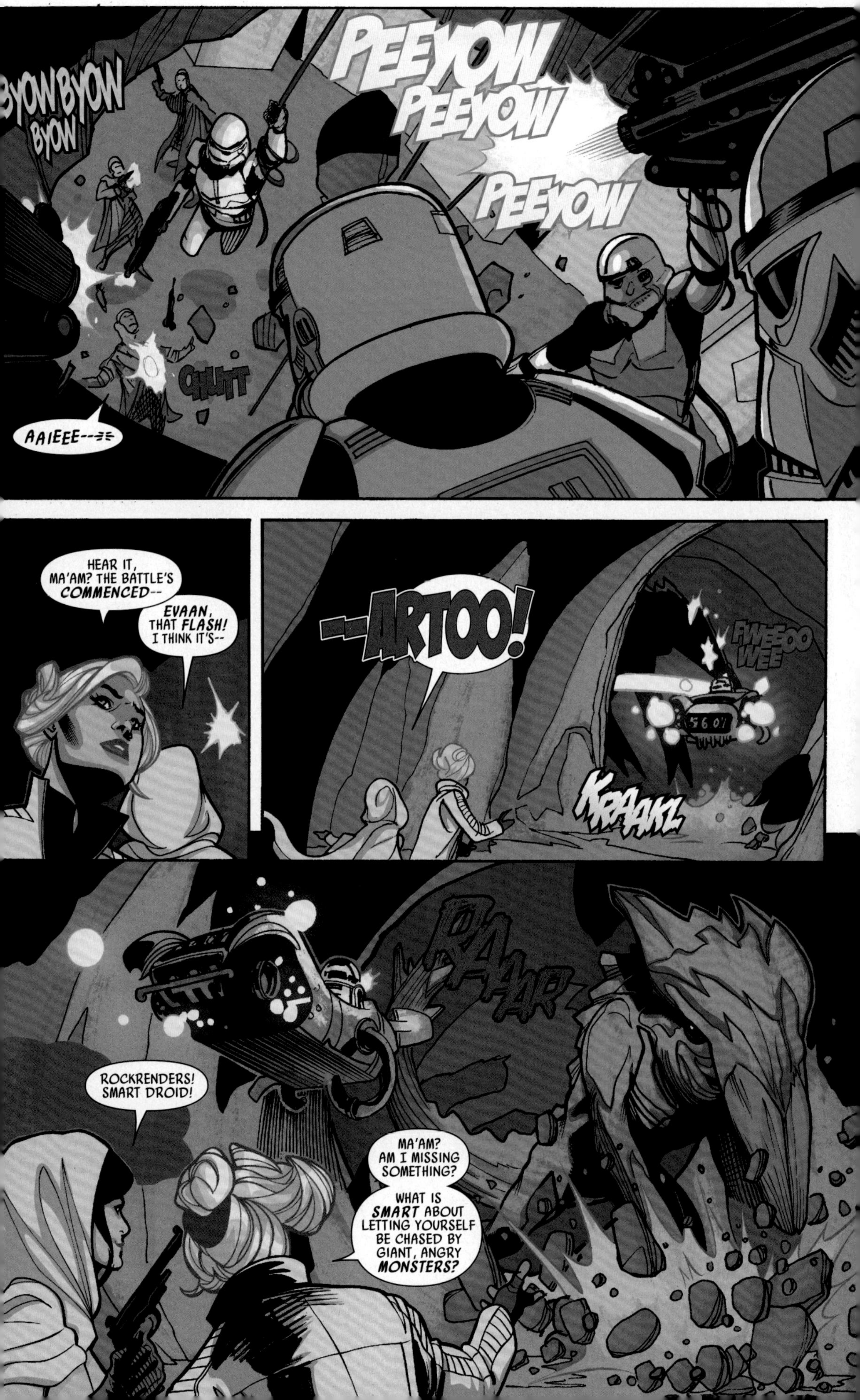

BYOW BYOW BYOW
PEEYOW PEEYOW
PEEYOW
CHUTT
AAIEEE--
HEAR IT, MA'AM? THE BATTLE'S COMMENCED--
EVAAN, THAT FLASH! I THINK IT'S--
--ARTOO!
FWEEOO WEE
KRAAKL
RAAAR
ROCKRENDERS! SMART DROID!
MA'AM? AM I MISSING SOMETHING?
WHAT IS SMART ABOUT LETTING YOURSELF BE CHASED BY GIANT, ANGRY MONSTERS?

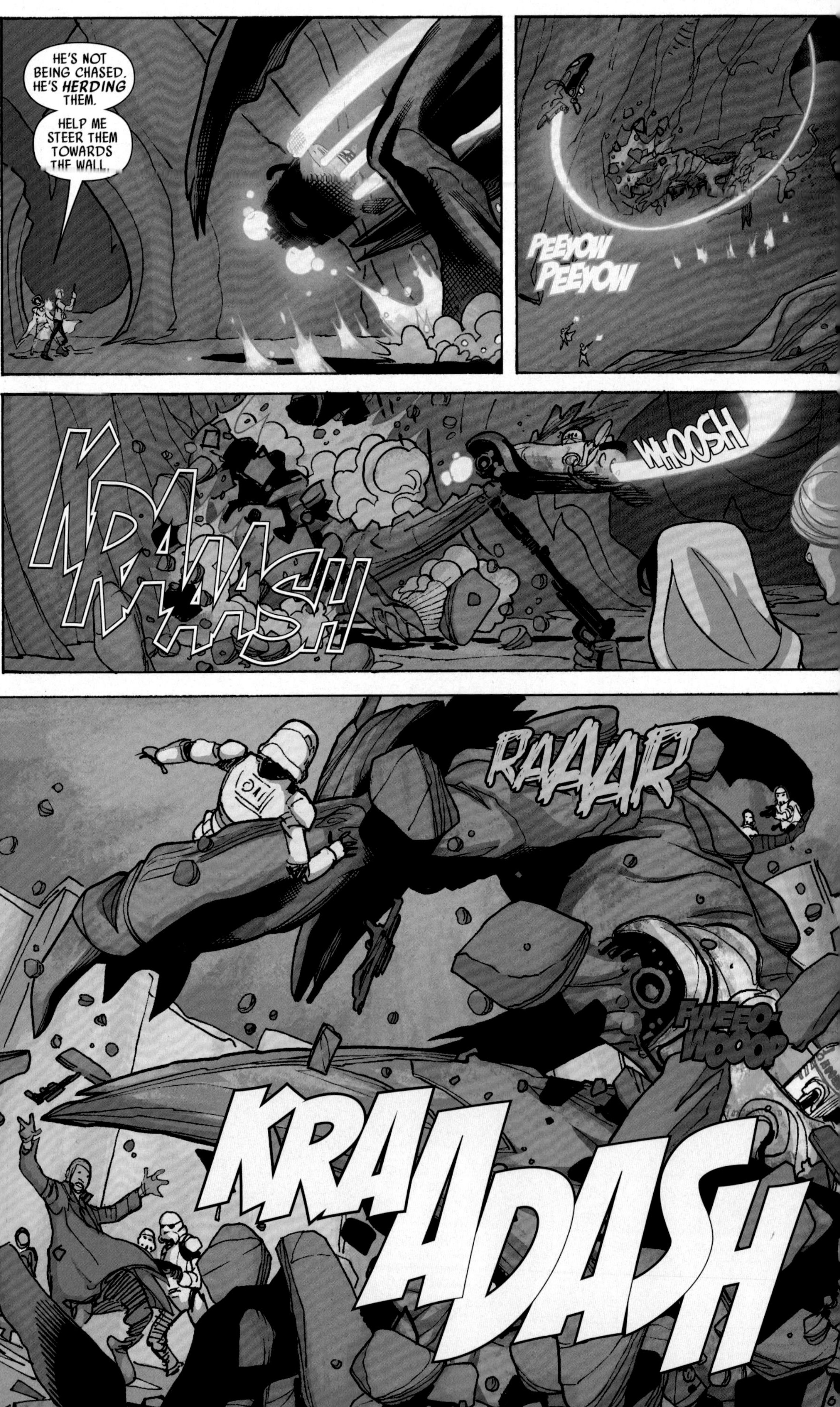

HE'S NOT BEING CHASED. HE'S *HERDING* THEM.
HELP ME STEER THEM TOWARDS THE WALL.
PEEYOW PEEYOW
KRAAASH
WHOOSH
RAAAR
FWEEO-WOOOP
KRAADASH

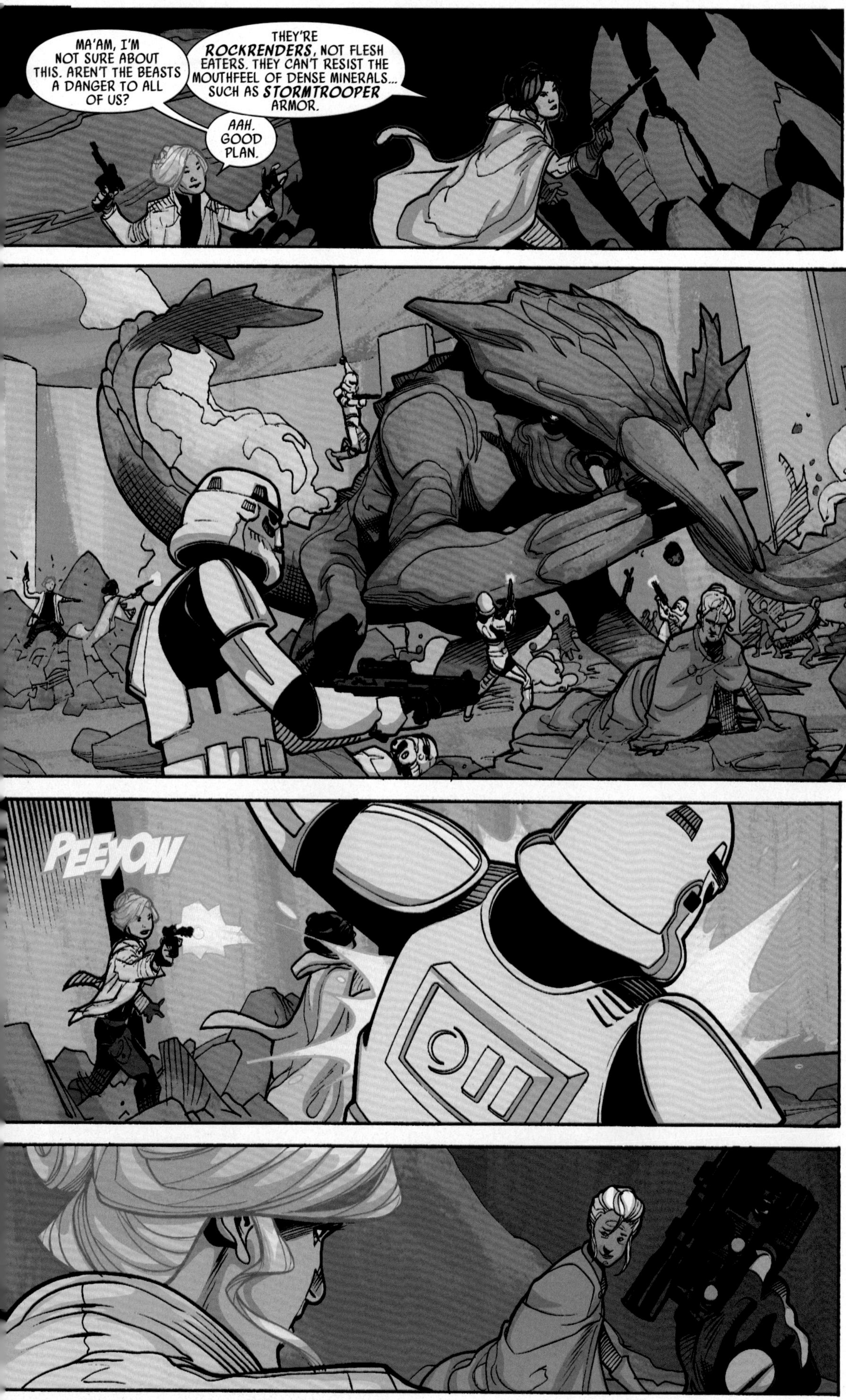
MA'AM, I'M NOT SURE ABOUT THIS. AREN'T THE BEASTS A DANGER TO ALL OF US?
THEY'RE ROCKRENDERS, NOT FLESH EATERS. THEY CAN'T RESIST THE MOUTHFEEL OF DENSE MINERALS... SUCH AS STORMTROOPER ARMOR.
AAH. GOOD PLAN.
PEEYOW

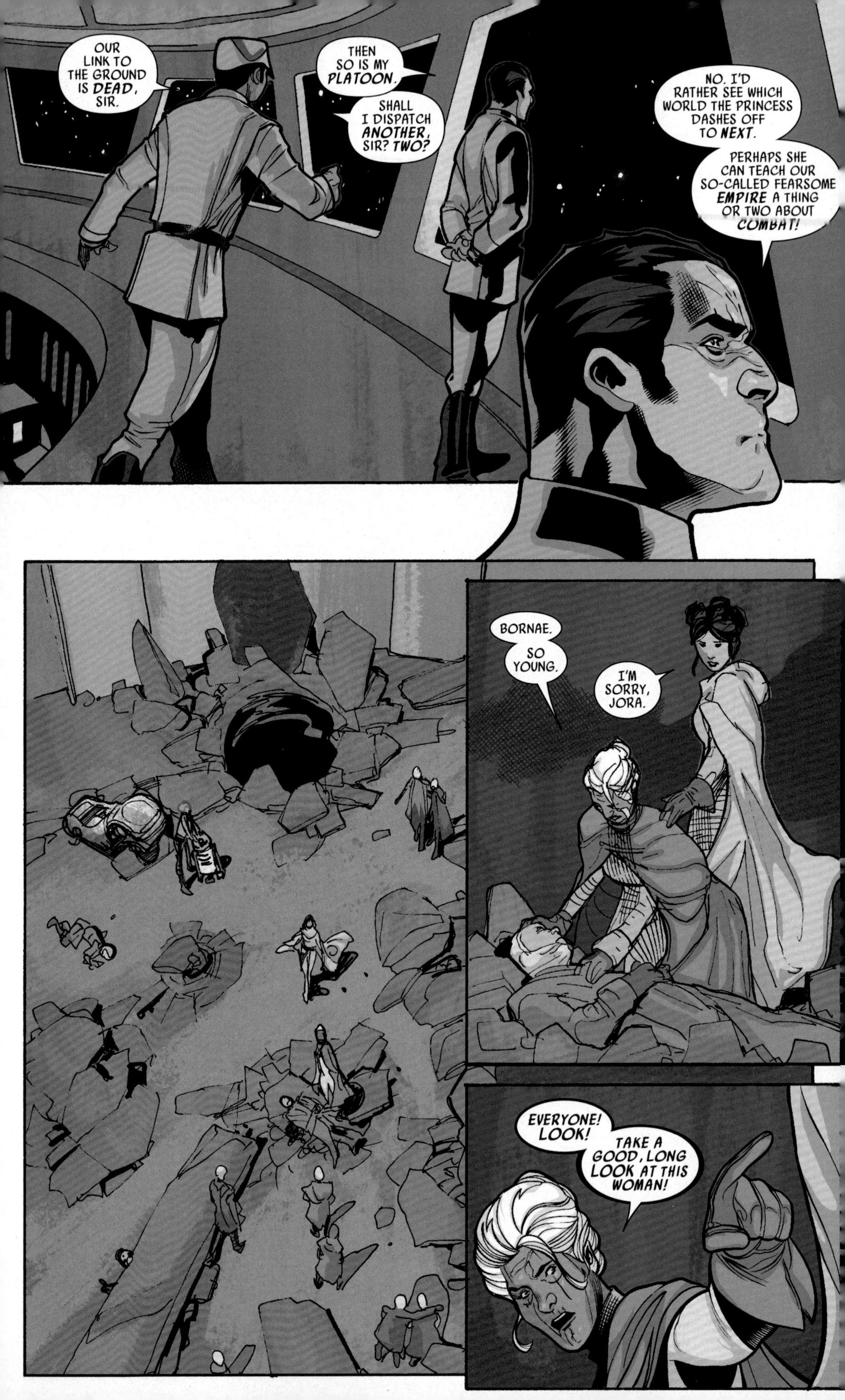
OUR LINK TO THE GROUND IS DEAD, SIR.
THEN SO IS MY PLATOON.
SHALL I DISPATCH ANOTHER, SIR? TWO?
NO. I'D RATHER SEE WHICH WORLD THE PRINCESS DASHES OFF TO NEXT.
PERHAPS SHE CAN TEACH OUR SO-CALLED FEARSOME EMPIRE A THING OR TWO ABOUT COMBAT!
BORNAE. SO YOUNG.
I'M SORRY, JORA.
EVERYONE! LOOK!
TAKE A GOOD, LONG LOOK AT THIS WOMAN!

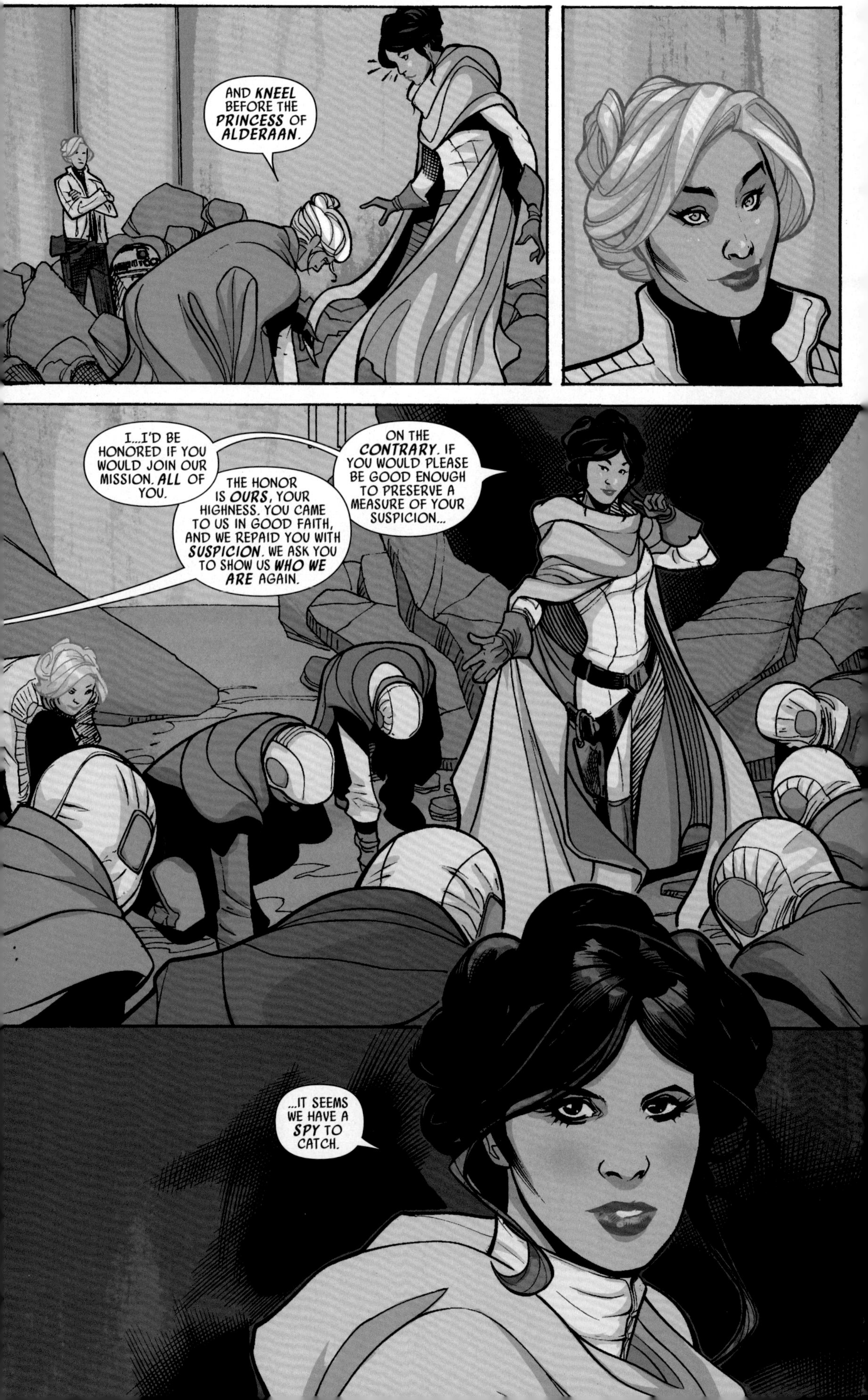
AND KNEEL BEFORE THE PRINCESS OF ALDERAAN.
I...I'D BE HONORED IF YOU WOULD JOIN OUR MISSION. ALL OF YOU.
THE HONOR IS OURS, YOUR HIGHNESS. YOU CAME TO US IN GOOD FAITH, AND WE REPAID YOU WITH SUSPICION. WE ASK YOU TO SHOW US WHO WE ARE AGAIN.
ON THE CONTRARY. IF YOU WOULD PLEASE BE GOOD ENOUGH TO PRESERVE A MEASURE OF YOUR SUSPICION...
...IT SEEMS WE HAVE A SPY TO CATCH.

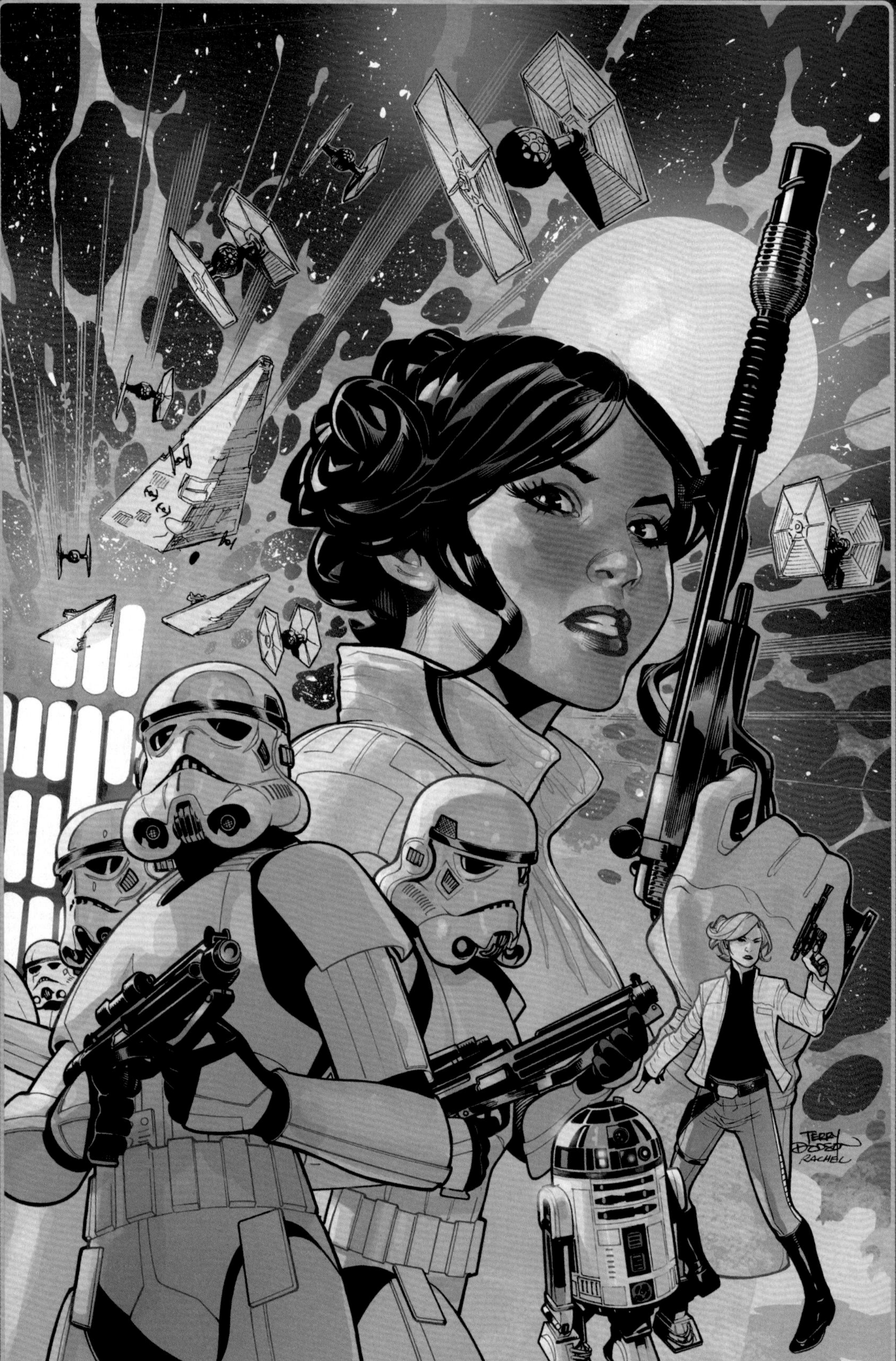

4

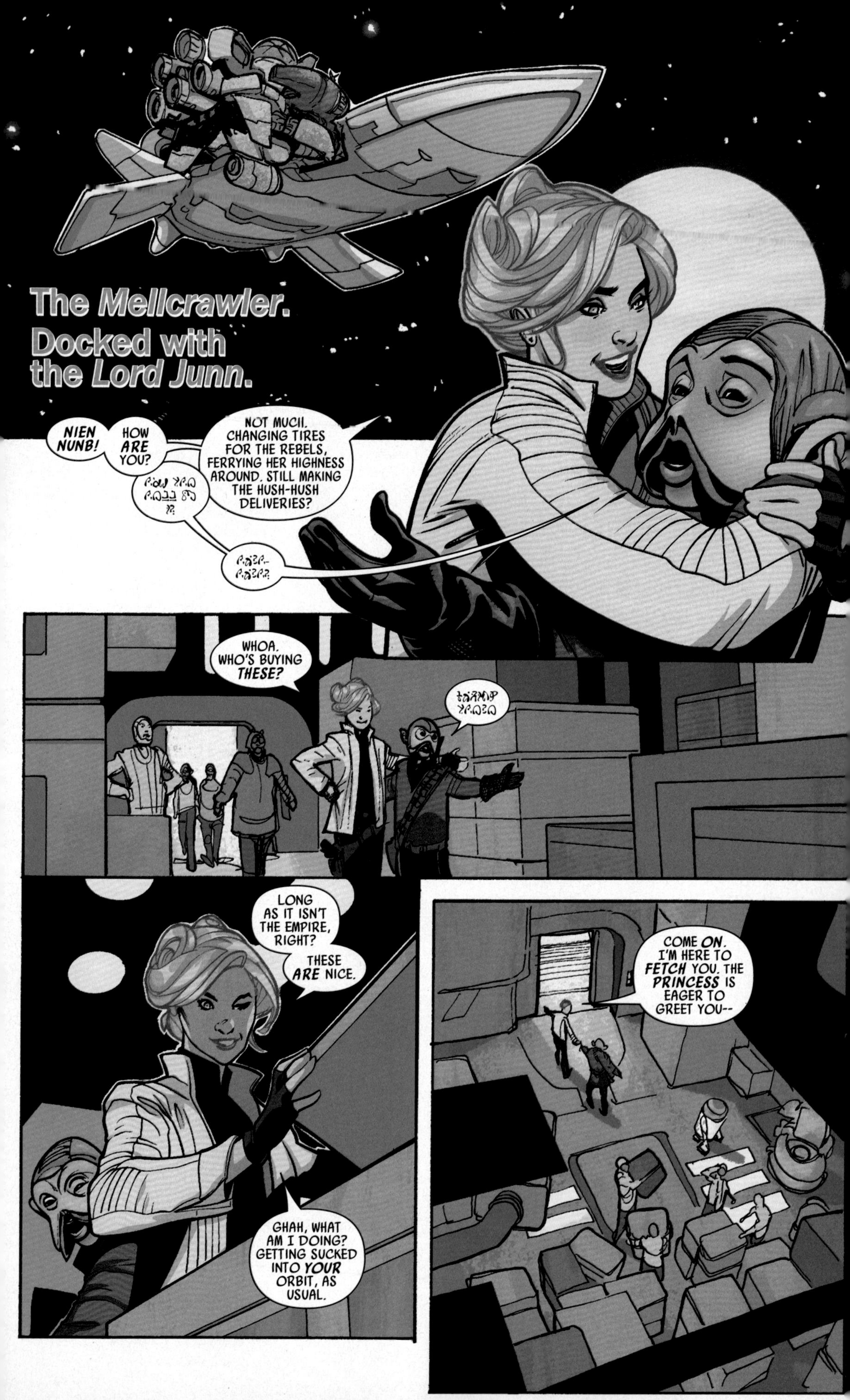

The Mellcrawler. Docked with the Lord Junn.
NIEN NUNB!
HOW ARE YOU?
NOT MUCH. CHANGING TIRES FOR THE REBELS, FERRYING HER HIGHNESS AROUND. STILL MAKING THE HUSH-HUSH DELIVERIES?
WHOA. WHO'S BUYING THESE?
LONG AS IT ISN'T THE EMPIRE, RIGHT?
THESE ARE NICE.
GHAH, WHAT AM I DOING? GETTING SUCKED INTO YOUR ORBIT, AS USUAL.
COME ON. I'M HERE TO FETCH YOU. THE PRINCESS IS EAGER TO GREET YOU--

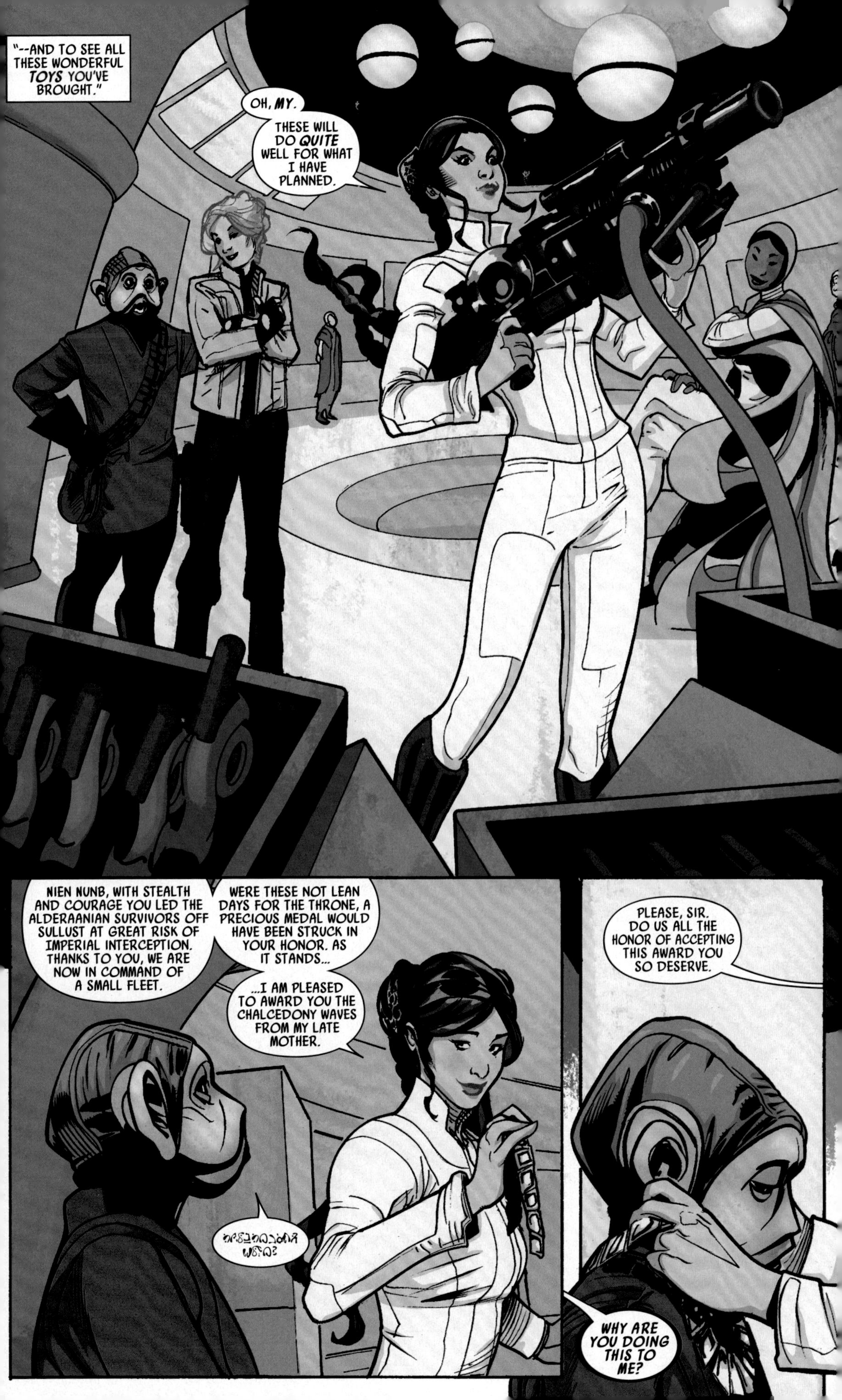
"--AND TO SEE ALL THESE WONDERFUL TOYS YOU'VE BROUGHT."
OH, MY.
THESE WILL DO QUITE WELL FOR WHAT I HAVE PLANNED.
NIEN NUNB, WITH STEALTH AND COURAGE YOU LED THE ALDERAANIAN SURVIVORS OFF SULLUST AT GREAT RISK OF IMPERIAL INTERCEPTION. THANKS TO YOU, WE ARE NOW IN COMMAND OF A SMALL FLEET.
WERE THESE NOT LEAN DAYS FOR THE THRONE, A PRECIOUS MEDAL WOULD HAVE BEEN STRUCK IN YOUR HONOR. AS IT STANDS...
...I AM PLEASED TO AWARD YOU THE CHALCEDONY WAVES FROM MY LATE MOTHER.
PLEASE, SIR. DO US ALL THE HONOR OF ACCEPTING THIS AWARD YOU SO DESERVE.
WHY ARE YOU DOING THIS TO ME?

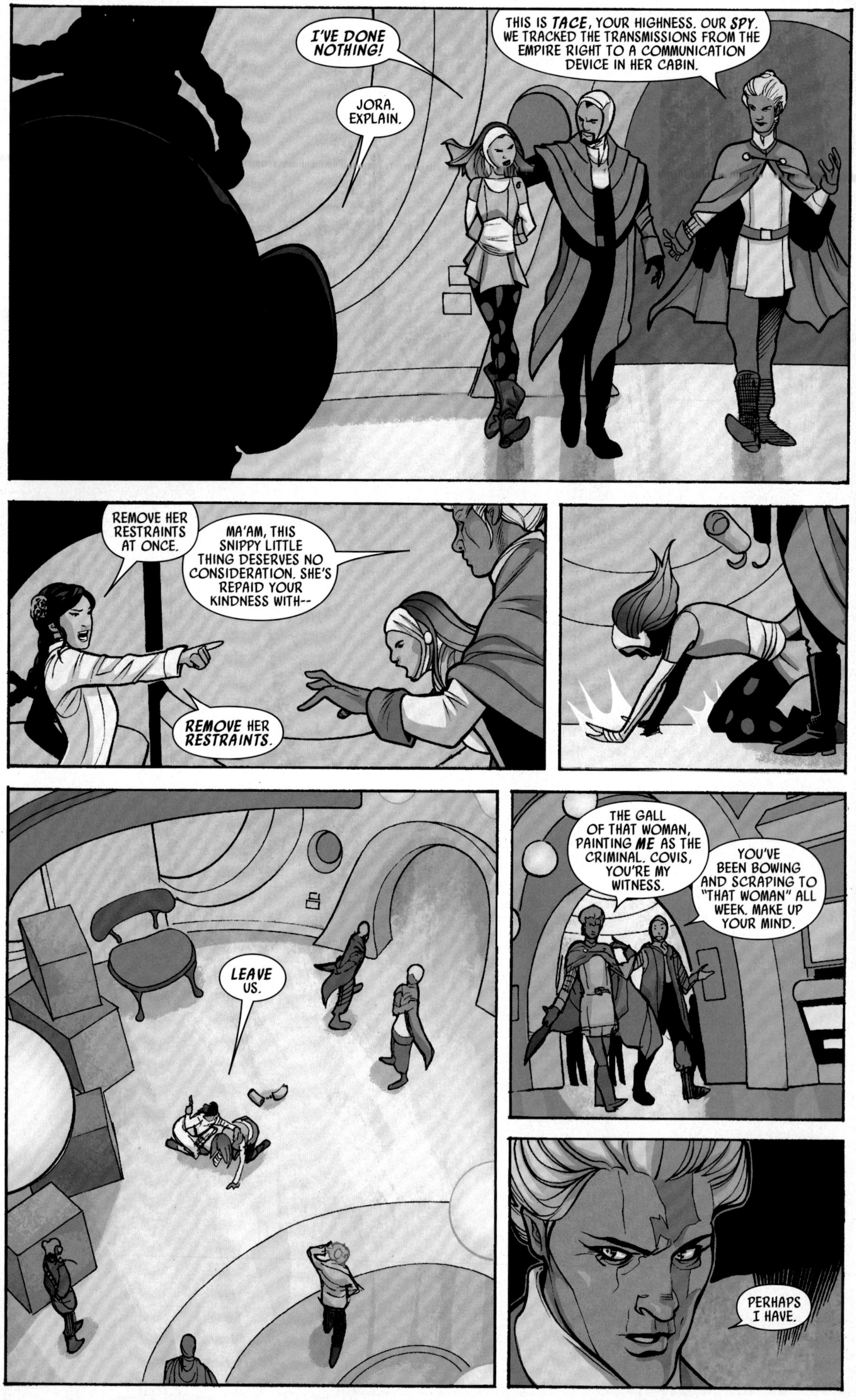

I'VE DONE NOTHING!
JORA. EXPLAIN.
THIS IS TACE, YOUR HIGHNESS. OUR SPY. WE TRACKED THE TRANSMISSIONS FROM THE EMPIRE RIGHT TO A COMMUNICATION DEVICE IN HER CABIN.
REMOVE HER RESTRAINTS AT ONCE.
MA'AM, THIS SNIPPY LITTLE THING DESERVES NO CONSIDERATION. SHE'S REPAID YOUR KINDNESS WITH--
REMOVE HER RESTRAINTS.
LEAVE US.
THE GALL OF THAT WOMAN, PAINTING ME AS THE CRIMINAL. COVIS, YOU'RE MY WITNESS.
YOU'VE BEEN BOWING AND SCRAPING TO "THAT WOMAN" ALL WEEK. MAKE UP YOUR MIND.
PERHAPS I HAVE.

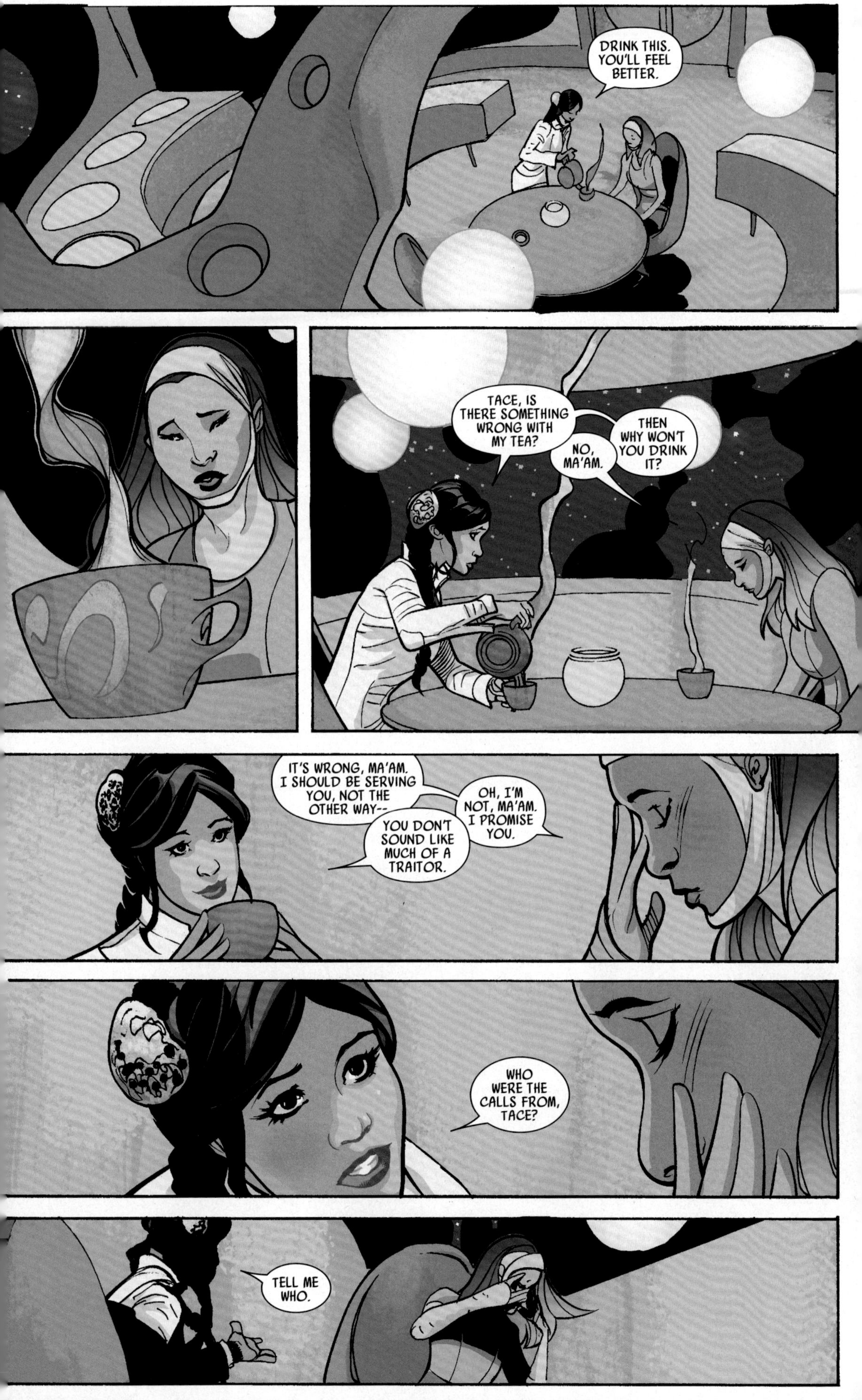
DRINK THIS. YOU'LL FEEL BETTER.
TACE, IS THERE SOMETHING WRONG WITH MY TEA?
NO, MA'AM.
THEN WHY WON'T YOU DRINK IT?
IT'S WRONG, MA'AM. I SHOULD BE SERVING YOU, NOT THE OTHER WAY--
YOU DON'T SOUND LIKE MUCH OF A TRAITOR.
OH, I'M NOT, MA'AM. I PROMISE YOU.
WHO WERE THE CALLS FROM, TACE?
TELL ME WHO.

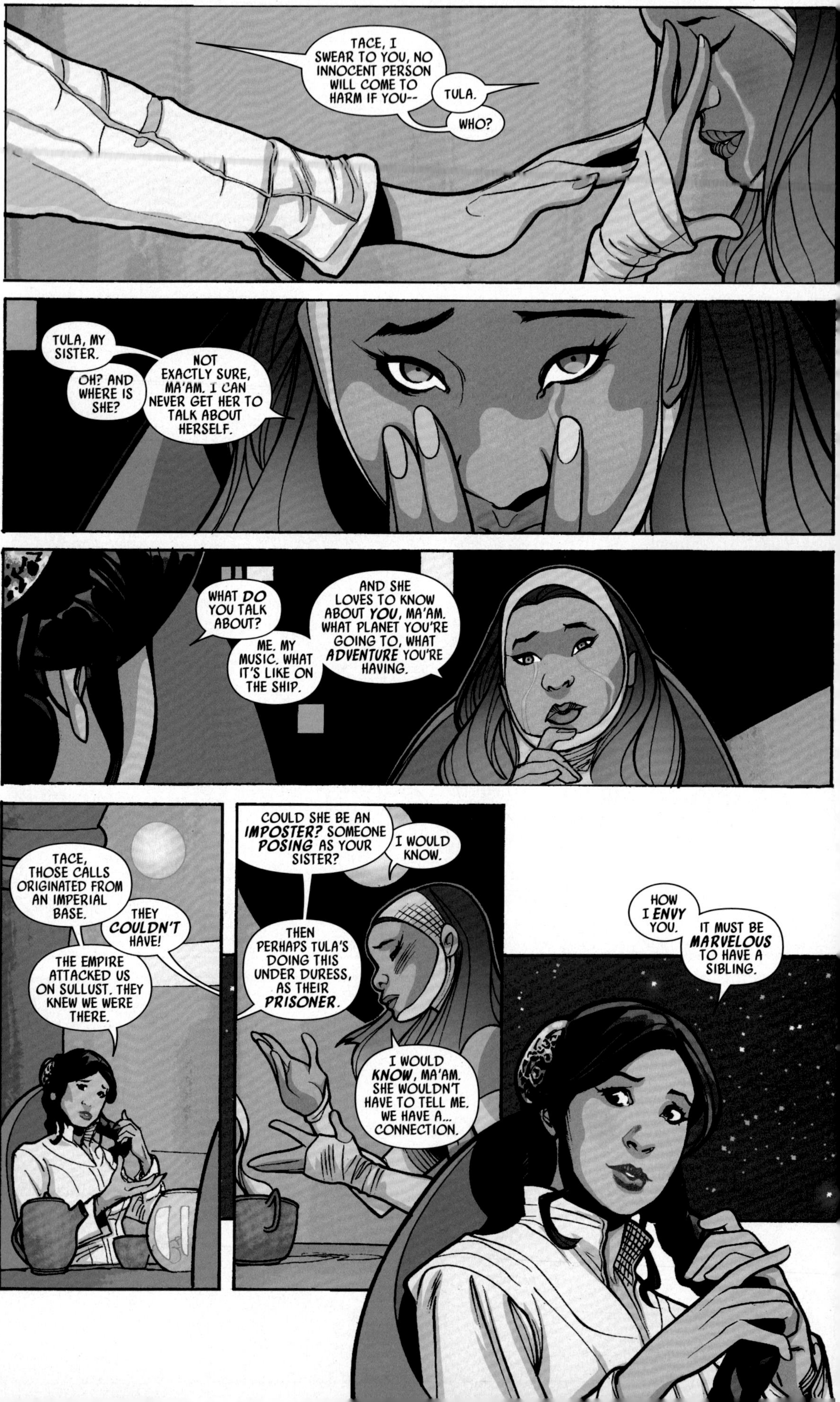

TACE, I SWEAR TO YOU, NO INNOCENT PERSON WILL COME TO HARM IF YOU--
TULA.
WHO?
TULA, MY SISTER.
OH? AND WHERE IS SHE?
NOT EXACTLY SURE, MA'AM. I CAN NEVER GET HER TO TALK ABOUT HERSELF.
WHAT DO YOU TALK ABOUT?
ME. MY MUSIC. WHAT IT'S LIKE ON THE SHIP.
AND SHE LOVES TO KNOW ABOUT YOU, MA'AM. WHAT PLANET YOU'RE GOING TO, WHAT ADVENTURE YOU'RE HAVING.
TACE, THOSE CALLS ORIGINATED FROM AN IMPERIAL BASE.
THEY COULDN'T HAVE!
THE EMPIRE ATTACKED US ON SULLUST. THEY KNEW WE WERE THERE.
COULD SHE BE AN IMPOSTER? SOMEONE POSING AS YOUR SISTER?
I WOULD KNOW.
THEN PERHAPS TULA'S DOING THIS UNDER DURESS, AS THEIR PRISONER.
I WOULD KNOW, MA'AM. SHE WOULDN'T HAVE TO TELL ME. WE HAVE A... CONNECTION.
HOW I ENVY YOU.
IT MUST BE MARVELOUS TO HAVE A SIBLING.

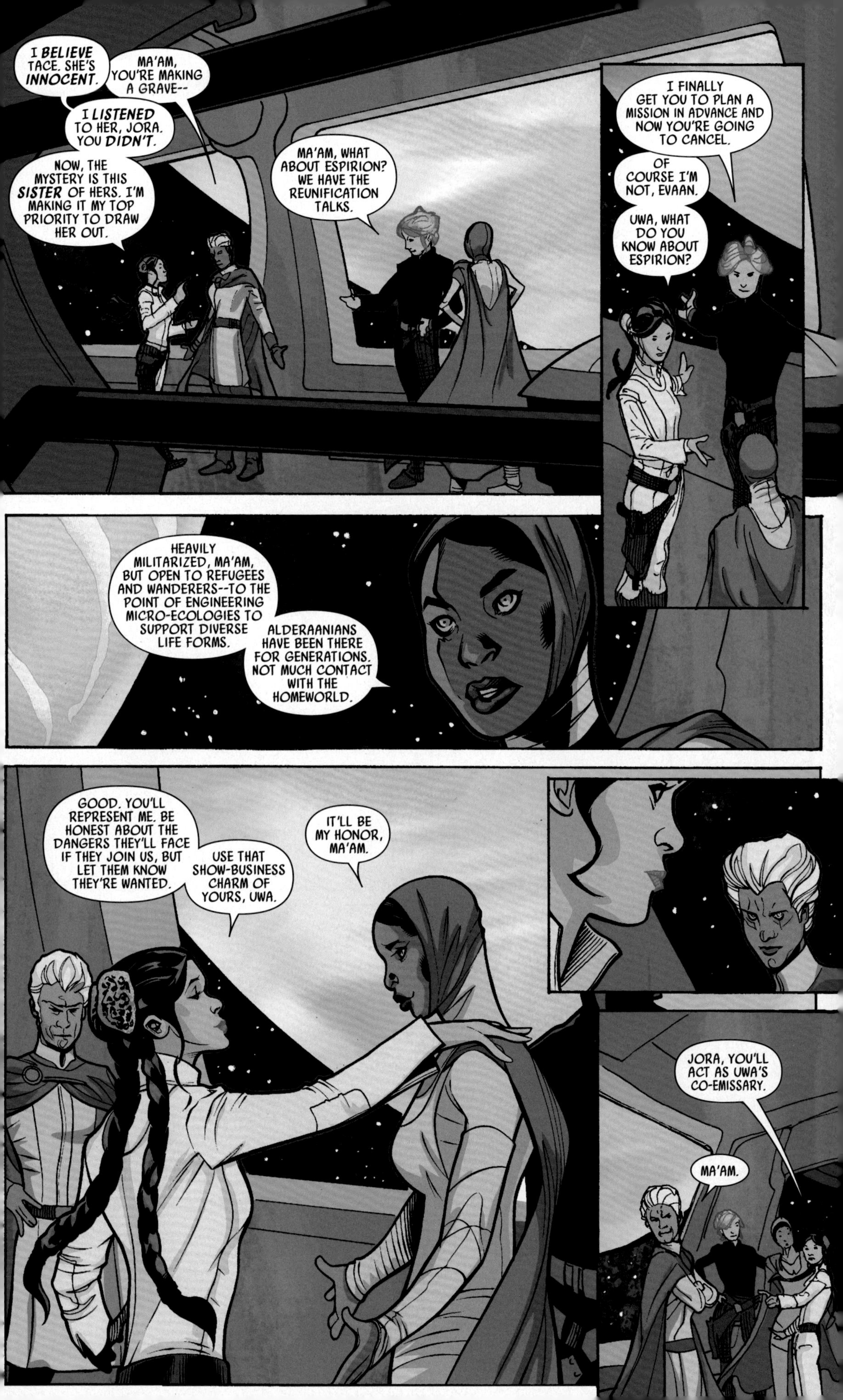
I BELIEVE TACE. SHE'S INNOCENT.
MA'AM, YOU'RE MAKING A GRAVE--
I LISTENED TO HER, JORA. YOU DIDN'T.
NOW, THE MYSTERY IS THIS SISTER OF HERS. I'M MAKING IT MY TOP PRIORITY TO DRAW HER OUT.
MA'AM, WHAT ABOUT ESPIRION? WE HAVE THE REUNIFICATION TALKS.
I FINALLY GET YOU TO PLAN A MISSION IN ADVANCE AND NOW YOU'RE GOING TO CANCEL.
OF COURSE I'M NOT, EVAAN.
UWA, WHAT DO YOU KNOW ABOUT ESPIRION?
HEAVILY MILITARIZED, MA'AM, BUT OPEN TO REFUGEES AND WANDERERS--TO THE POINT OF ENGINEERING MICRO-ECOLOGIES TO SUPPORT DIVERSE LIFE FORMS.
ALDERAANIANS HAVE BEEN THERE FOR GENERATIONS. NOT MUCH CONTACT WITH THE HOMEWORLD.
GOOD. YOU'LL REPRESENT ME. BE HONEST ABOUT THE DANGERS THEY'LL FACE IF THEY JOIN US, BUT LET THEM KNOW THEY'RE WANTED.
USE THAT SHOW-BUSINESS CHARM OF YOURS, UWA.
IT'LL BE MY HONOR, MA'AM.
JORA, YOU'LL ACT AS UWA'S CO-EMISSARY.
MA'AM.

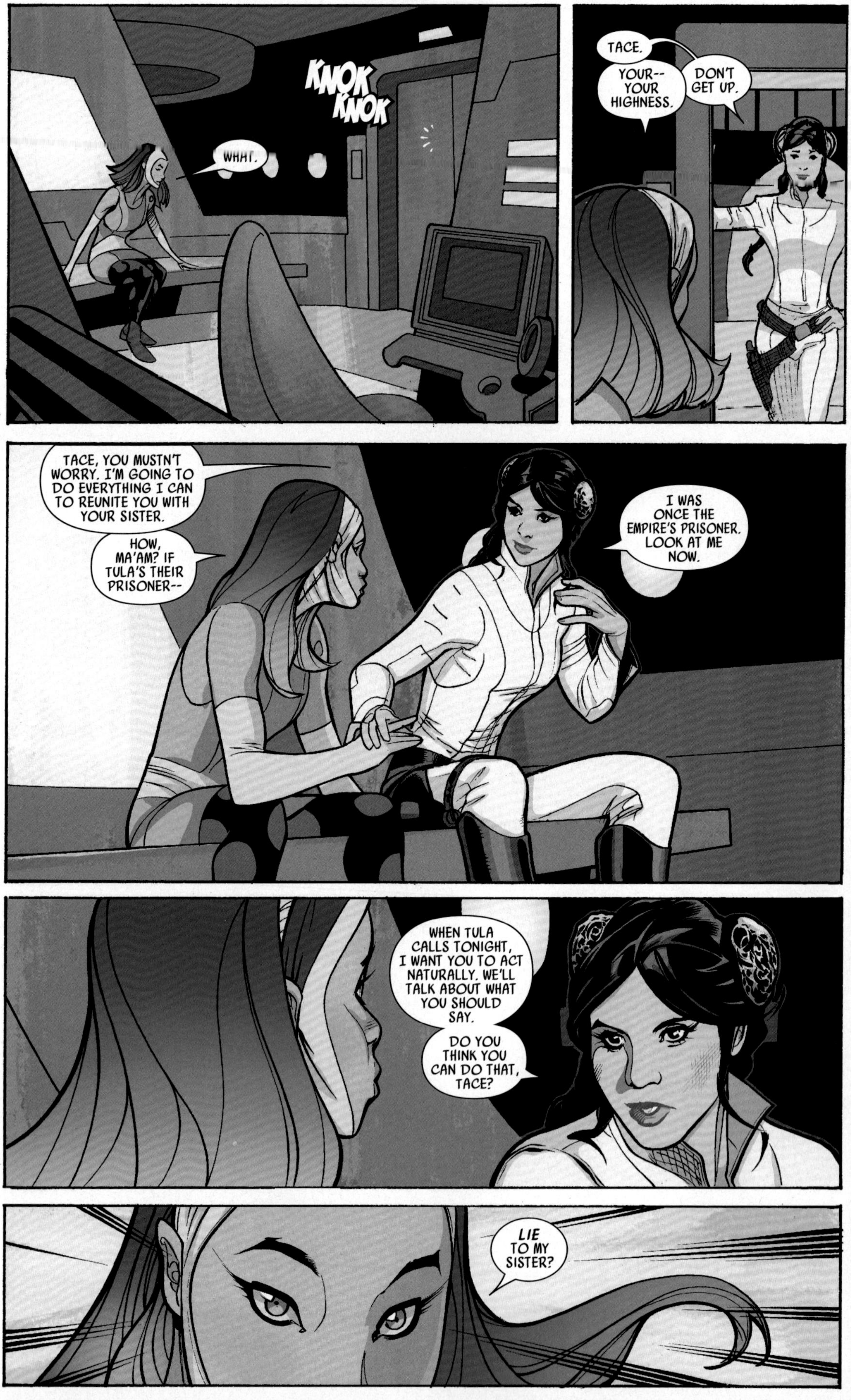
KNOK KNOK
WHAT.
TACE.
YOUR-- YOUR HIGHNESS.
DON'T GET UP.
TACE, YOU MUSTN'T WORRY. I'M GOING TO DO EVERYTHING I CAN TO REUNITE YOU WITH YOUR SISTER.
HOW, MA'AM? IF TULA'S THEIR PRISONER--
I WAS ONCE THE EMPIRE'S PRISONER. LOOK AT ME NOW.
WHEN TULA CALLS TONIGHT, I WANT YOU TO ACT NATURALLY. WE'LL TALK ABOUT WHAT YOU SHOULD SAY.
DO YOU THINK YOU CAN DO THAT, TACE?
LIE TO MY SISTER?

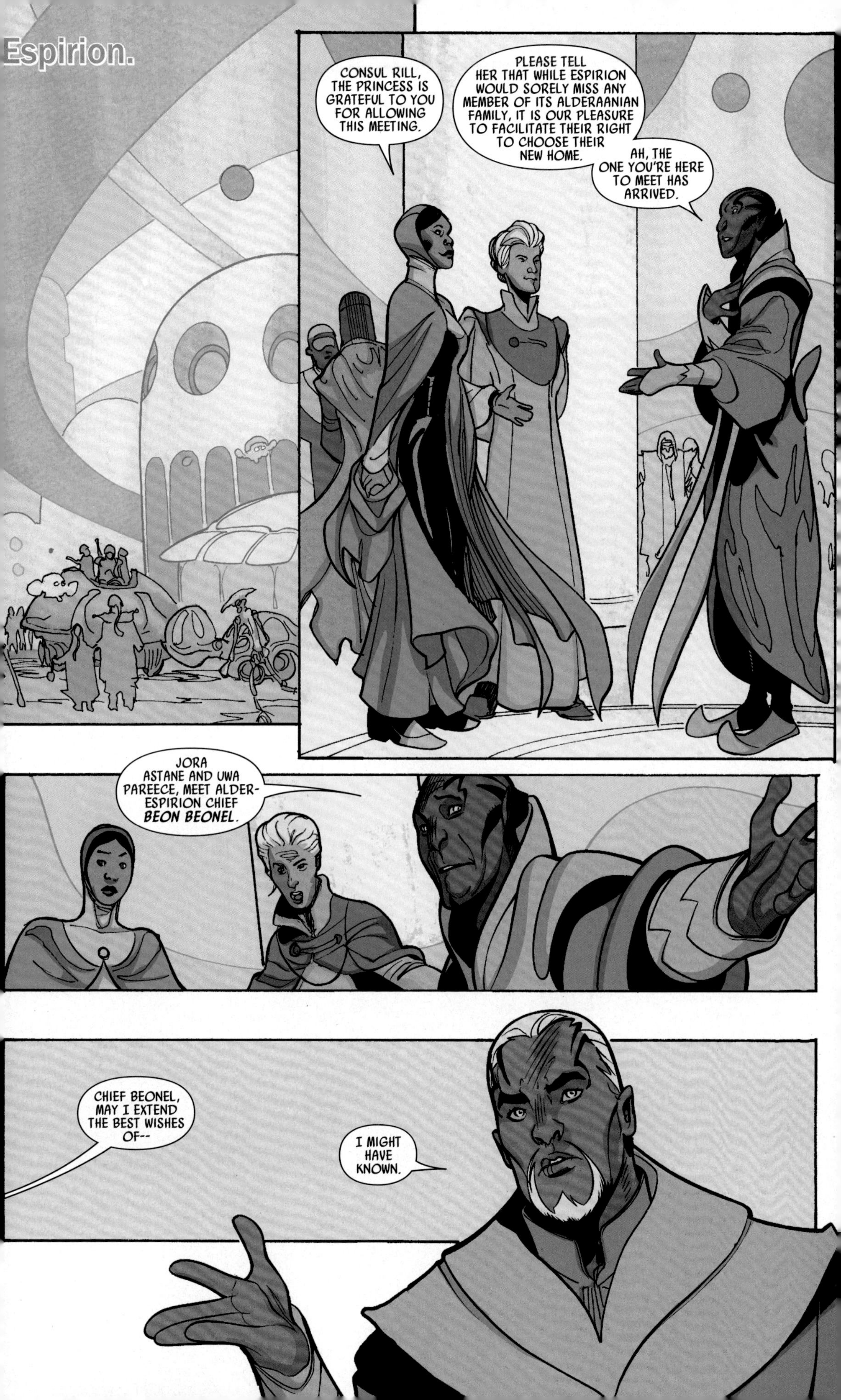
Espirion.
CONSUL RILL, THE PRINCESS IS GRATEFUL TO YOU FOR ALLOWING THIS MEETING.
PLEASE TELL HER THAT WHILE ESPIRION WOULD SORELY MISS ANY MEMBER OF ITS ALDERAANIAN FAMILY, IT IS OUR PLEASURE TO FACILITATE THEIR RIGHT TO CHOOSE THEIR NEW HOME.
AH, THE ONE YOU'RE HERE TO MEET HAS ARRIVED.
JORA ASTANE AND UWA PAREECE, MEET ALDER-ESPIRION CHIEF *BEON BEONEL*.
CHIEF BEONEL, MAY I EXTEND THE BEST WISHES OF--
I MIGHT HAVE KNOWN.

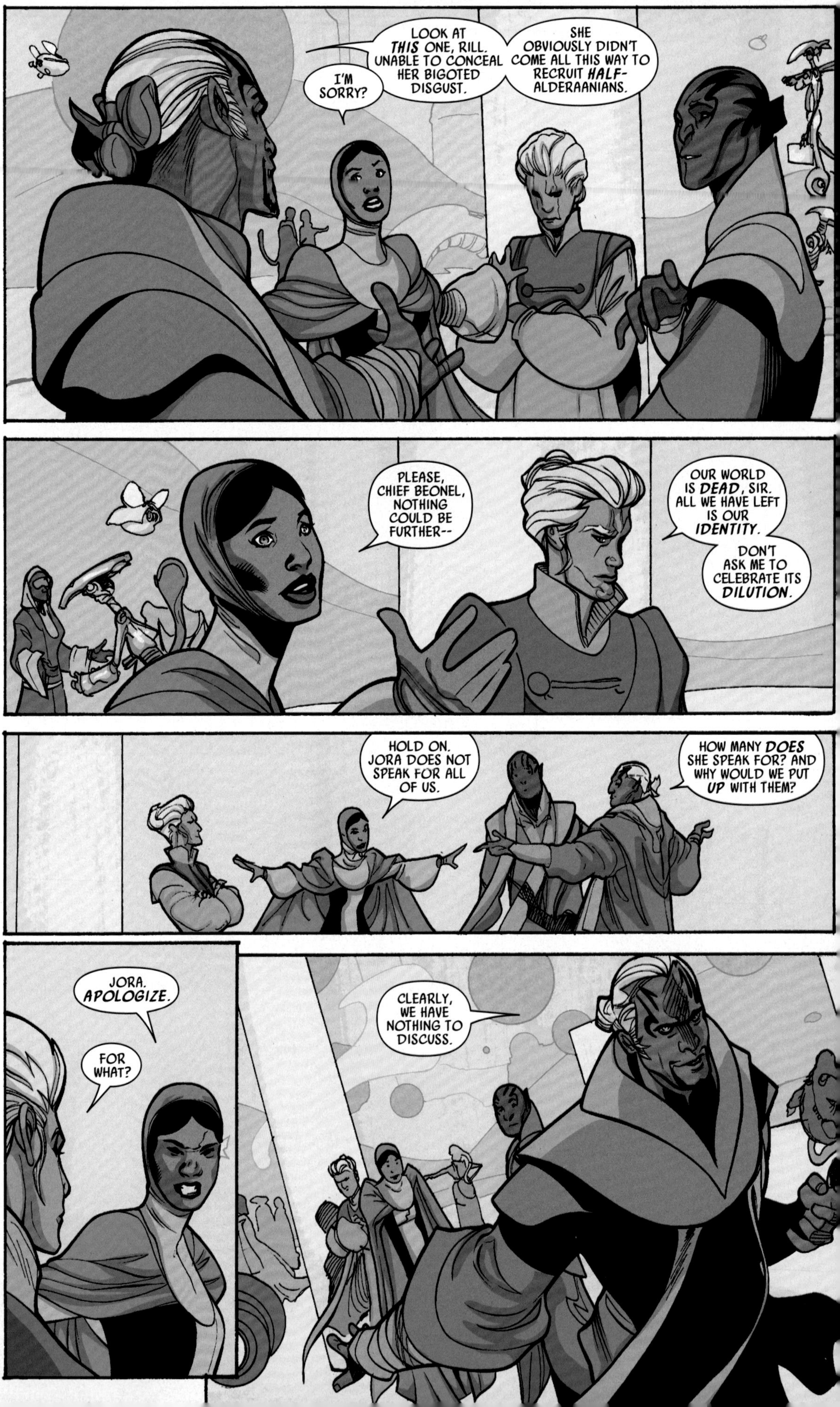

LOOK AT THIS ONE, RILL. UNABLE TO CONCEAL HER BIGOTED DISGUST.
I'M SORRY?
SHE OBVIOUSLY DIDN'T COME ALL THIS WAY TO RECRUIT HALF-ALDERAANIANS.
PLEASE, CHIEF BEONEL, NOTHING COULD BE FURTHER--
OUR WORLD IS DEAD, SIR. ALL WE HAVE LEFT IS OUR IDENTITY.
DON'T ASK ME TO CELEBRATE ITS DILUTION.
HOLD ON. JORA DOES NOT SPEAK FOR ALL OF US.
HOW MANY DOES SHE SPEAK FOR? AND WHY WOULD WE PUT UP WITH THEM?
JORA. APOLOGIZE.
FOR WHAT?
CLEARLY, WE HAVE NOTHING TO DISCUSS.

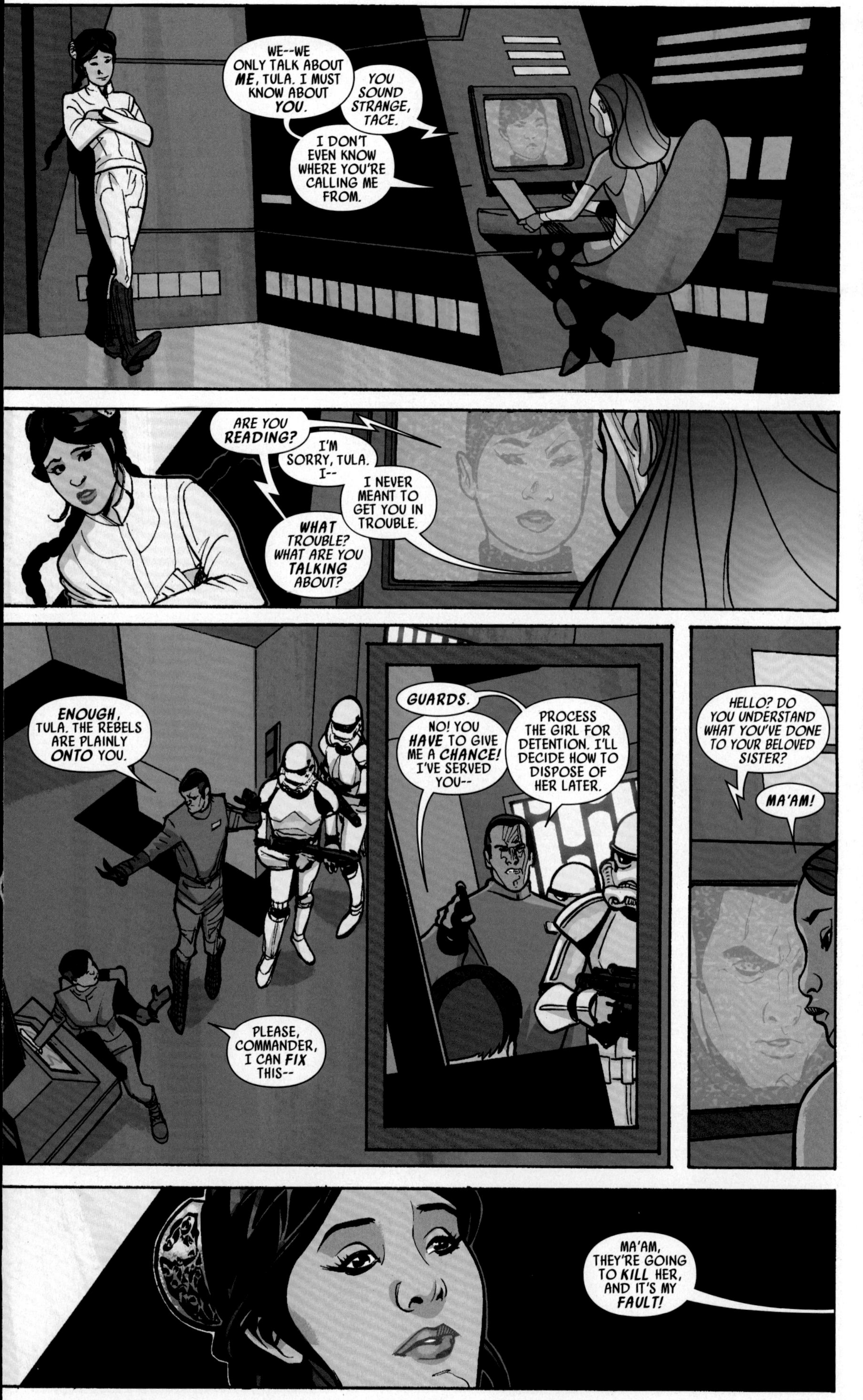
WE--WE ONLY TALK ABOUT ME, TULA. I MUST KNOW ABOUT YOU.
YOU SOUND STRANGE, TACE.
I DON'T EVEN KNOW WHERE YOU'RE CALLING ME FROM.
ARE YOU READING?
I'M SORRY, TULA. I--
I NEVER MEANT TO GET YOU IN TROUBLE.
WHAT TROUBLE? WHAT ARE YOU TALKING ABOUT?
ENOUGH, TULA. THE REBELS ARE PLAINLY ONTO YOU.
PLEASE, COMMANDER, I CAN FIX THIS--
GUARDS.
NO! YOU HAVE TO GIVE ME A CHANCE! I'VE SERVED YOU--
PROCESS THE GIRL FOR DETENTION. I'LL DECIDE HOW TO DISPOSE OF HER LATER.
HELLO? DO YOU UNDERSTAND WHAT YOU'VE DONE TO YOUR BELOVED SISTER?
MA'AM!
MA'AM, THEY'RE GOING TO KILL HER, AND IT'S MY FAULT!

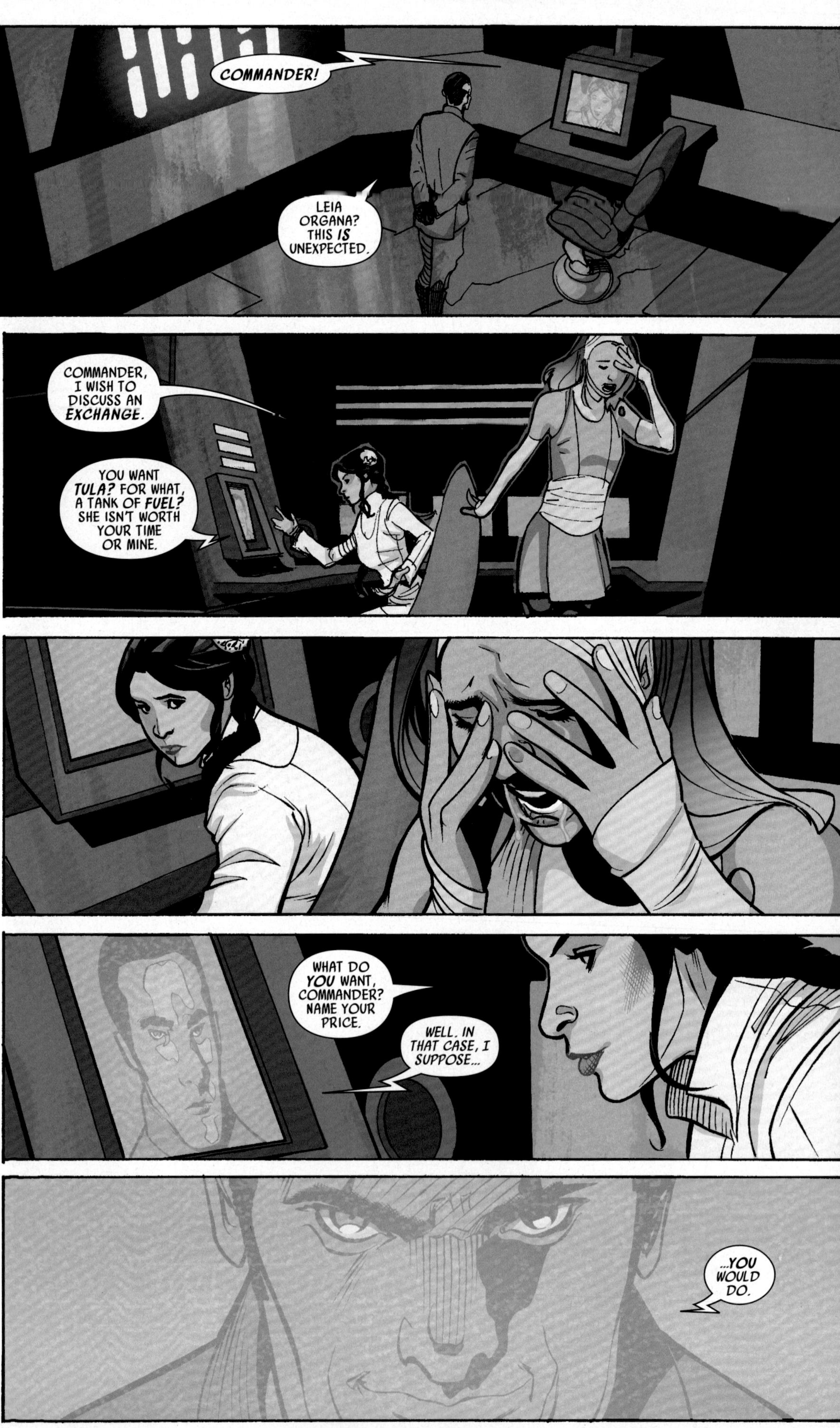
COMMANDER!
LEIA ORGANA? THIS IS UNEXPECTED.
COMMANDER, I WISH TO DISCUSS AN EXCHANGE.
YOU WANT TULA? FOR WHAT, A TANK OF FUEL? SHE ISN'T WORTH YOUR TIME OR MINE.
WHAT DO YOU WANT, COMMANDER? NAME YOUR PRICE.
WELL. IN THAT CASE, I SUPPOSE...
...YOU WOULD DO.

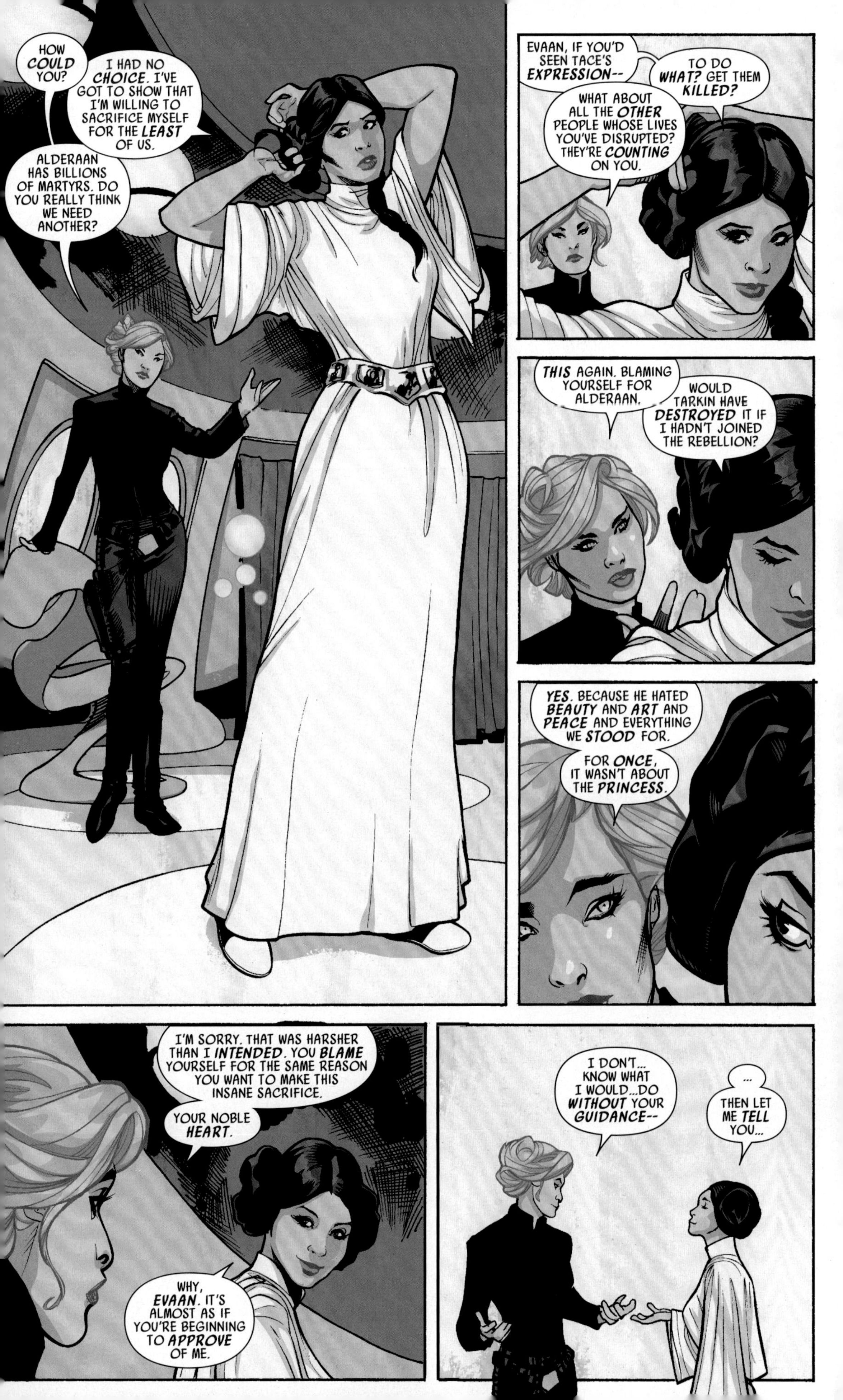

HOW COULD YOU?
I HAD NO CHOICE. I'VE GOT TO SHOW THAT I'M WILLING TO SACRIFICE MYSELF FOR THE LEAST OF US.
ALDERAAN HAS BILLIONS OF MARTYRS. DO YOU REALLY THINK WE NEED ANOTHER?
EVAAN, IF YOU'D SEEN TACE'S EXPRESSION--
TO DO WHAT? GET THEM KILLED?
WHAT ABOUT ALL THE OTHER PEOPLE WHOSE LIVES YOU'VE DISRUPTED? THEY'RE COUNTING ON YOU.
THIS AGAIN. BLAMING YOURSELF FOR ALDERAAN.
WOULD TARKIN HAVE DESTROYED IT IF I HADN'T JOINED THE REBELLION?
YES. BECAUSE HE HATED BEAUTY AND ART AND PEACE AND EVERYTHING WE STOOD FOR.
FOR ONCE, IT WASN'T ABOUT THE PRINCESS.
I'M SORRY. THAT WAS HARSHER THAN I INTENDED. YOU BLAME YOURSELF FOR THE SAME REASON YOU WANT TO MAKE THIS INSANE SACRIFICE.
YOUR NOBLE HEART.
WHY, EVAAN. IT'S ALMOST AS IF YOU'RE BEGINNING TO APPROVE OF ME.
I DON'T... KNOW WHAT I WOULD...DO WITHOUT YOUR GUIDANCE--
...
THEN LET ME TELL YOU...

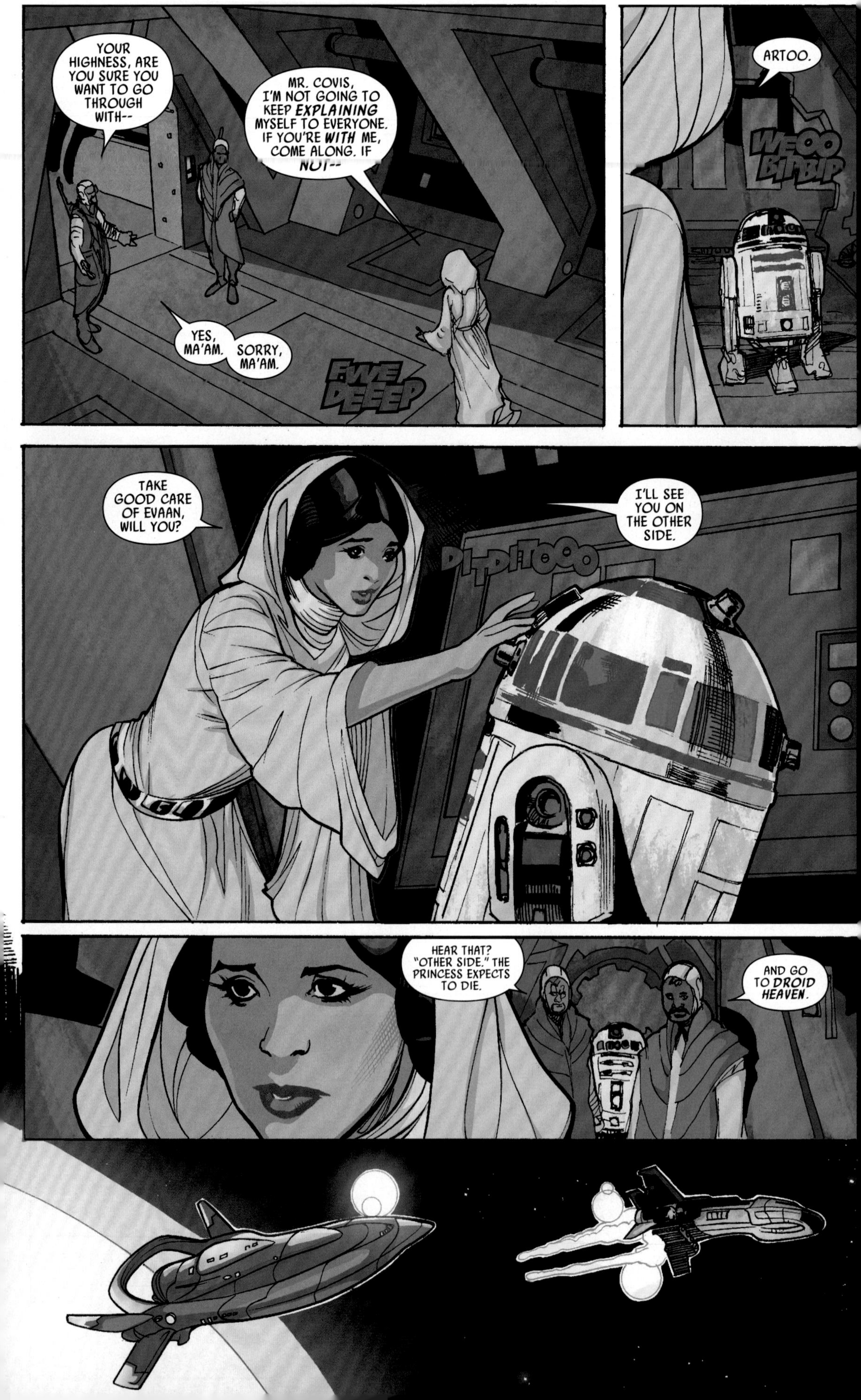

YOUR HIGHNESS, ARE YOU SURE YOU WANT TO GO THROUGH WITH--
MR. COVIS, I'M NOT GOING TO KEEP EXPLAINING MYSELF TO EVERYONE. IF YOU'RE WITH ME, COME ALONG. IF NOT--
YES, MA'AM.
SORRY, MA'AM.
FWE DEEEP
ARTOO.
WEOO BIPBIP
TAKE GOOD CARE OF EVAAN, WILL YOU?
I'LL SEE YOU ON THE OTHER SIDE.
DI-DI-TOOO
HEAR THAT? "OTHER SIDE." THE PRINCESS EXPECTS TO DIE.
AND GO TO DROID HEAVEN.

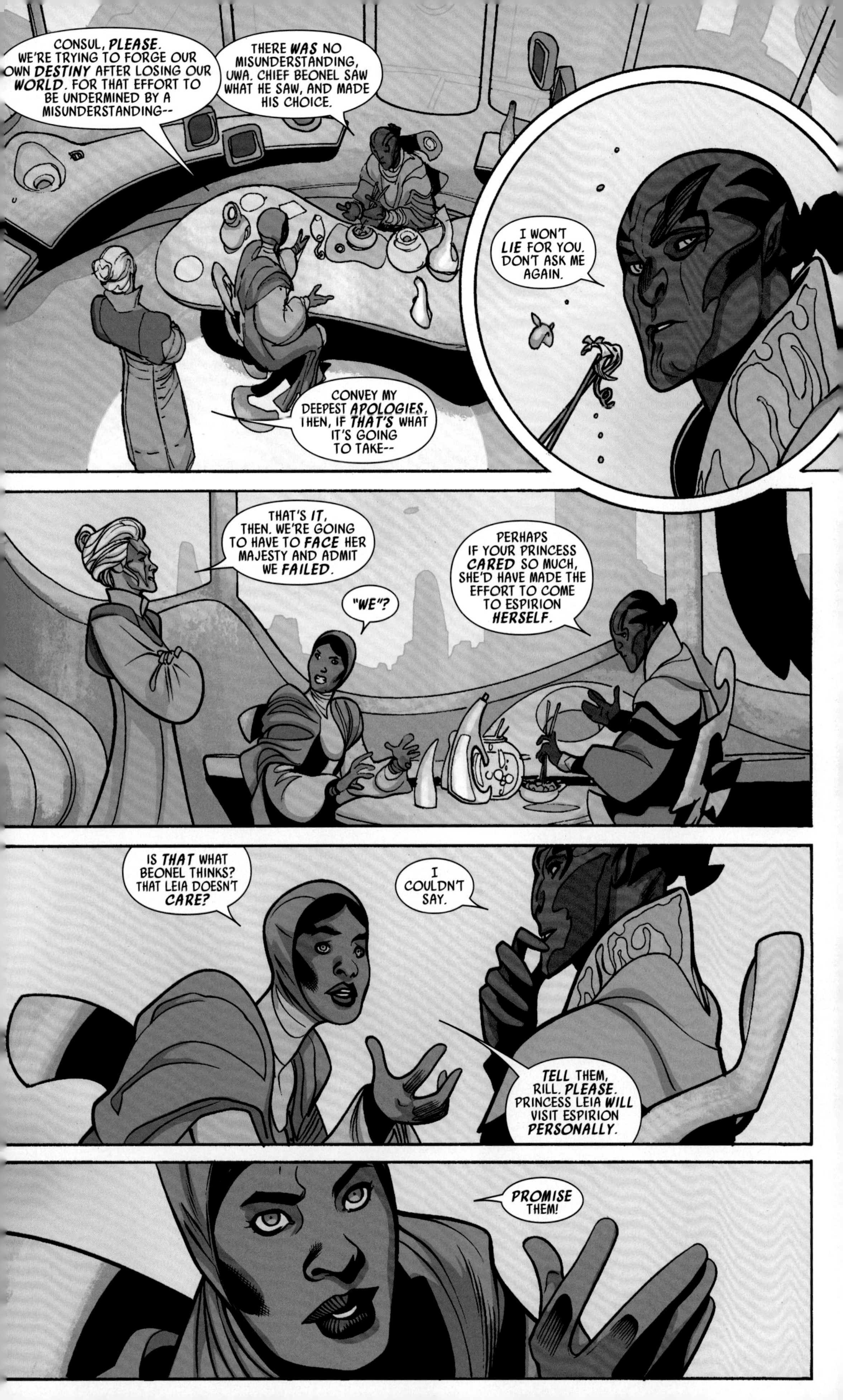
CONSUL, PLEASE. WE'RE TRYING TO FORGE OUR OWN DESTINY AFTER LOSING OUR WORLD. FOR THAT EFFORT TO BE UNDERMINED BY A MISUNDERSTANDING--
THERE WAS NO MISUNDERSTANDING, UWA. CHIEF BEONEL SAW WHAT HE SAW, AND MADE HIS CHOICE.
CONVEY MY DEEPEST APOLOGIES, THEN, IF THAT'S WHAT IT'S GOING TO TAKE--
I WON'T LIE FOR YOU. DON'T ASK ME AGAIN.
THAT'S IT, THEN. WE'RE GOING TO HAVE TO FACE HER MAJESTY AND ADMIT WE FAILED.
"WE"?
PERHAPS IF YOUR PRINCESS CARED SO MUCH, SHE'D HAVE MADE THE EFFORT TO COME TO ESPIRION HERSELF.
IS THAT WHAT BEONEL THINKS? THAT LEIA DOESN'T CARE?
I COULDN'T SAY.
TELL THEM, RILL. PLEASE. PRINCESS LEIA WILL VISIT ESPIRION PERSONALLY.
PROMISE THEM!

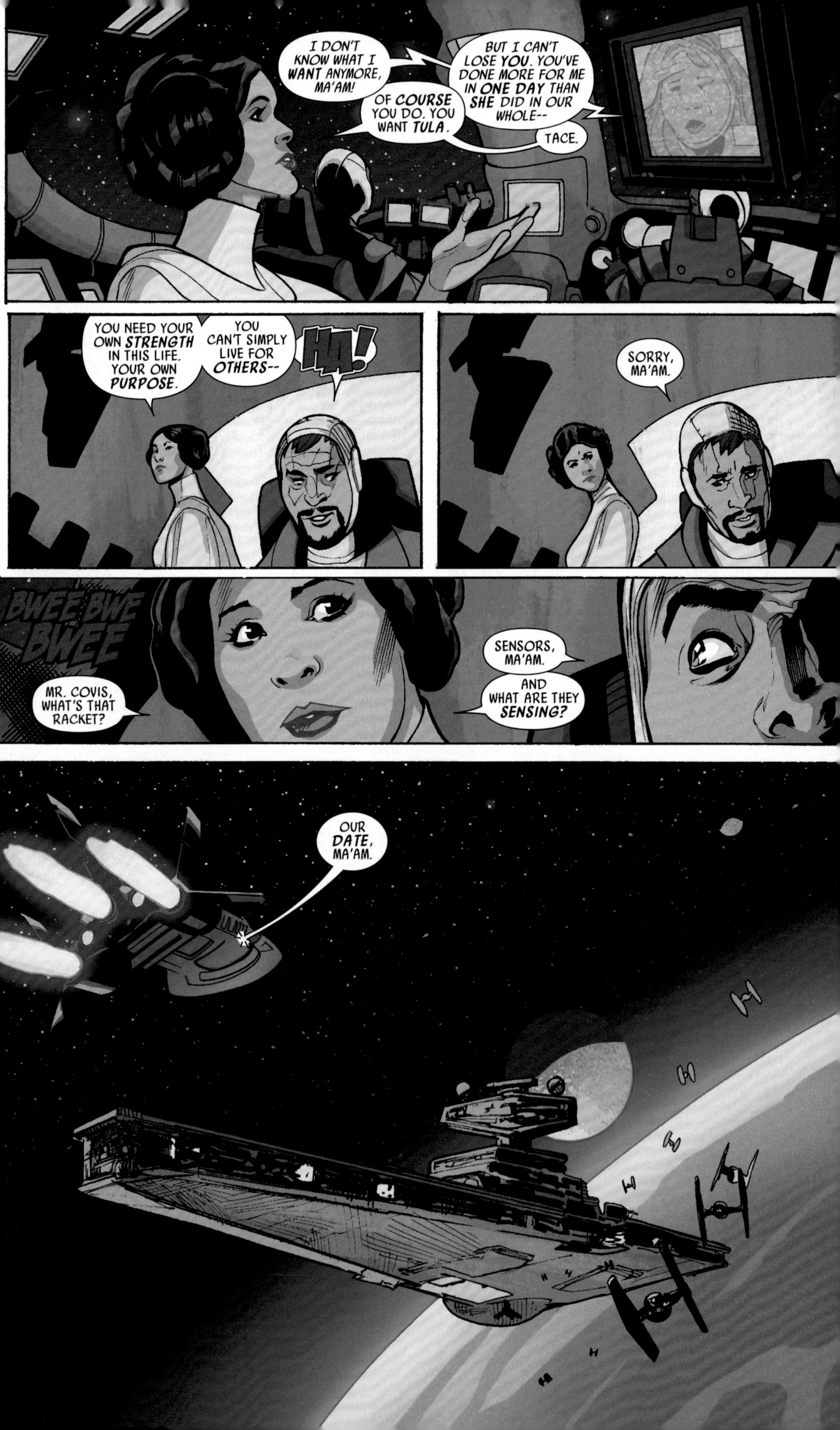
I DON'T KNOW WHAT I WANT ANYMORE, MA'AM!
OF COURSE YOU DO. YOU WANT TULA.
BUT I CAN'T LOSE YOU. YOU'VE DONE MORE FOR ME IN ONE DAY THAN SHE DID IN OUR WHOLE--
TACE.
YOU NEED YOUR OWN STRENGTH IN THIS LIFE. YOUR OWN PURPOSE.
YOU CAN'T SIMPLY LIVE FOR OTHERS--
HA!
SORRY, MA'AM.
BWEE BWE BWEE
MR. COVIS, WHAT'S THAT RACKET?
SENSORS, MA'AM.
AND WHAT ARE THEY SENSING?
OUR DATE, MA'AM.

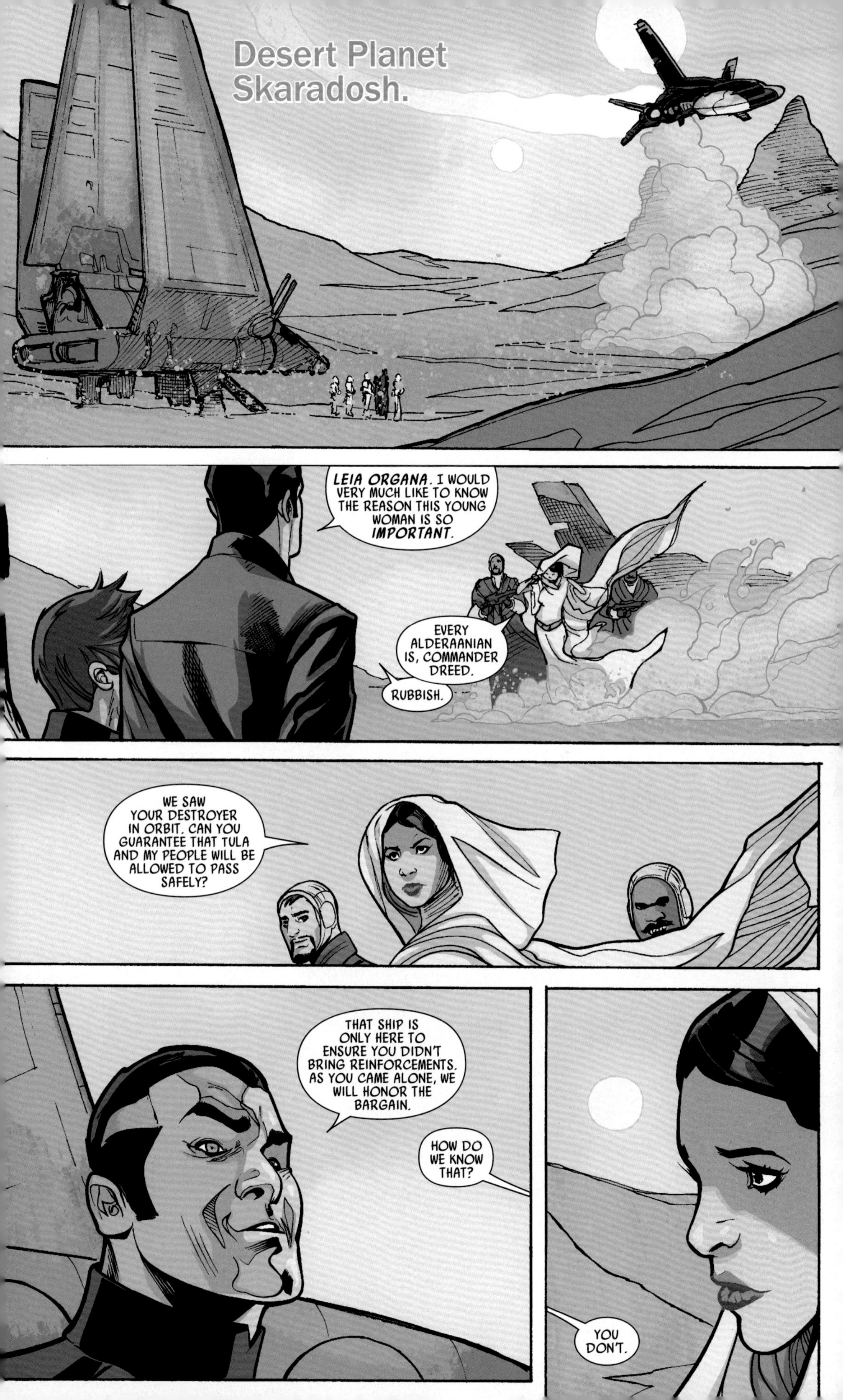
Desert Planet Skaradosh.
LEIA ORGANA. I WOULD VERY MUCH LIKE TO KNOW THE REASON THIS YOUNG WOMAN IS SO IMPORTANT.
EVERY ALDERAANIAN IS, COMMANDER DREED.
RUBBISH.
WE SAW YOUR DESTROYER IN ORBIT. CAN YOU GUARANTEE THAT TULA AND MY PEOPLE WILL BE ALLOWED TO PASS SAFELY?
THAT SHIP IS ONLY HERE TO ENSURE YOU DIDN'T BRING REINFORCEMENTS. AS YOU CAME ALONE, WE WILL HONOR THE BARGAIN.
HOW DO WE KNOW THAT?
YOU DON'T.

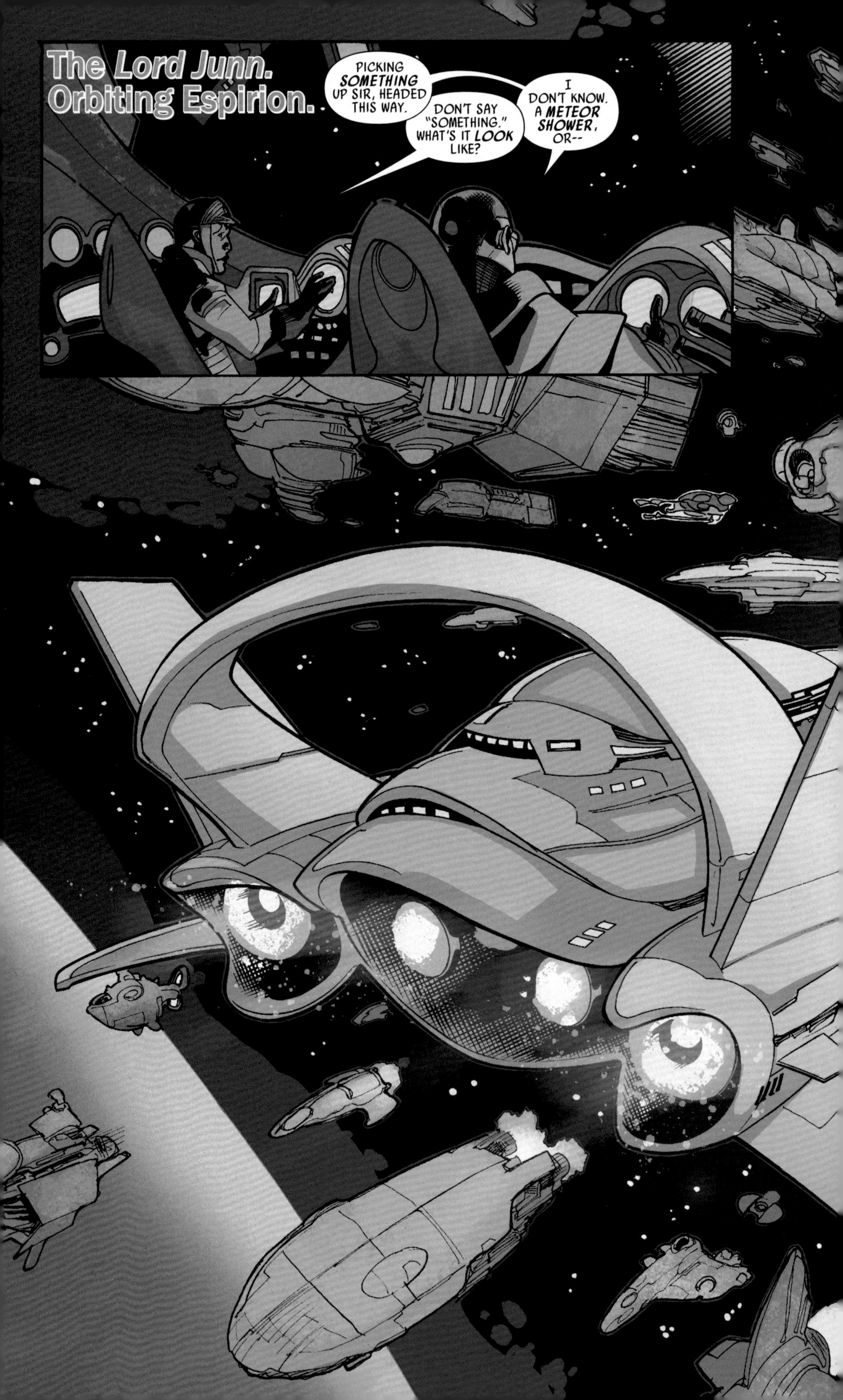
The Lord Junn. Orbiting Espirion.
PICKING SOMETHING UP SIR, HEADED THIS WAY.
DON'T SAY "SOMETHING." WHAT'S IT LOOK LIKE?
I DON'T KNOW. A METEOR SHOWER, OR--

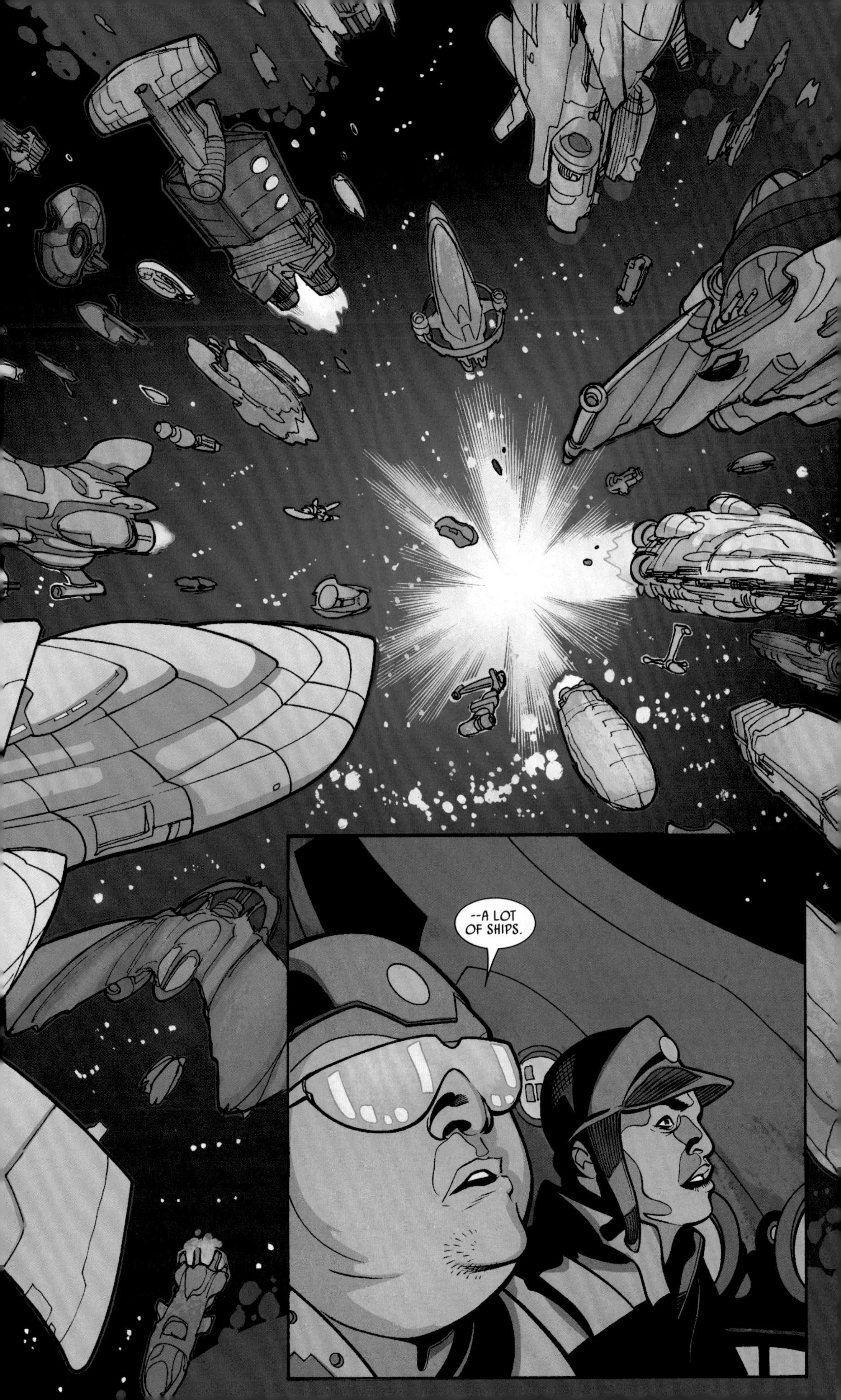
--A LOT OF SHIPS.

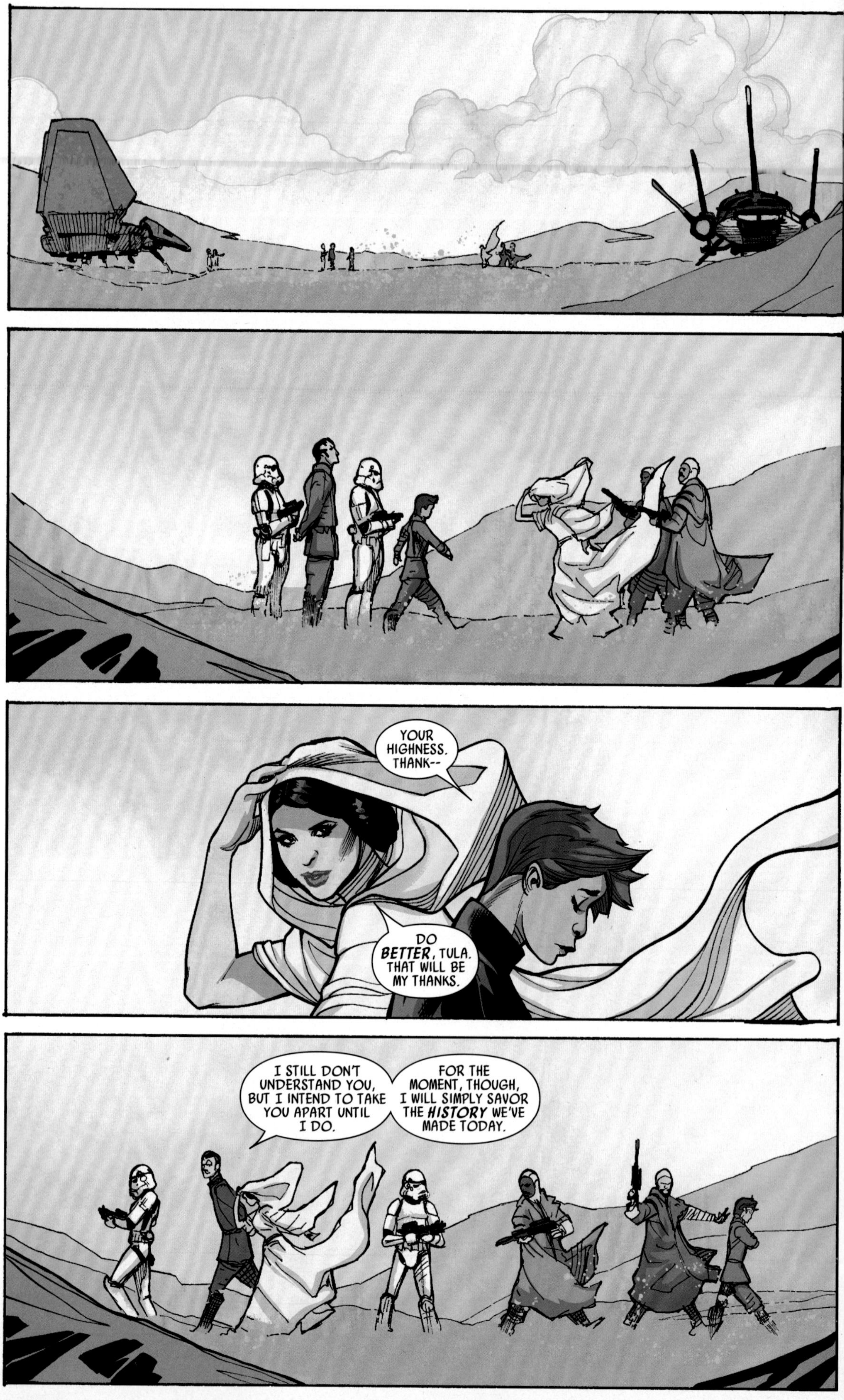
YOUR HIGHNESS. THANK--
DO BETTER, TULA. THAT WILL BE MY THANKS.
I STILL DON'T UNDERSTAND YOU, BUT I INTEND TO TAKE YOU APART UNTIL I DO.
FOR THE MOMENT, THOUGH, I WILL SIMPLY SAVOR THE HISTORY WE'VE MADE TODAY.

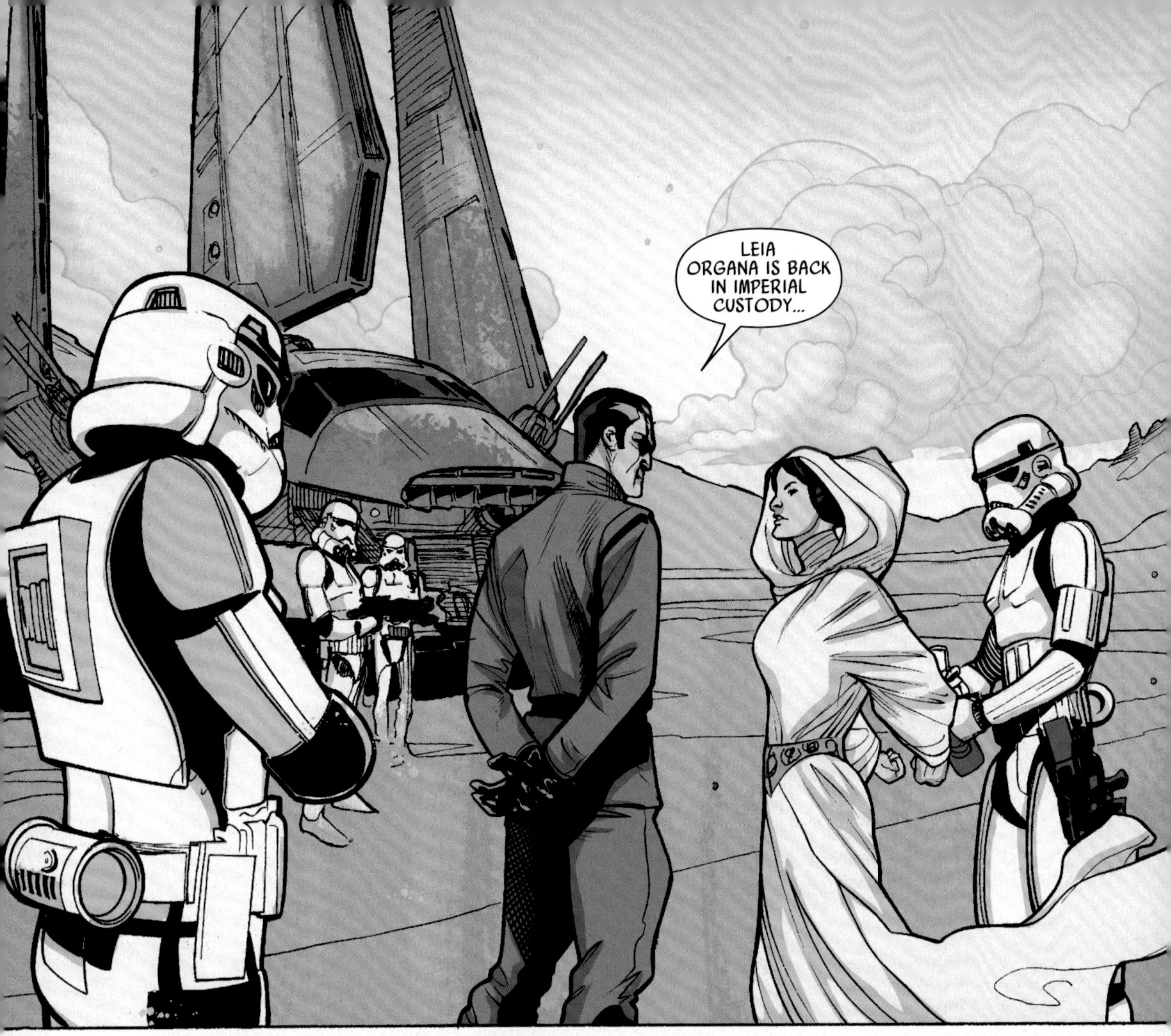
LEIA ORGANA IS BACK IN IMPERIAL CUSTODY...

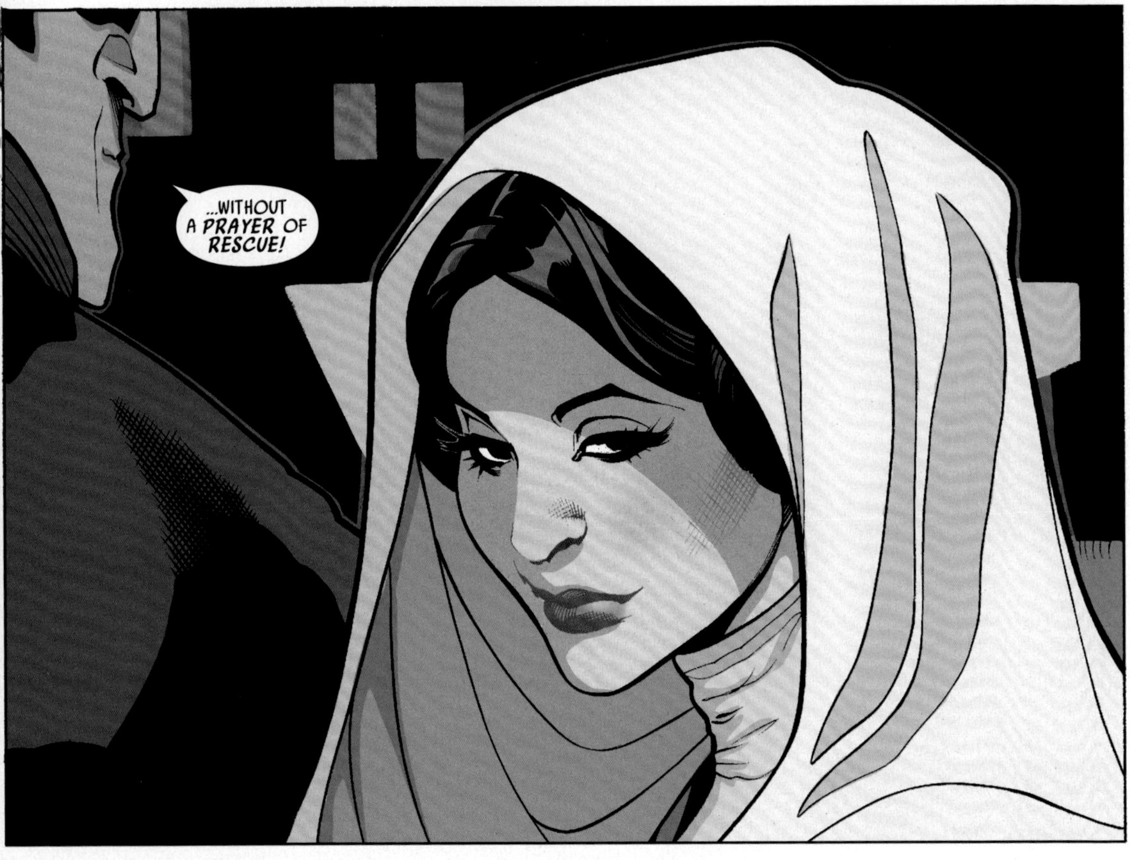
...WITHOUT A PRAYER OF RESCUE!

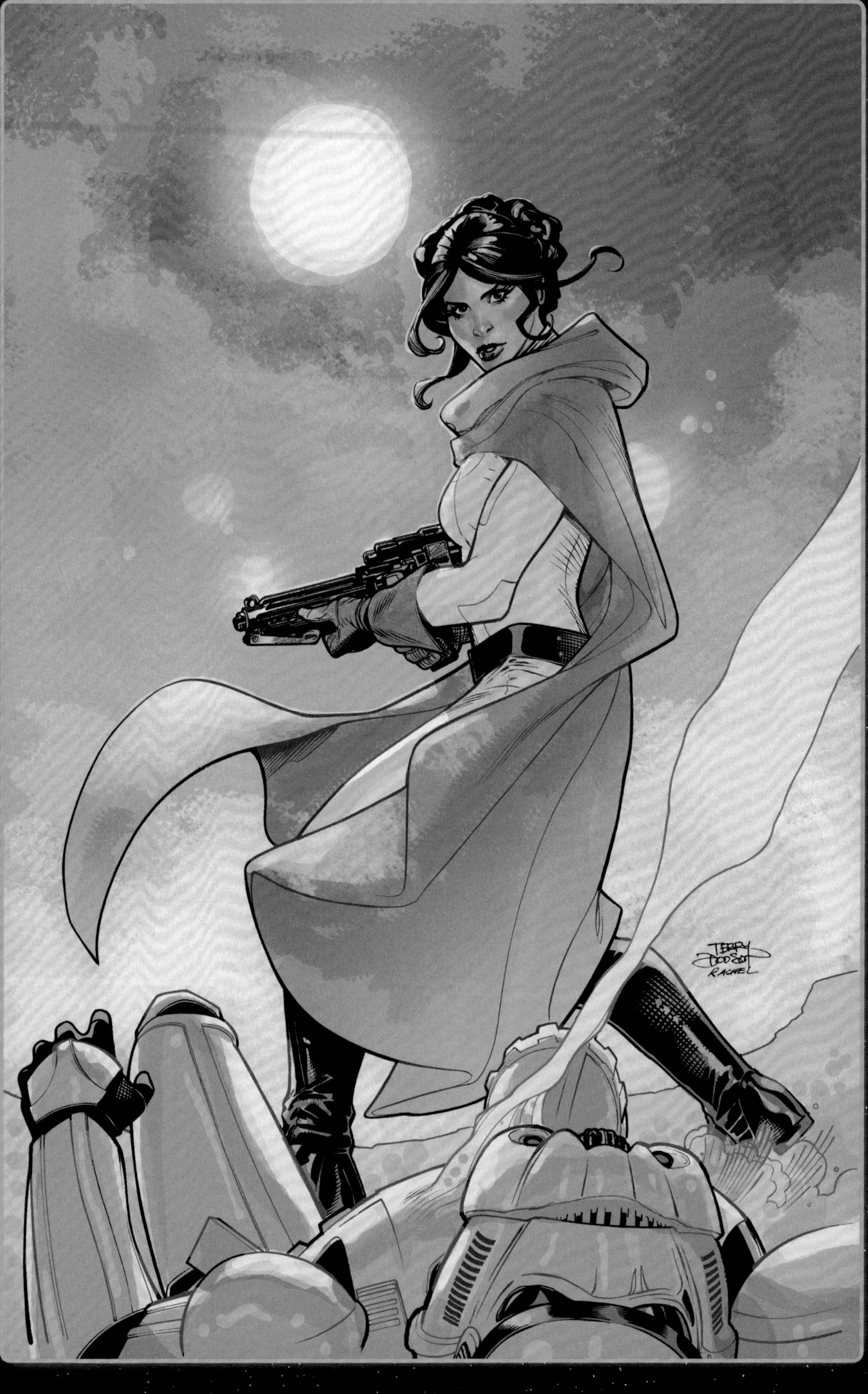
TERRY DODSON
RACHEL

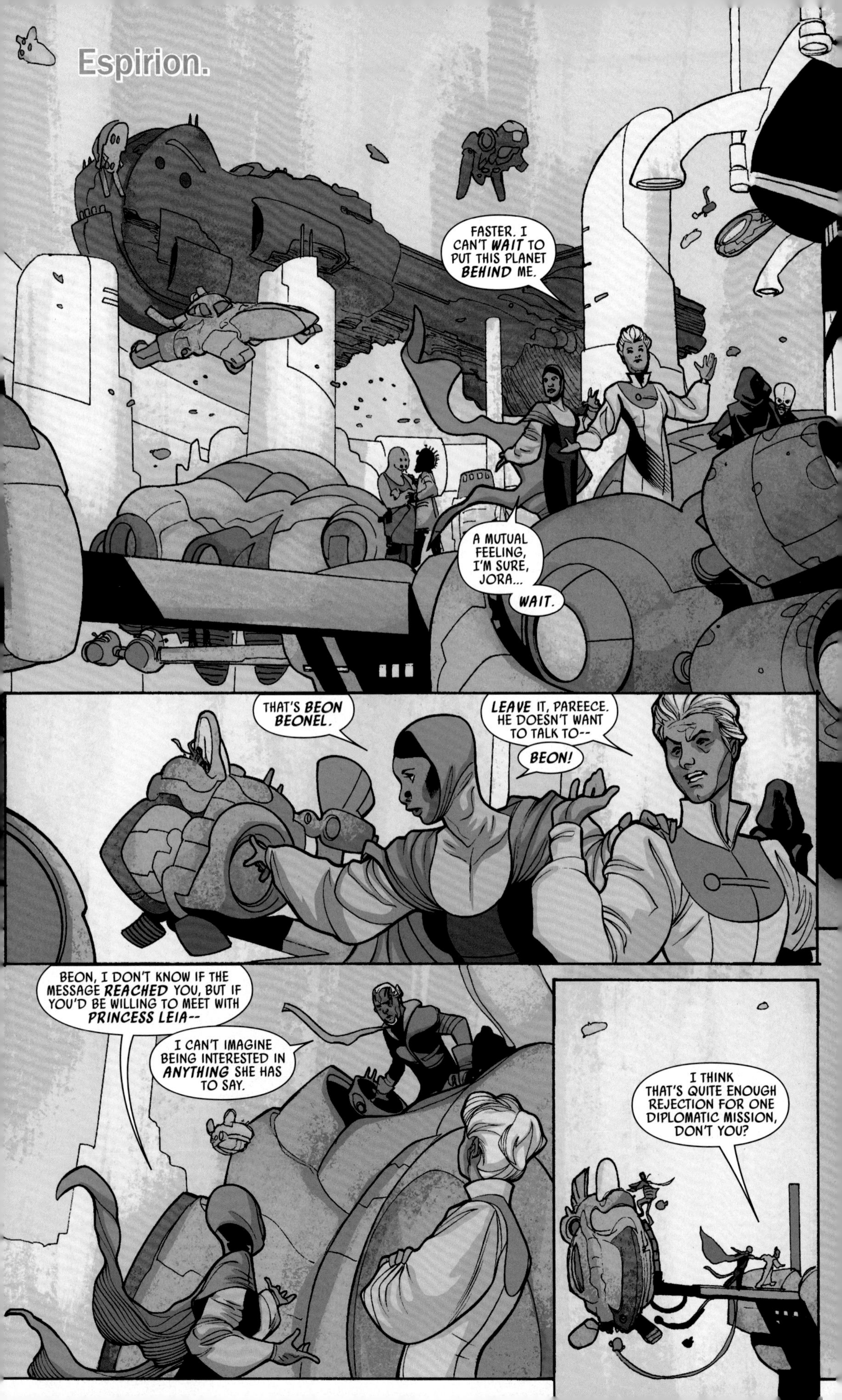
Espirion.
FASTER. I CAN'T WAIT TO PUT THIS PLANET BEHIND ME.
A MUTUAL FEELING, I'M SURE, JORA...
WAIT.
THAT'S BEON BEONEL.
LEAVE IT, PAREECE. HE DOESN'T WANT TO TALK TO--
BEON!
BEON, I DON'T KNOW IF THE MESSAGE REACHED YOU, BUT IF YOU'D BE WILLING TO MEET WITH PRINCESS LEIA--
I CAN'T IMAGINE BEING INTERESTED IN ANYTHING SHE HAS TO SAY.
I THINK THAT'S QUITE ENOUGH REJECTION FOR ONE DIPLOMATIC MISSION, DON'T YOU?

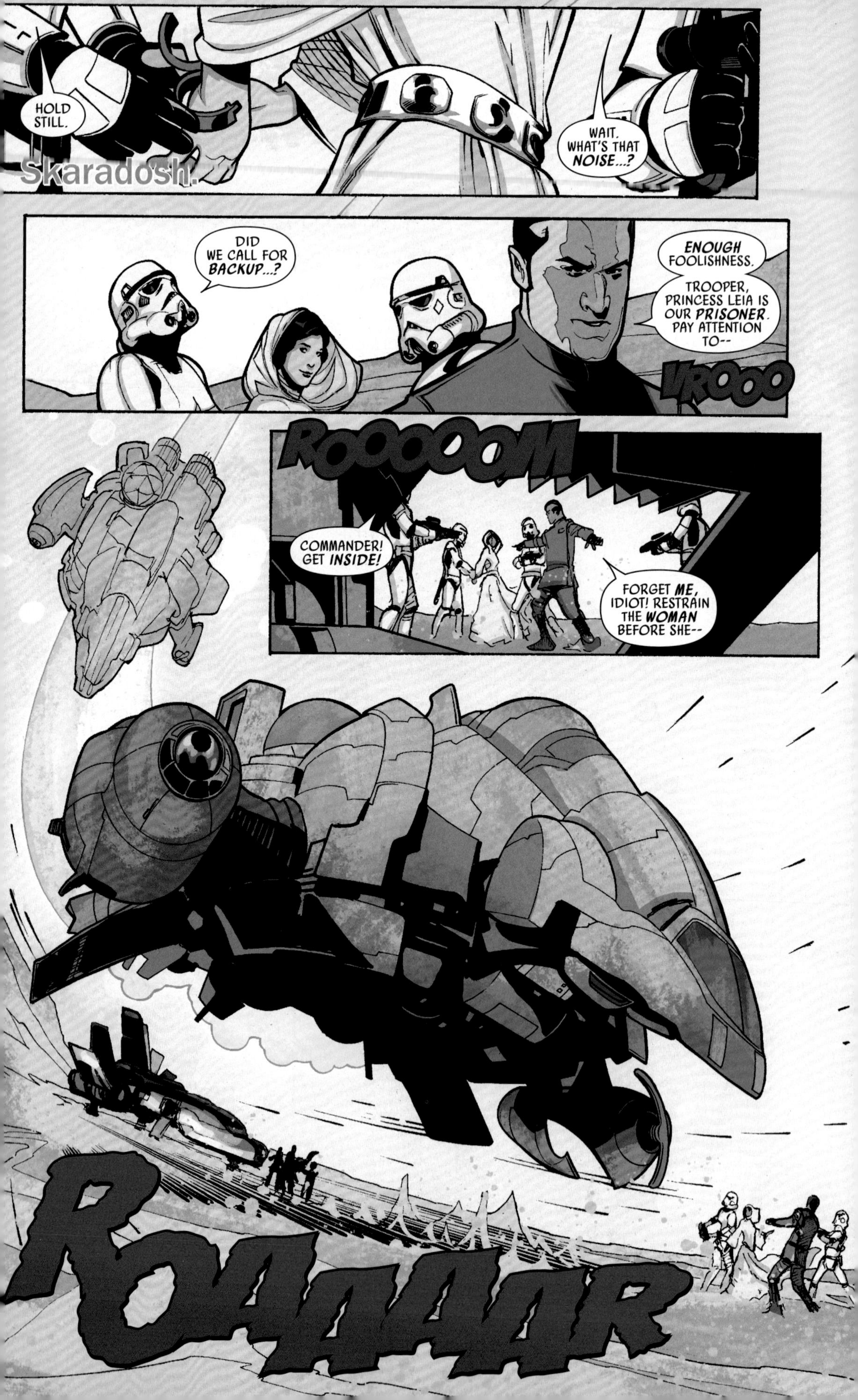
HOLD STILL.
WAIT. WHAT'S THAT NOISE...?
DID WE CALL FOR BACKUP...?
ENOUGH FOOLISHNESS.
TROOPER, PRINCESS LEIA IS OUR PRISONER. PAY ATTENTION TO--
VROOO
ROOOOOOM
COMMANDER! GET INSIDE!
FORGET ME, IDIOT! RESTRAIN THE WOMAN BEFORE SHE--
ROAAAAR

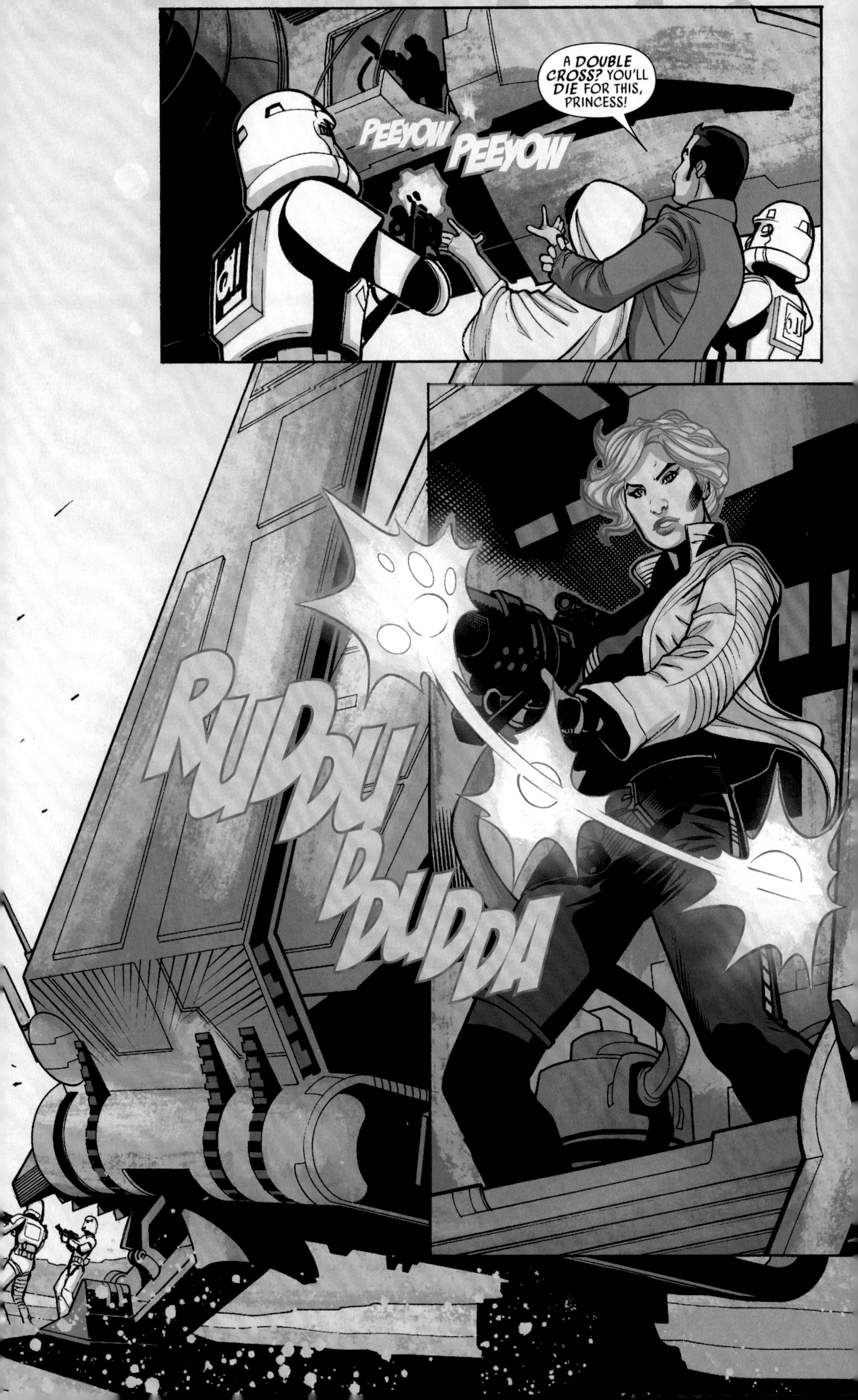
A DOUBLE CROSS? YOU'LL DIE FOR THIS, PRINCESS!
PEEYOW PEEYOW
RUDDU DDUDDA

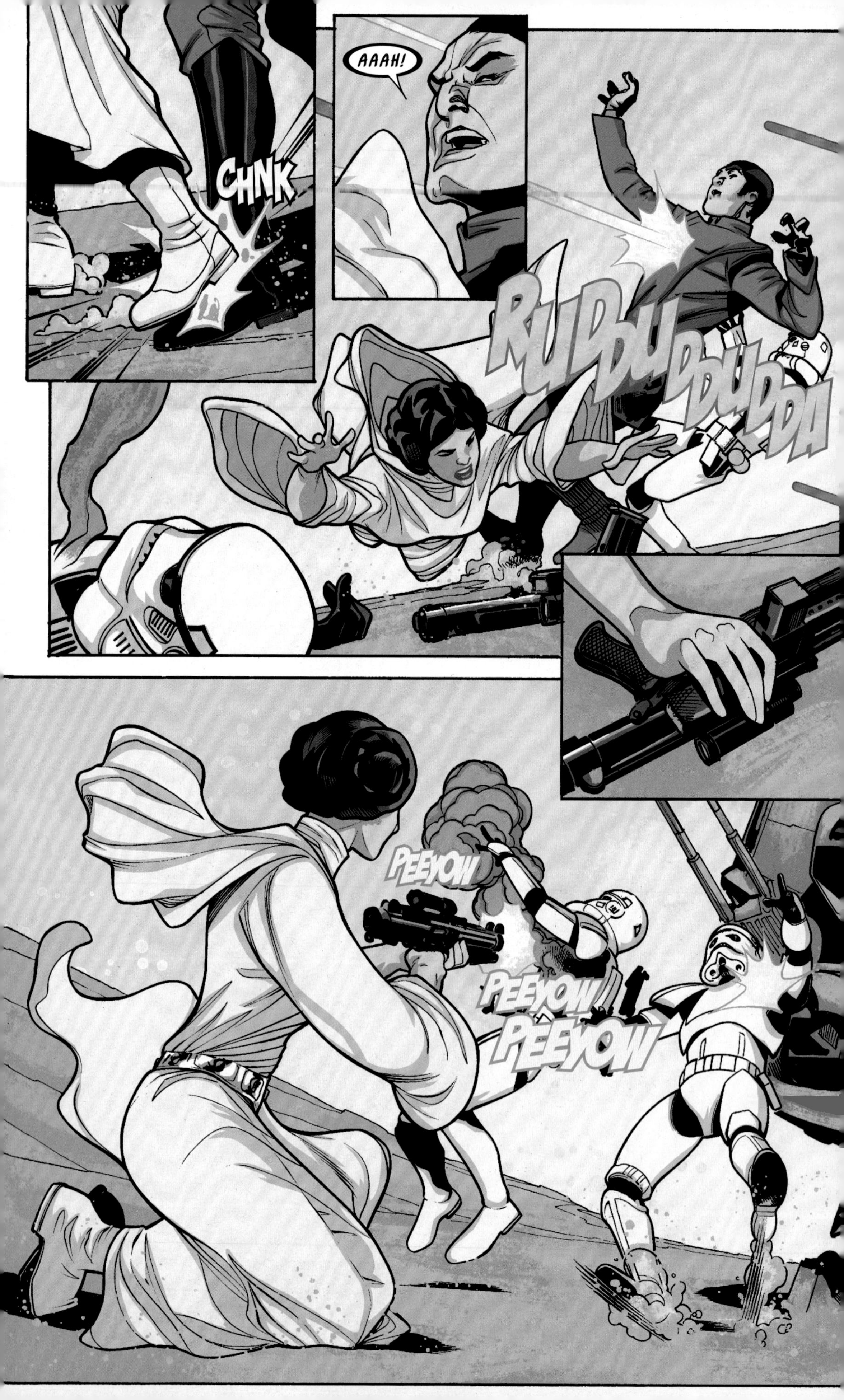
CHNK
AAAH!
RUDDUDDUDDA
PEEYOW
PEEYOW
PEEYOW

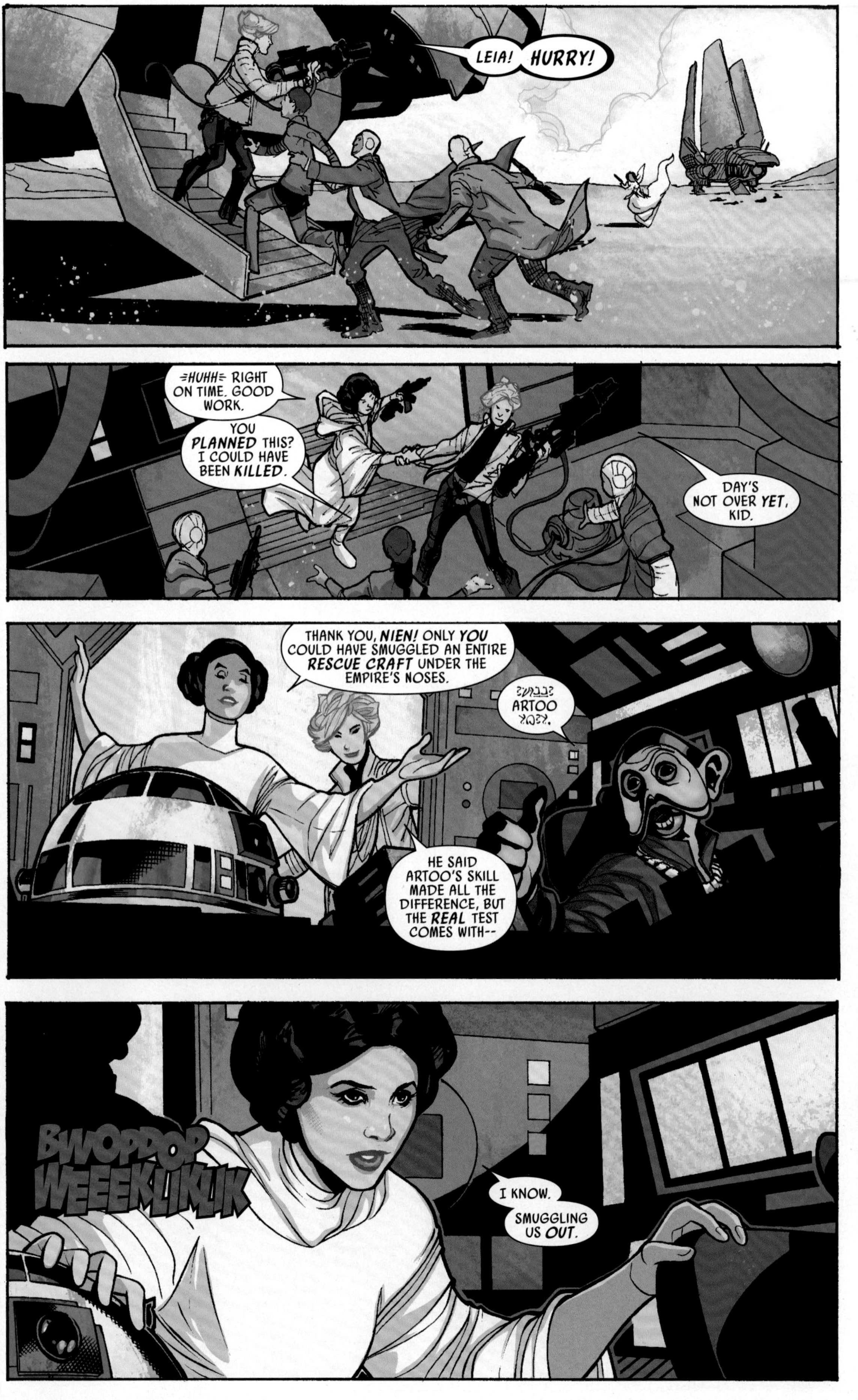
LEIA! HURRY!
=HUHH= RIGHT ON TIME. GOOD WORK.
YOU PLANNED THIS? I COULD HAVE BEEN KILLED.
DAY'S NOT OVER YET, KID.
THANK YOU, NIEN! ONLY YOU COULD HAVE SMUGGLED AN ENTIRE RESCUE CRAFT UNDER THE EMPIRE'S NOSES.
ARTOO
HE SAID ARTOO'S SKILL MADE ALL THE DIFFERENCE, BUT THE REAL TEST COMES WITH--
BWOPDOP WEEEKLIKLIK
I KNOW.
SMUGGLING US OUT.

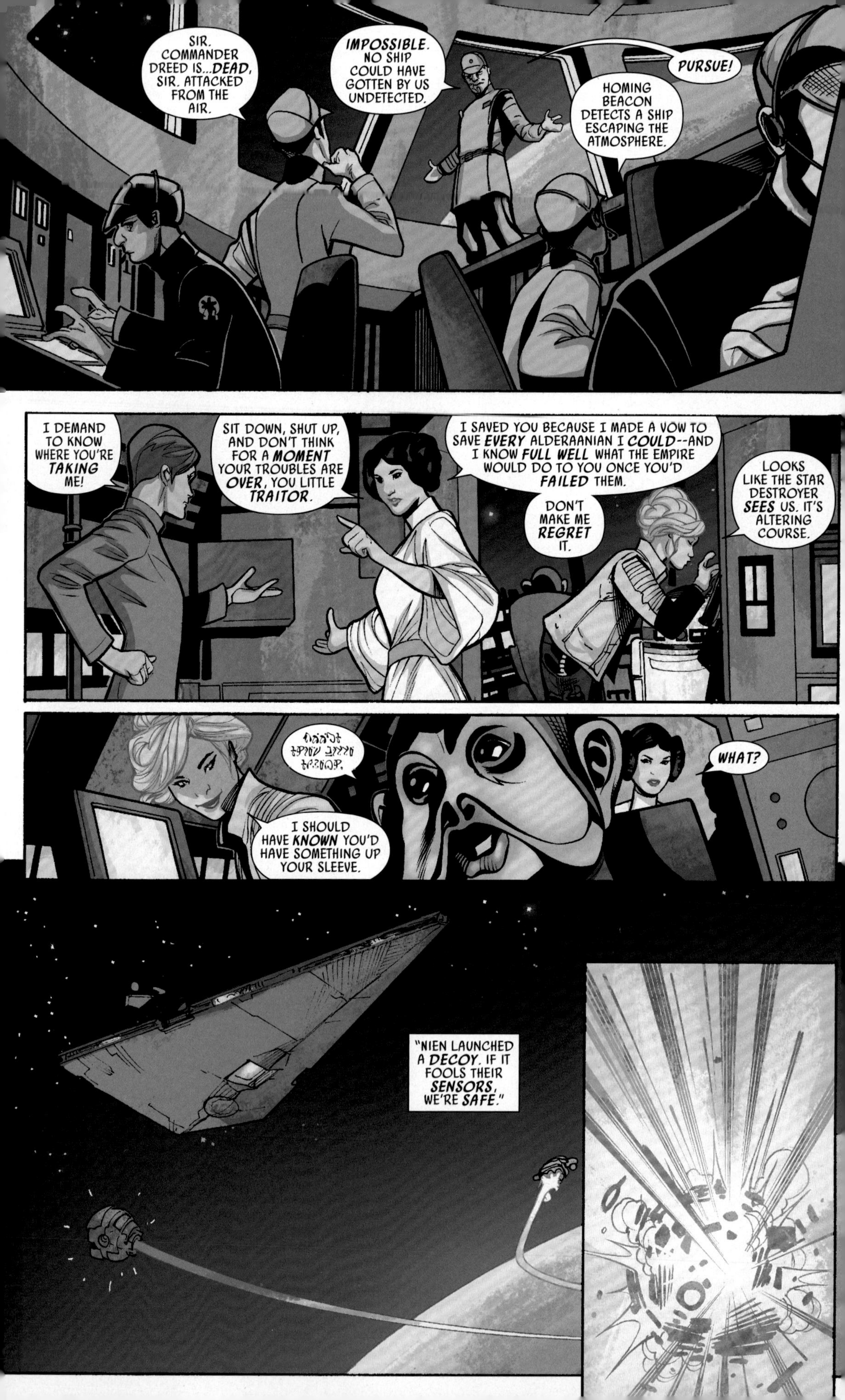
SIR. COMMANDER DREED IS...DEAD, SIR. ATTACKED FROM THE AIR.
IMPOSSIBLE. NO SHIP COULD HAVE GOTTEN BY US UNDETECTED.
HOMING BEACON DETECTS A SHIP ESCAPING THE ATMOSPHERE.
PURSUE!
I DEMAND TO KNOW WHERE YOU'RE TAKING ME!
SIT DOWN, SHUT UP, AND DON'T THINK FOR A MOMENT YOUR TROUBLES ARE OVER, YOU LITTLE TRAITOR.
I SAVED YOU BECAUSE I MADE A VOW TO SAVE EVERY ALDERAANIAN I COULD--AND I KNOW FULL WELL WHAT THE EMPIRE WOULD DO TO YOU ONCE YOU'D FAILED THEM.
DON'T MAKE ME REGRET IT.
LOOKS LIKE THE STAR DESTROYER SEES US. IT'S ALTERING COURSE.
WHAT?
I SHOULD HAVE KNOWN YOU'D HAVE SOMETHING UP YOUR SLEEVE.
"NIEN LAUNCHED A DECOY. IF IT FOOLS THEIR SENSORS, WE'RE SAFE."

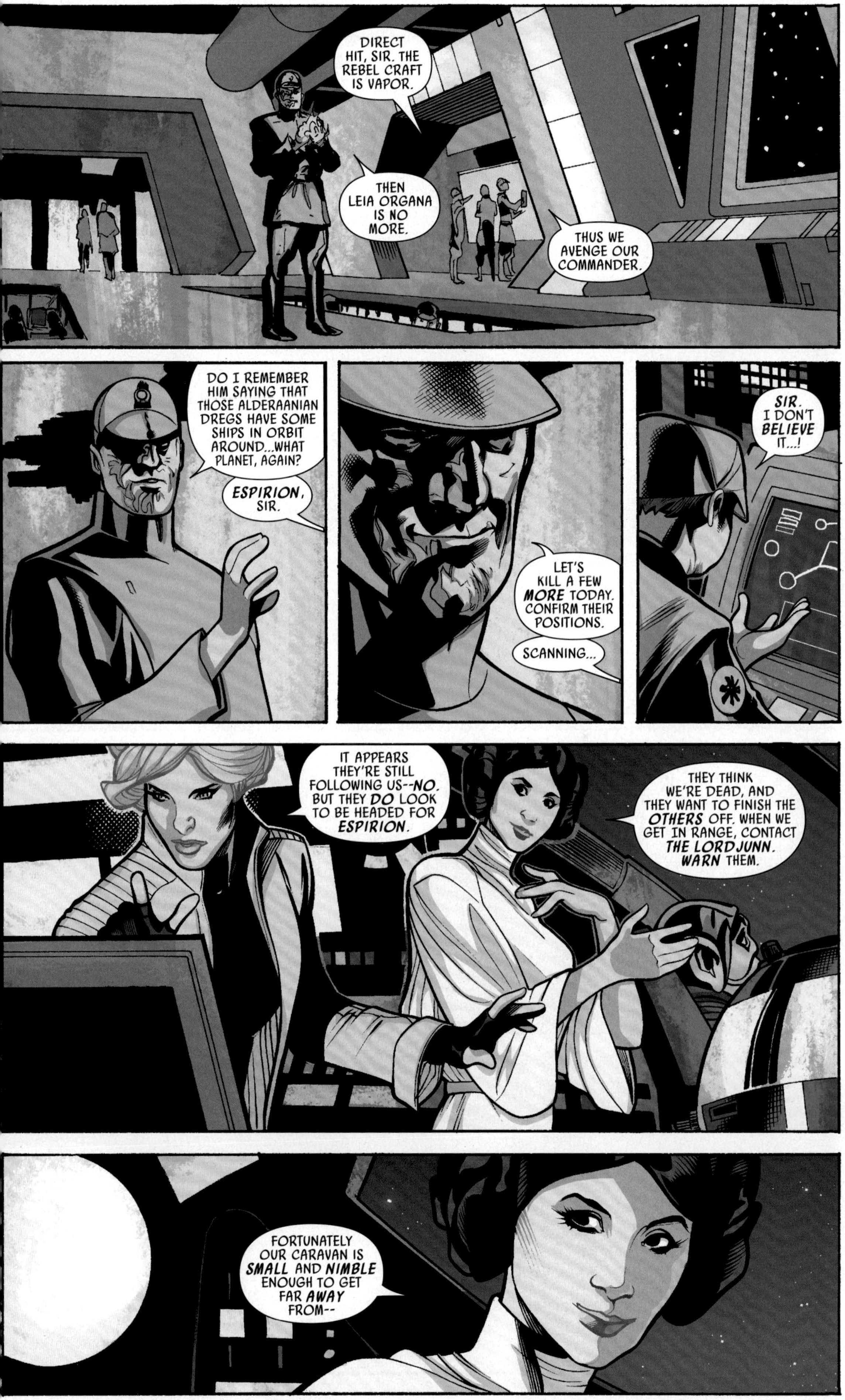
DIRECT HIT, SIR. THE REBEL CRAFT IS VAPOR.
THEN LEIA ORGANA IS NO MORE.
THUS WE AVENGE OUR COMMANDER.
DO I REMEMBER HIM SAYING THAT THOSE ALDERAANIAN DREGS HAVE SOME SHIPS IN ORBIT AROUND...WHAT PLANET, AGAIN?
ESPIRION, SIR.
LET'S KILL A FEW MORE TODAY. CONFIRM THEIR POSITIONS.
SCANNING...
SIR. I DON'T BELIEVE IT...!
IT APPEARS THEY'RE STILL FOLLOWING US--NO. BUT THEY DO LOOK TO BE HEADED FOR ESPIRION.
THEY THINK WE'RE DEAD, AND THEY WANT TO FINISH THE OTHERS OFF. WHEN WE GET IN RANGE, CONTACT THE LORDJUNN. WARN THEM.
FORTUNATELY OUR CARAVAN IS SMALL AND NIMBLE ENOUGH TO GET FAR AWAY FROM--

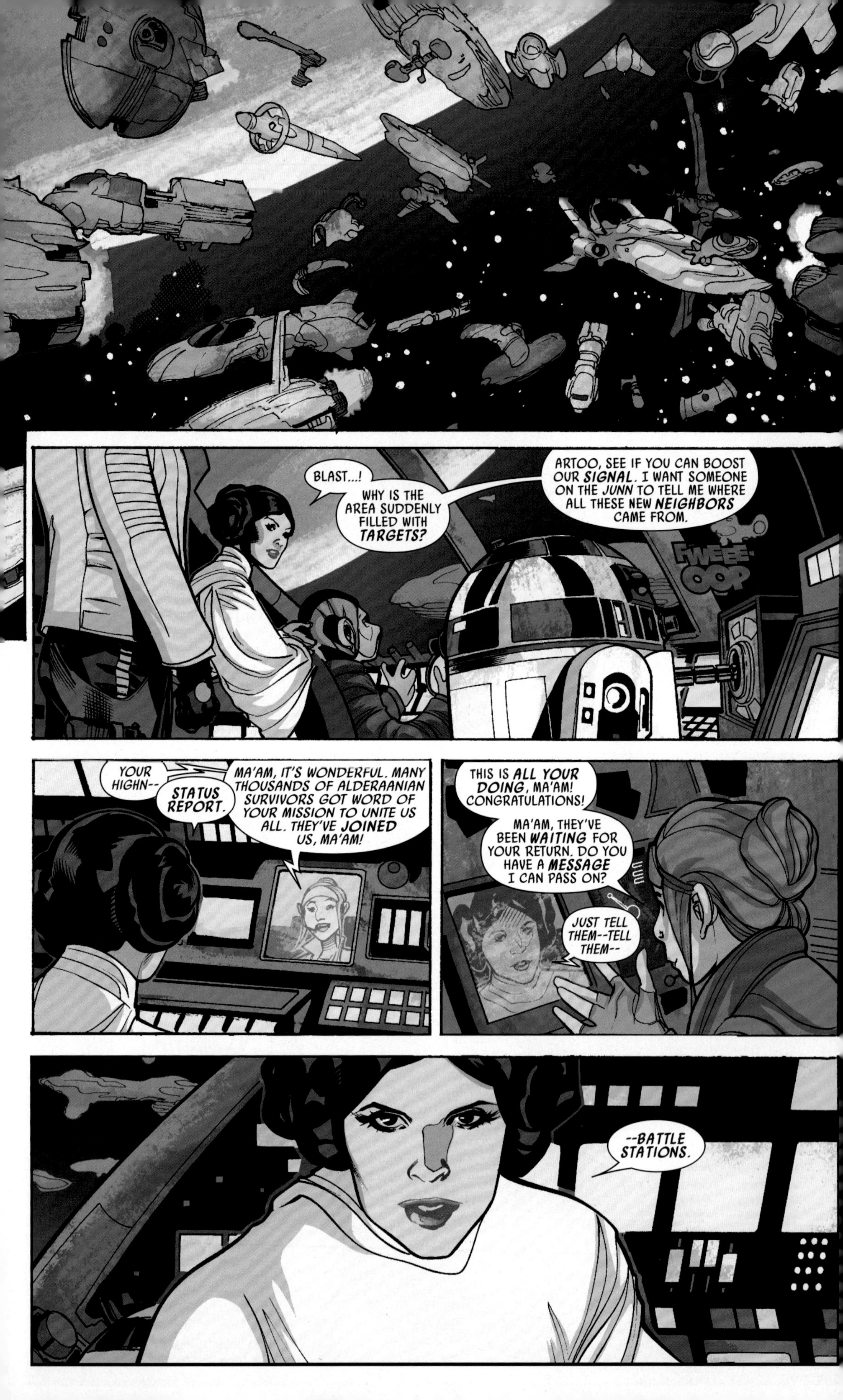
BLAST...!
WHY IS THE AREA SUDDENLY FILLED WITH TARGETS?
ARTOO, SEE IF YOU CAN BOOST OUR SIGNAL. I WANT SOMEONE ON THE JUNN TO TELL ME WHERE ALL THESE NEW NEIGHBORS CAME FROM.
FWEEE-OOP
YOUR HIGHN--
STATUS REPORT.
MA'AM, IT'S WONDERFUL. MANY THOUSANDS OF ALDERAANIAN SURVIVORS GOT WORD OF YOUR MISSION TO UNITE US ALL. THEY'VE JOINED US, MA'AM!
THIS IS ALL YOUR DOING, MA'AM! CONGRATULATIONS!
MA'AM, THEY'VE BEEN WAITING FOR YOUR RETURN. DO YOU HAVE A MESSAGE I CAN PASS ON?
JUST TELL THEM--TELL THEM--
--BATTLE STATIONS.

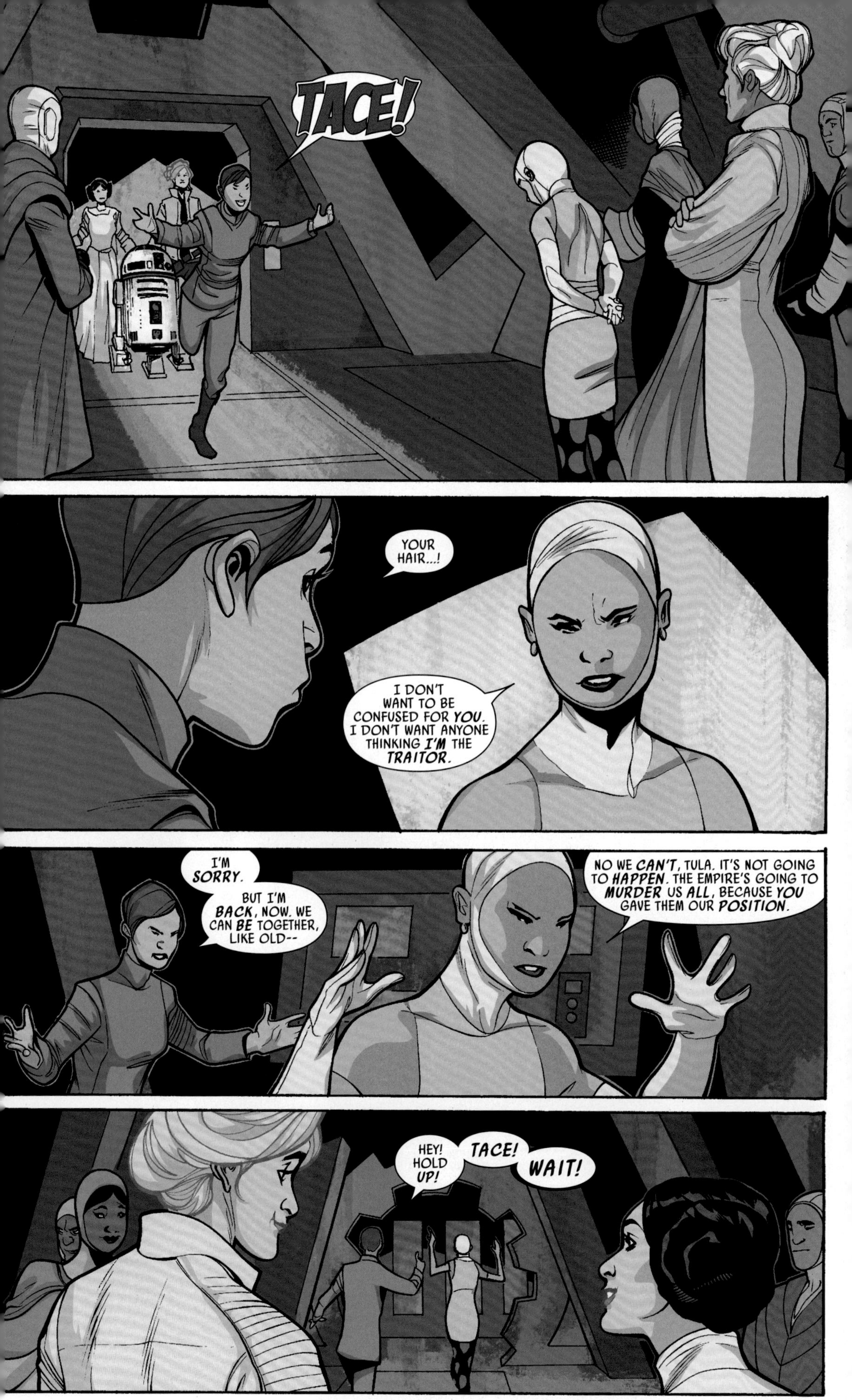
TACE!
YOUR HAIR...!
I DON'T WANT TO BE CONFUSED FOR YOU. I DON'T WANT ANYONE THINKING I'M THE TRAITOR.
I'M SORRY.
BUT I'M BACK, NOW. WE CAN BE TOGETHER, LIKE OLD--
NO WE CAN'T, TULA. IT'S NOT GOING TO HAPPEN. THE EMPIRE'S GOING TO MURDER US ALL, BECAUSE YOU GAVE THEM OUR POSITION.
HEY! HOLD UP!
TACE!
WAIT!

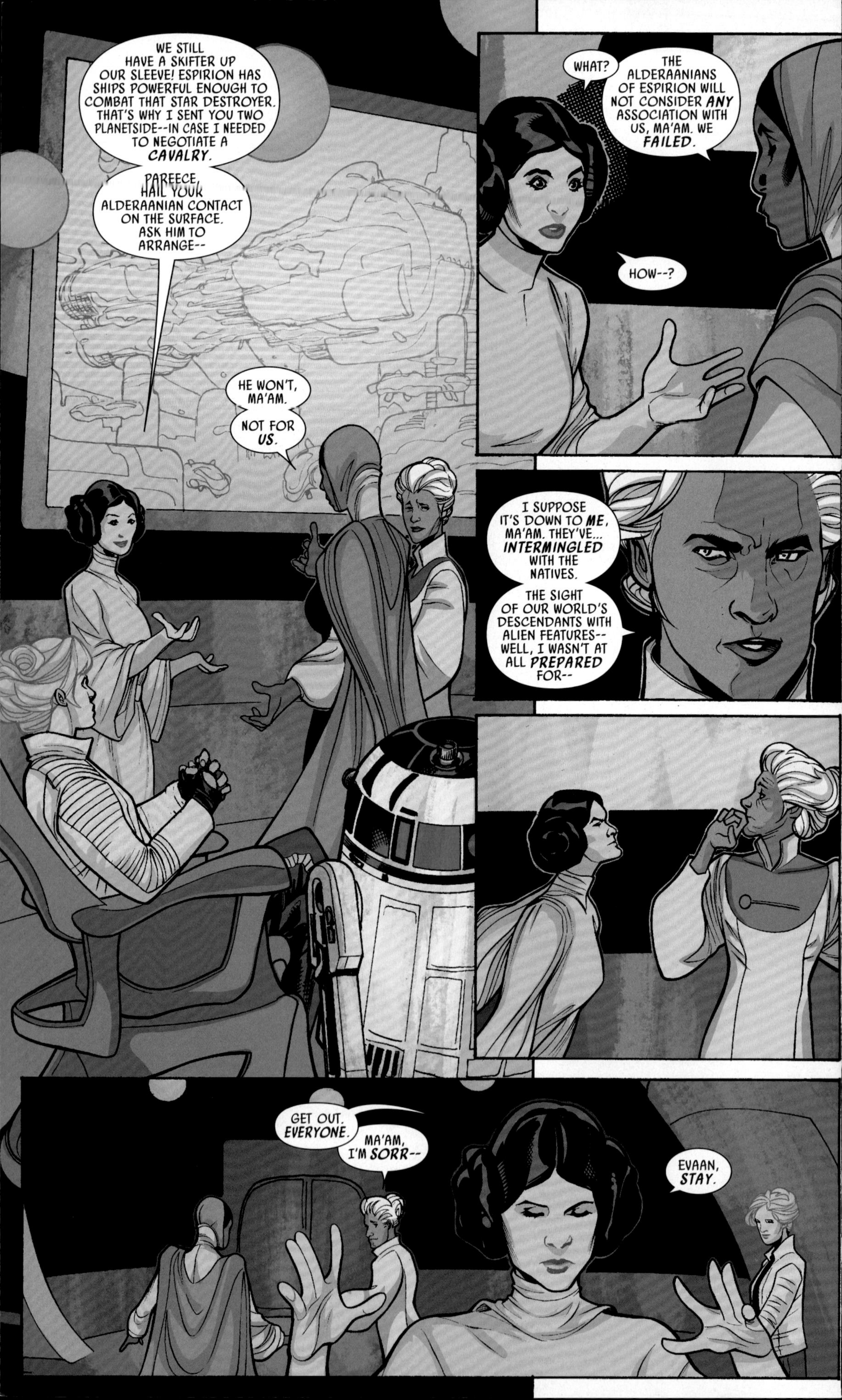

WE STILL HAVE A SKIFTER UP OUR SLEEVE! ESPIRION HAS SHIPS POWERFUL ENOUGH TO COMBAT THAT STAR DESTROYER. THAT'S WHY I SENT YOU TWO PLANETSIDE--IN CASE I NEEDED TO NEGOTIATE A CAVALRY.
PAREECE, HAIL YOUR ALDERAANIAN CONTACT ON THE SURFACE. ASK HIM TO ARRANGE--
HE WON'T, MA'AM.
NOT FOR US.
WHAT?
THE ALDERAANIANS OF ESPIRION WILL NOT CONSIDER ANY ASSOCIATION WITH US, MA'AM. WE FAILED.
HOW--?
I SUPPOSE IT'S DOWN TO ME, MA'AM. THEY'VE... INTERMINGLED WITH THE NATIVES.
THE SIGHT OF OUR WORLD'S DESCENDANTS WITH ALIEN FEATURES--WELL, I WASN'T AT ALL PREPARED FOR--
GET OUT. EVERYONE.
MA'AM, I'M SORR--
EVAAN, STAY.

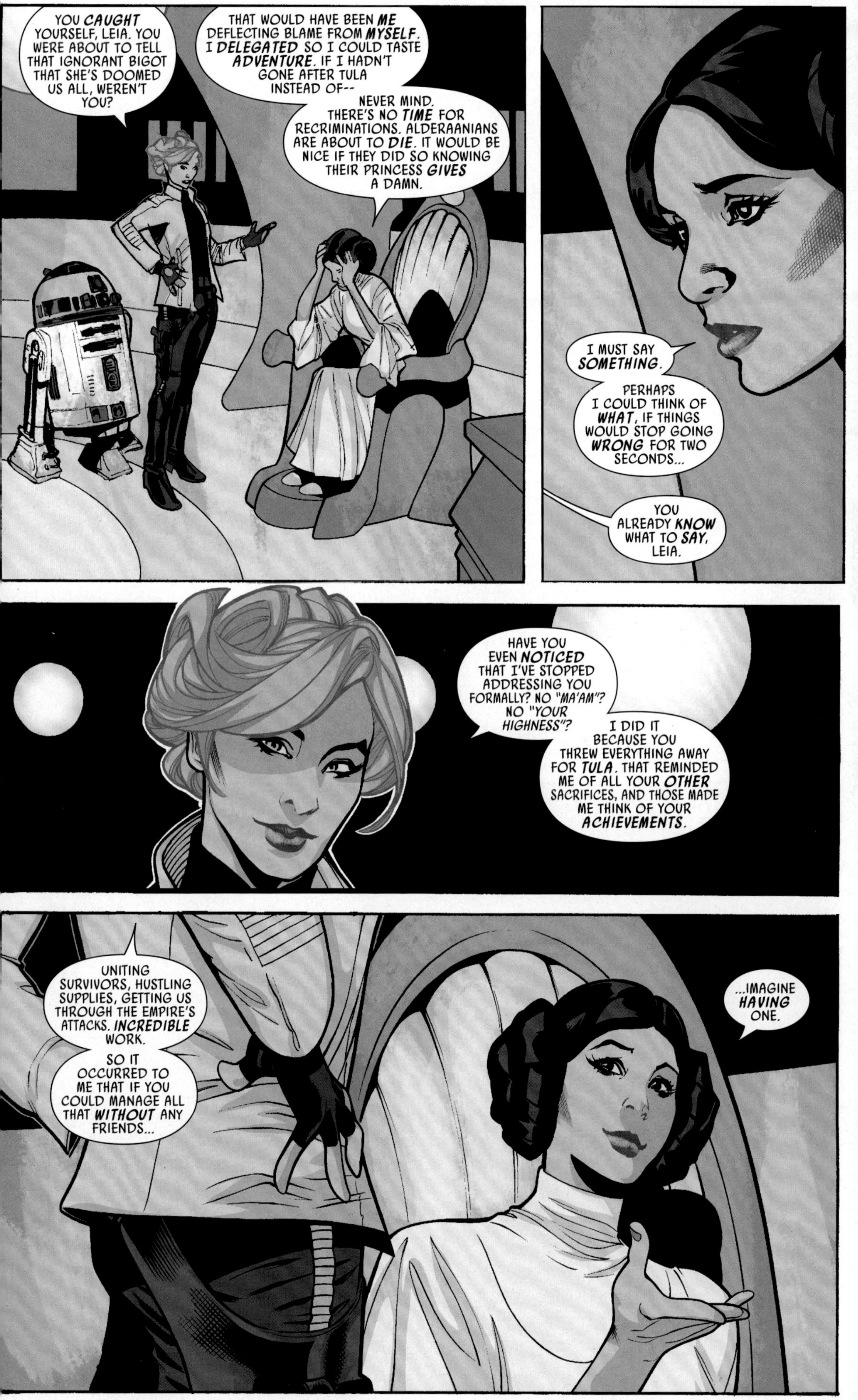

YOU CAUGHT YOURSELF, LEIA. YOU WERE ABOUT TO TELL THAT IGNORANT BIGOT THAT SHE'S DOOMED US ALL, WEREN'T YOU?
THAT WOULD HAVE BEEN ME DEFLECTING BLAME FROM MYSELF. I DELEGATED SO I COULD TASTE ADVENTURE. IF I HADN'T GONE AFTER TULA INSTEAD OF--
NEVER MIND. THERE'S NO TIME FOR RECRIMINATIONS. ALDERAANIANS ARE ABOUT TO DIE. IT WOULD BE NICE IF THEY DID SO KNOWING THEIR PRINCESS GIVES A DAMN.
I MUST SAY SOMETHING.
PERHAPS I COULD THINK OF WHAT, IF THINGS WOULD STOP GOING WRONG FOR TWO SECONDS...
YOU ALREADY KNOW WHAT TO SAY, LEIA.
HAVE YOU EVEN NOTICED THAT I'VE STOPPED ADDRESSING YOU FORMALLY? NO "MA'AM"? NO "YOUR HIGHNESS"?
I DID IT BECAUSE YOU THREW EVERYTHING AWAY FOR TULA. THAT REMINDED ME OF ALL YOUR OTHER SACRIFICES, AND THOSE MADE ME THINK OF YOUR ACHIEVEMENTS.
UNITING SURVIVORS, HUSTLING SUPPLIES, GETTING US THROUGH THE EMPIRE'S ATTACKS. INCREDIBLE WORK.
SO IT OCCURRED TO ME THAT IF YOU COULD MANAGE ALL THAT WITHOUT ANY FRIENDS...
...IMAGINE HAVING ONE.

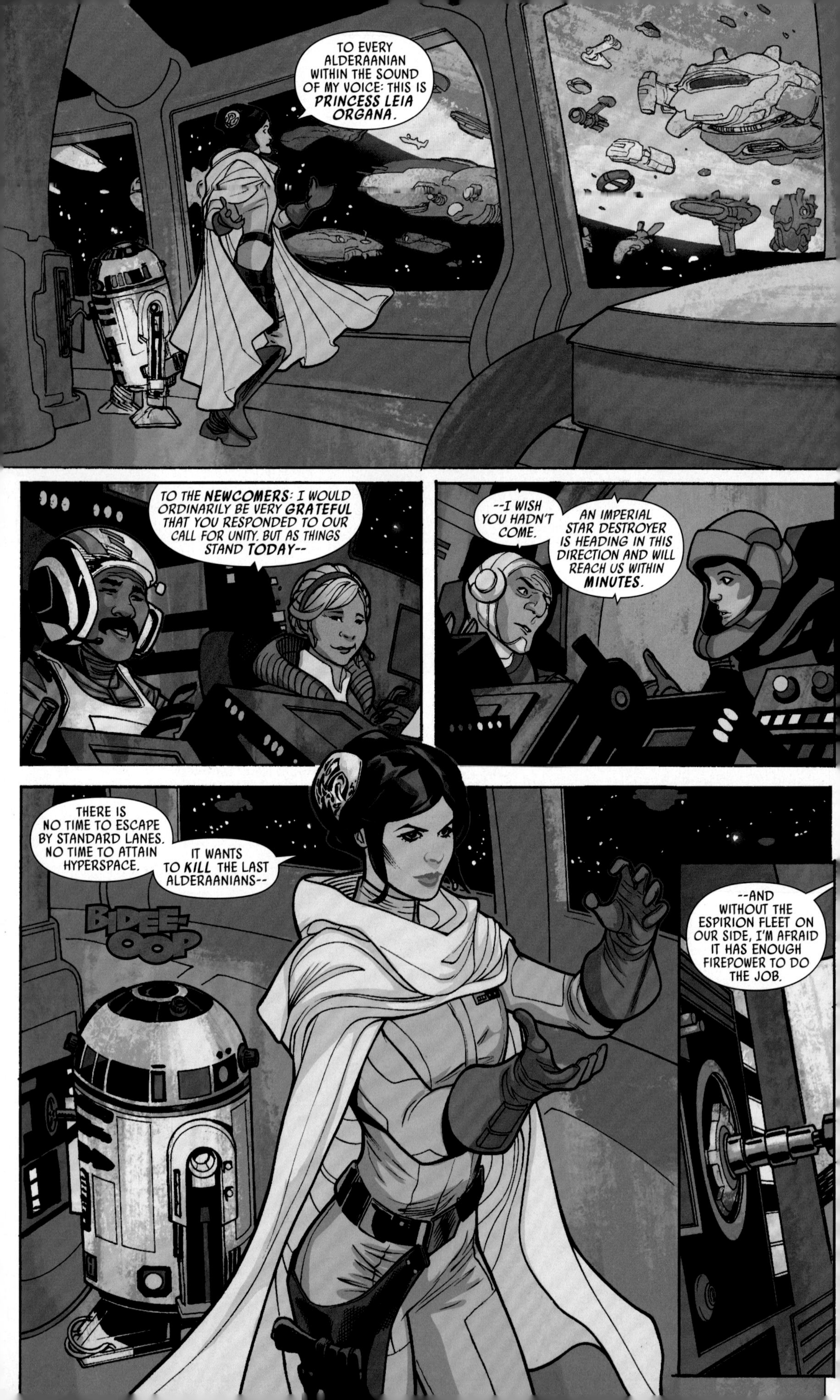
TO EVERY ALDERAANIAN WITHIN THE SOUND OF MY VOICE: THIS IS PRINCESS LEIA ORGANA.
TO THE NEWCOMERS: I WOULD ORDINARILY BE VERY GRATEFUL THAT YOU RESPONDED TO OUR CALL FOR UNITY. BUT AS THINGS STAND TODAY--
--I WISH YOU HADN'T COME.
AN IMPERIAL STAR DESTROYER IS HEADING IN THIS DIRECTION AND WILL REACH US WITHIN MINUTES.
THERE IS NO TIME TO ESCAPE BY STANDARD LANES. NO TIME TO ATTAIN HYPERSPACE.
IT WANTS TO KILL THE LAST ALDERAANIANS--
BIDEE-OOP
--AND WITHOUT THE ESPIRION FLEET ON OUR SIDE, I'M AFRAID IT HAS ENOUGH FIREPOWER TO DO THE JOB.

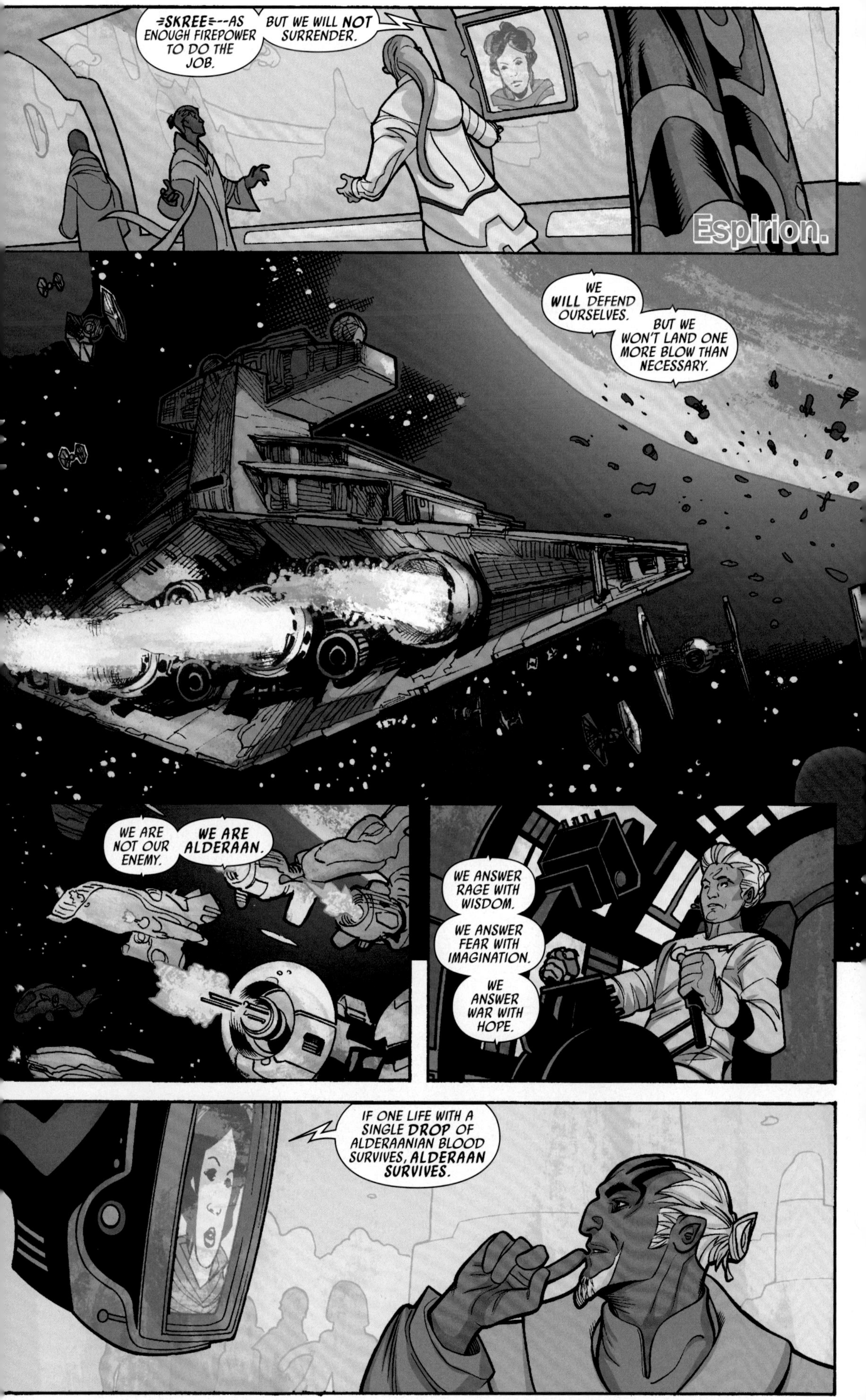

≡SKREE≡--AS ENOUGH FIREPOWER TO DO THE JOB.
BUT WE WILL NOT SURRENDER.
Espirion.
WE WILL DEFEND OURSELVES.
BUT WE WON'T LAND ONE MORE BLOW THAN NECESSARY.
WE ARE NOT OUR ENEMY.
WE ARE ALDERAAN.
WE ANSWER RAGE WITH WISDOM.
WE ANSWER FEAR WITH IMAGINATION.
WE ANSWER WAR WITH HOPE.
IF ONE LIFE WITH A SINGLE DROP OF ALDERAANIAN BLOOD SURVIVES, ALDERAAN SURVIVES.

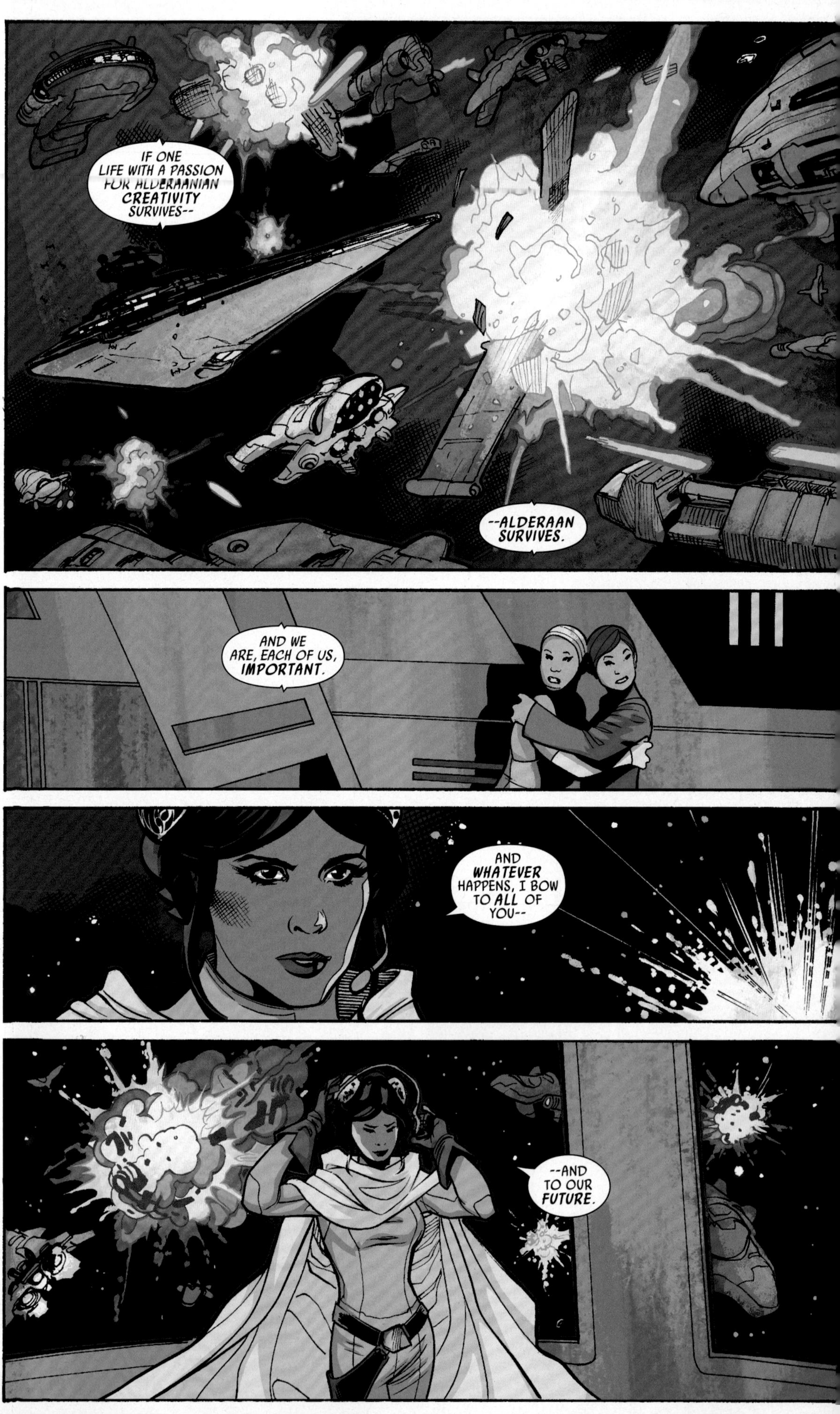
IF ONE LIFE WITH A PASSION FOR ALDERAANIAN CREATIVITY SURVIVES--
--ALDERAAN SURVIVES.
AND WE ARE, EACH OF US, IMPORTANT.
AND WHATEVER HAPPENS, I BOW TO ALL OF YOU--
--AND TO OUR FUTURE.

WHOOOM

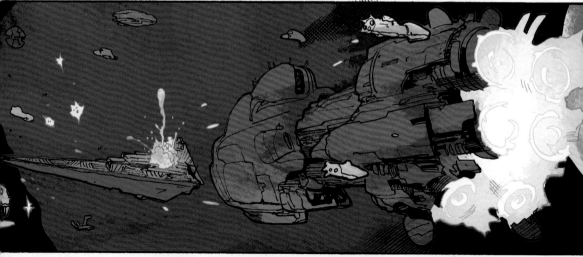

TO ALL OF OUR ALDERAANIAN SISTERS AND BROTHERS, THIS IS THE CAPTAIN OF THE *ESPIRION MULTI,* SAYING...

...STAY BACK. WE'VE GOT THIS.

NOT WITHOUT ME, CAPTAIN.

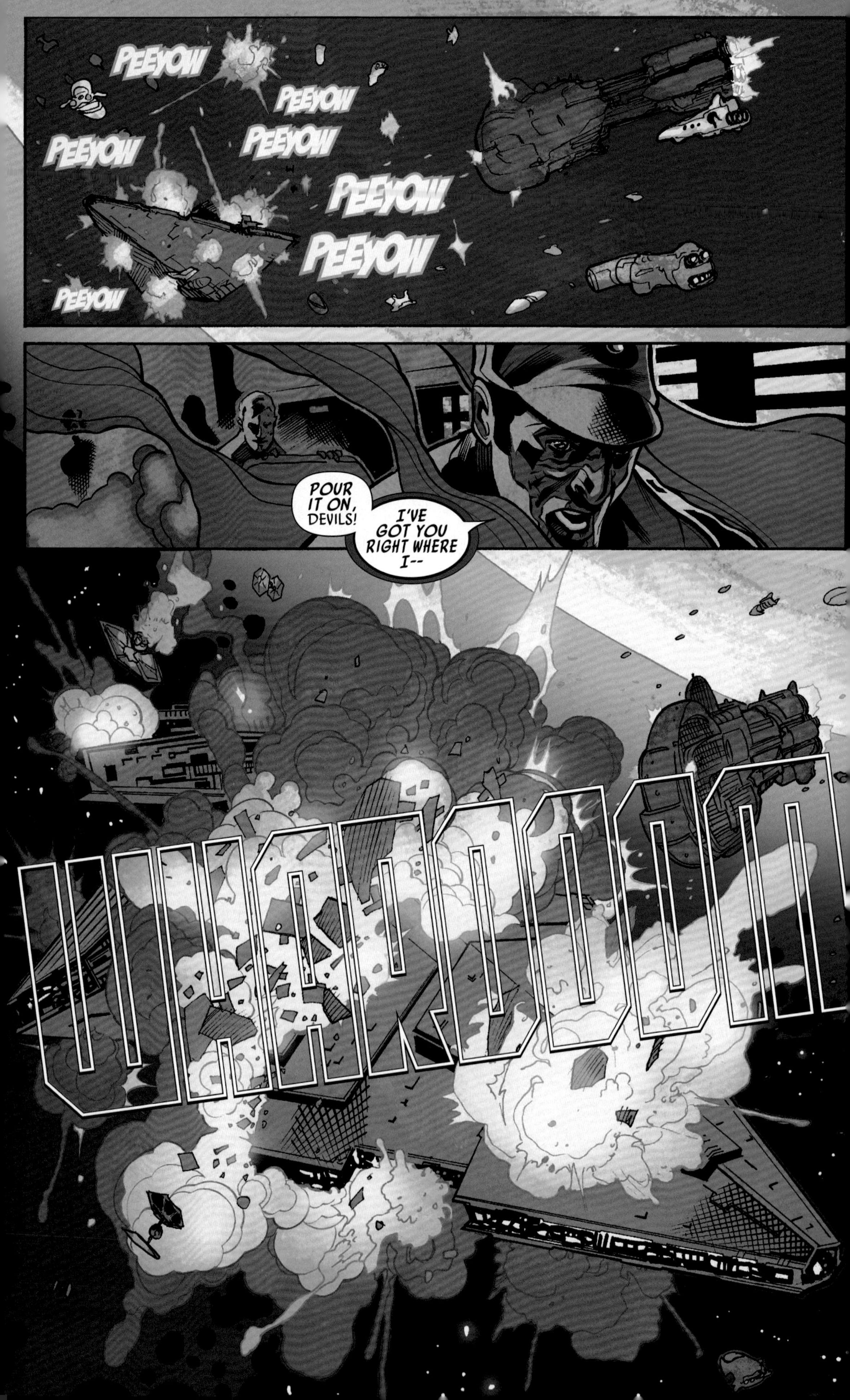
PEEYOW
PEEYOW
PEEYOW
PEEYOW
PEEYOW
PEEYOW
PEEYOW
POUR IT ON, DEVILS!
I'VE GOT YOU RIGHT WHERE I--

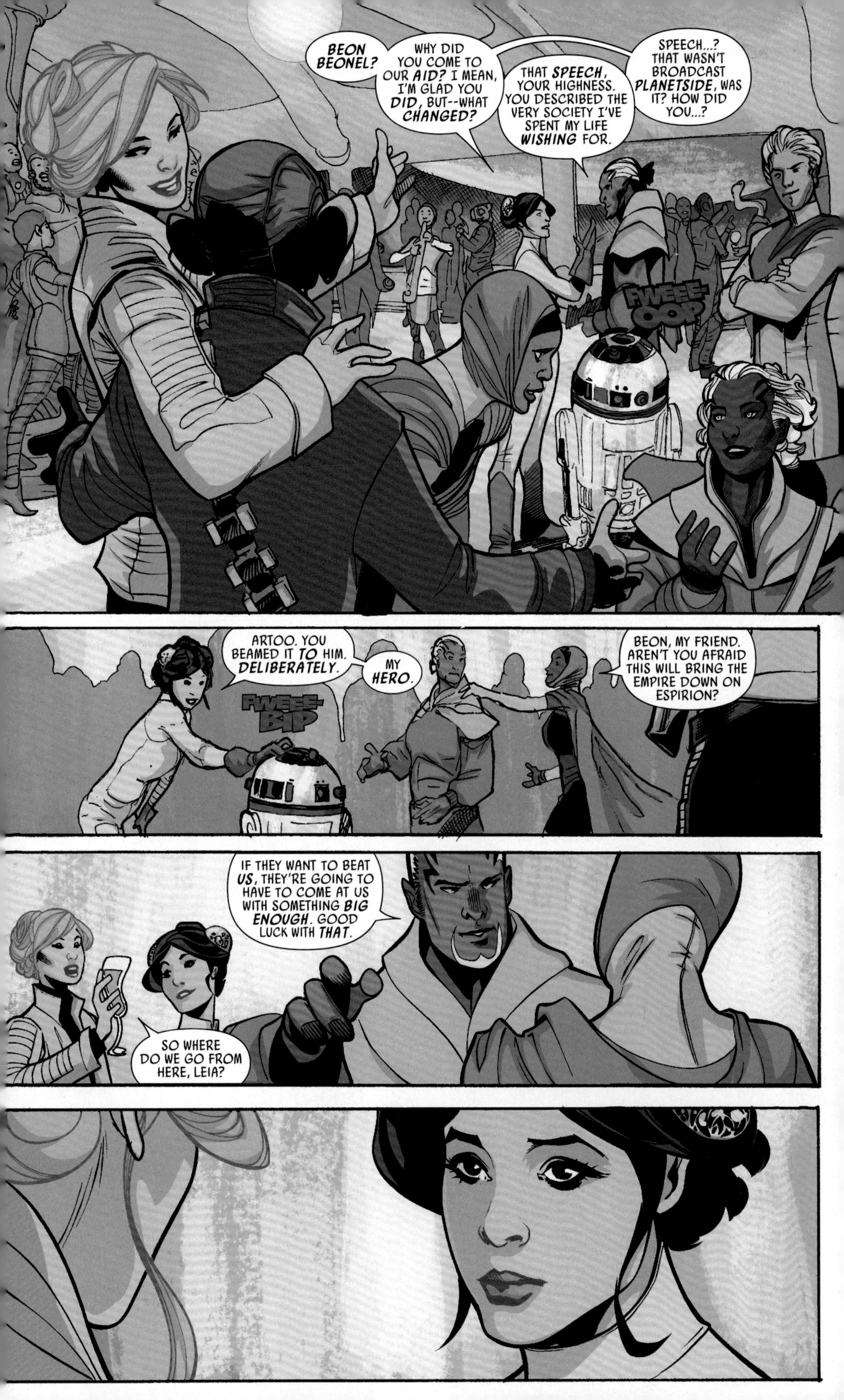
BEON BEONEL?
WHY DID YOU COME TO OUR AID? I MEAN, I'M GLAD YOU DID, BUT--WHAT CHANGED?
THAT SPEECH, YOUR HIGHNESS. YOU DESCRIBED THE VERY SOCIETY I'VE SPENT MY LIFE WISHING FOR.
SPEECH...? THAT WASN'T BROADCAST PLANETSIDE, WAS IT? HOW DID YOU...?
FWEEE-OOP
ARTOO. YOU BEAMED IT TO HIM. DELIBERATELY.
FWEEE-BIP
MY HERO.
BEON, MY FRIEND. AREN'T YOU AFRAID THIS WILL BRING THE EMPIRE DOWN ON ESPIRION?
IF THEY WANT TO BEAT US, THEY'RE GOING TO HAVE TO COME AT US WITH SOMETHING BIG ENOUGH. GOOD LUCK WITH THAT.
SO WHERE DO WE GO FROM HERE, LEIA?

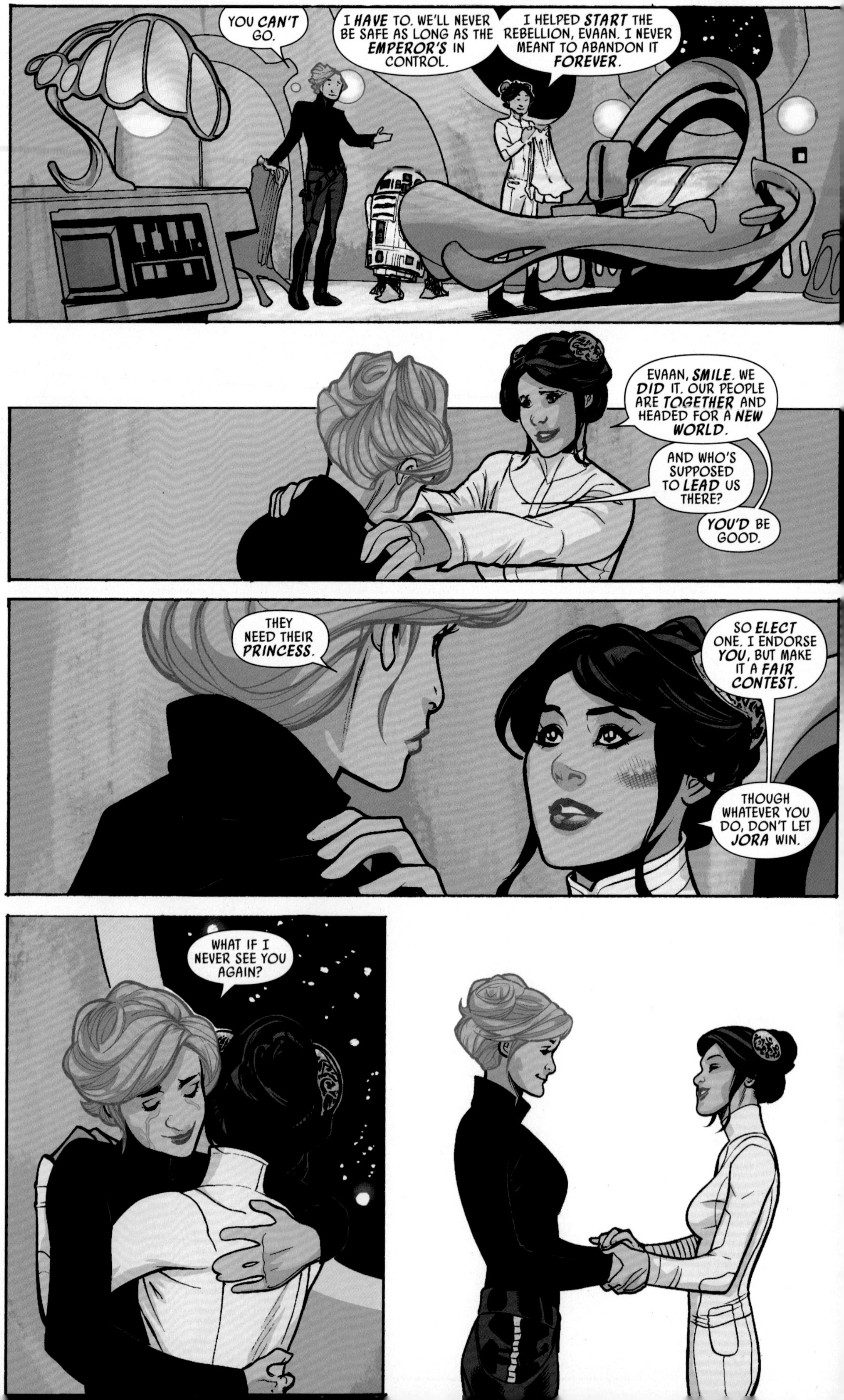

YOU CAN'T GO.
I HAVE TO. WE'LL NEVER BE SAFE AS LONG AS THE EMPEROR'S IN CONTROL.
I HELPED START THE REBELLION, EVAAN. I NEVER MEANT TO ABANDON IT FOREVER.
EVAAN, SMILE. WE DID IT. OUR PEOPLE ARE TOGETHER AND HEADED FOR A NEW WORLD.
AND WHO'S SUPPOSED TO LEAD US THERE?
YOU'D BE GOOD.
THEY NEED THEIR PRINCESS.
SO ELECT ONE. I ENDORSE YOU, BUT MAKE IT A FAIR CONTEST.
THOUGH WHATEVER YOU DO, DON'T LET JORA WIN.
WHAT IF I NEVER SEE YOU AGAIN?

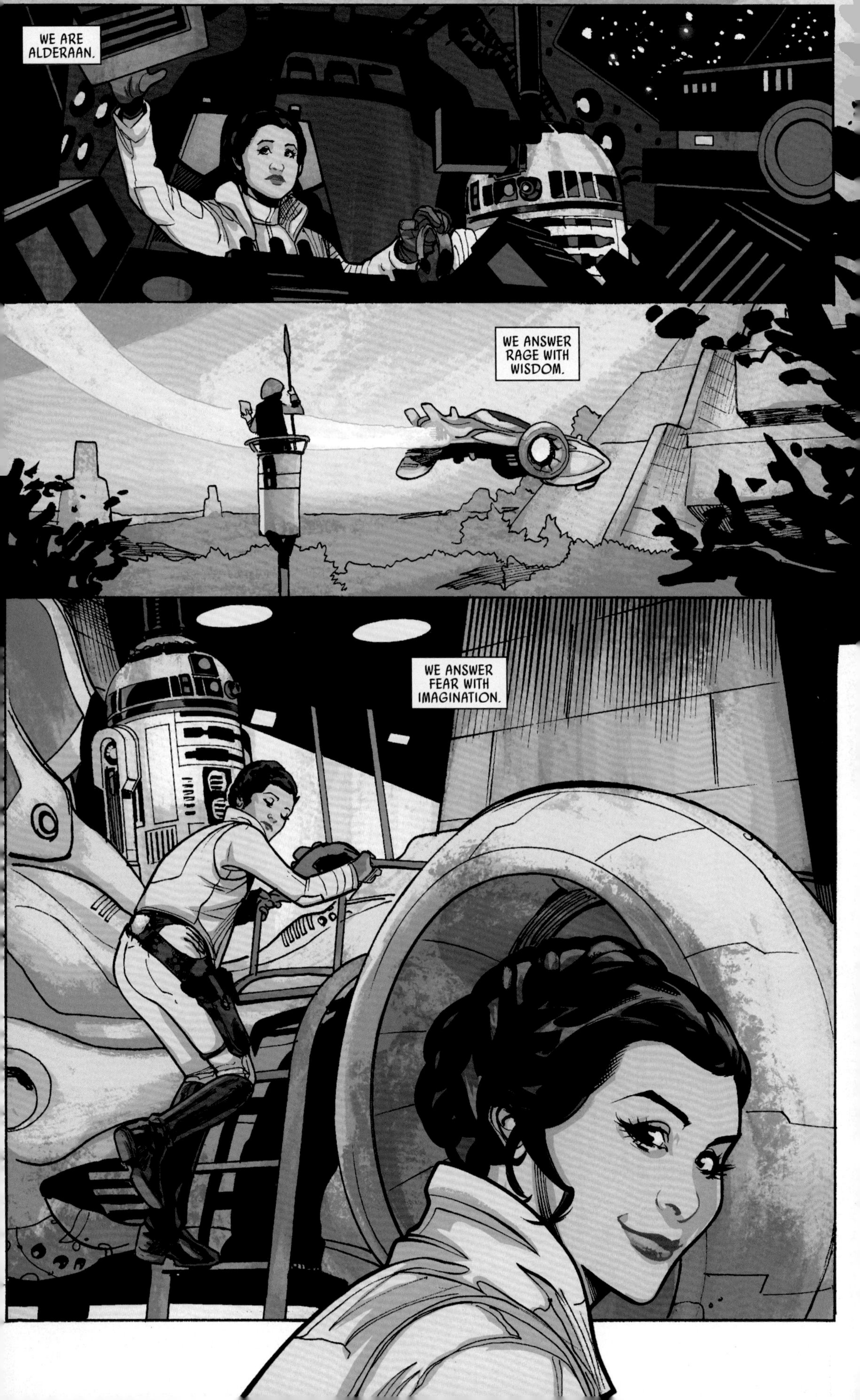
WE ARE ALDERAAN.
WE ANSWER RAGE WITH WISDOM.
WE ANSWER FEAR WITH IMAGINATION.

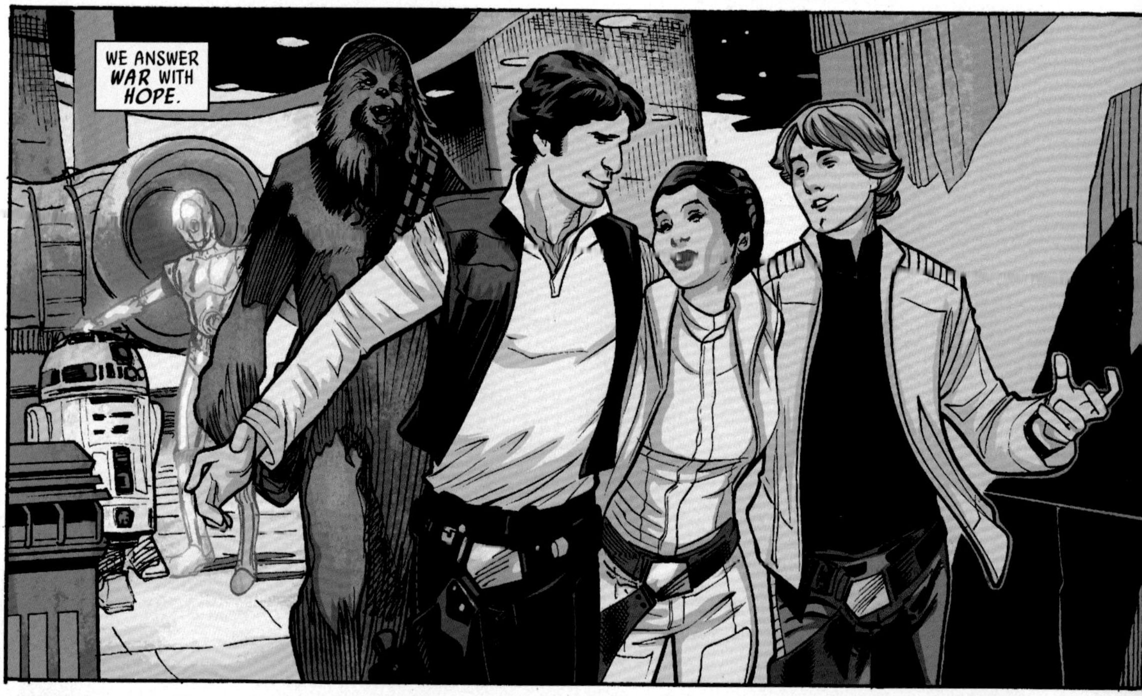
WE ANSWER WAR WITH HOPE.
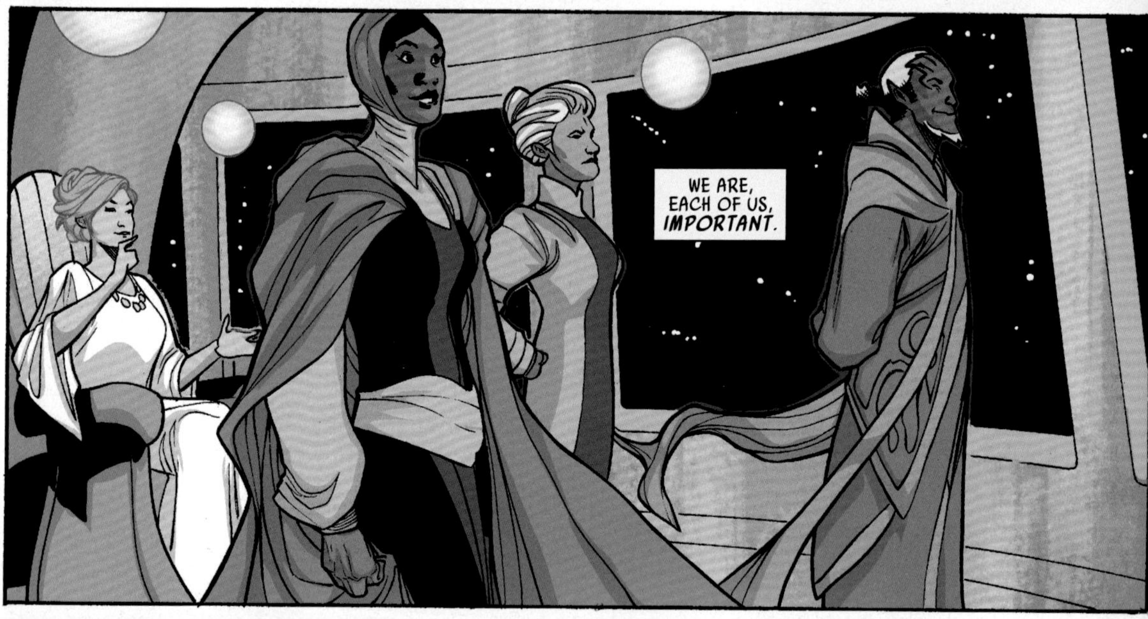
WE ARE, EACH OF US, IMPORTANT.
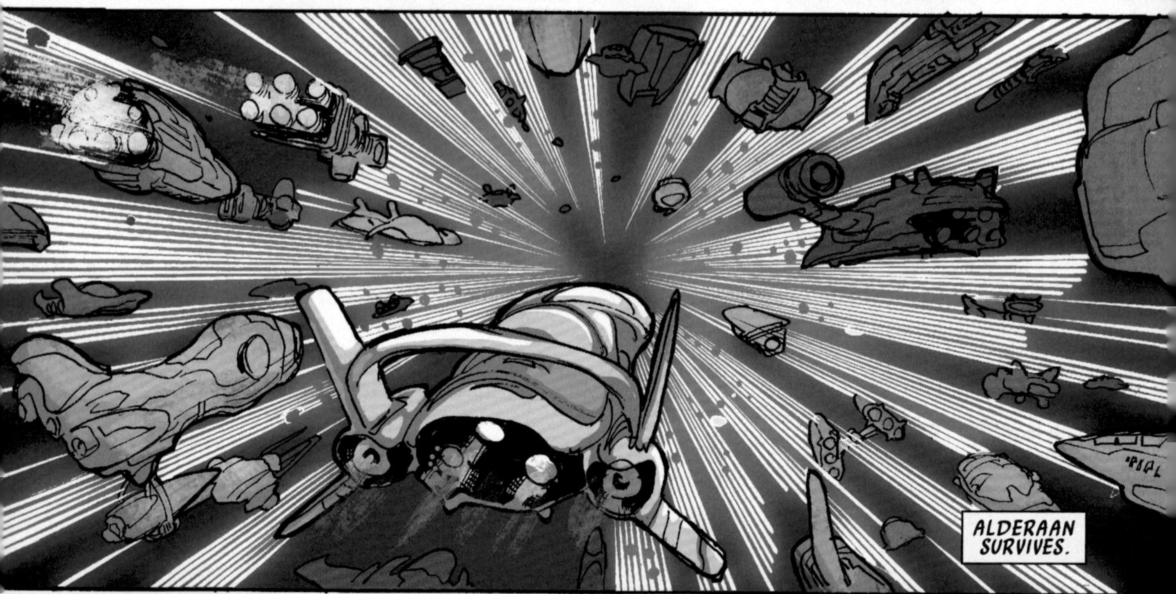
ALDERAAN SURVIVES.

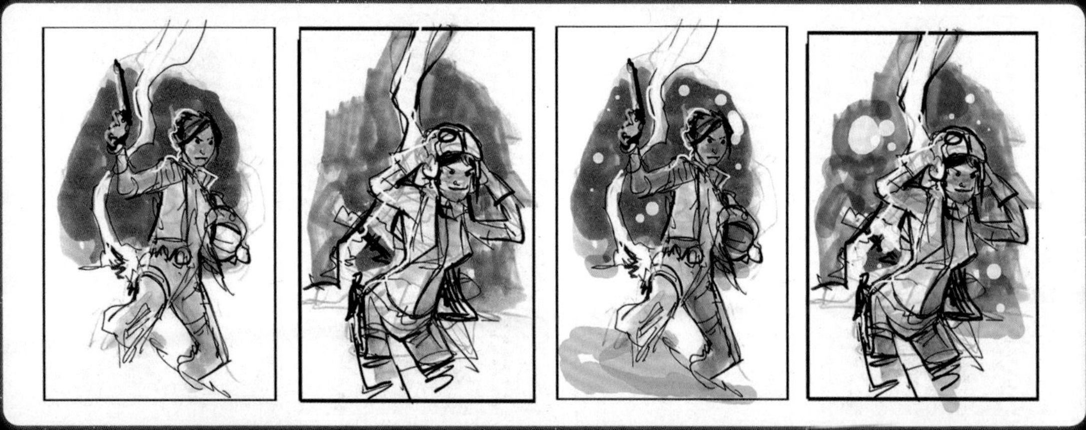

***PRINCESS LEIA* 1 Cover Sketches**

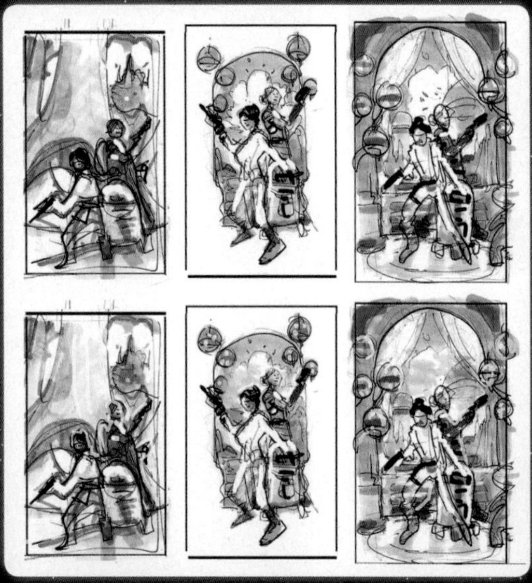

***PRINCESS LEIA* 2**
Cover Sketches

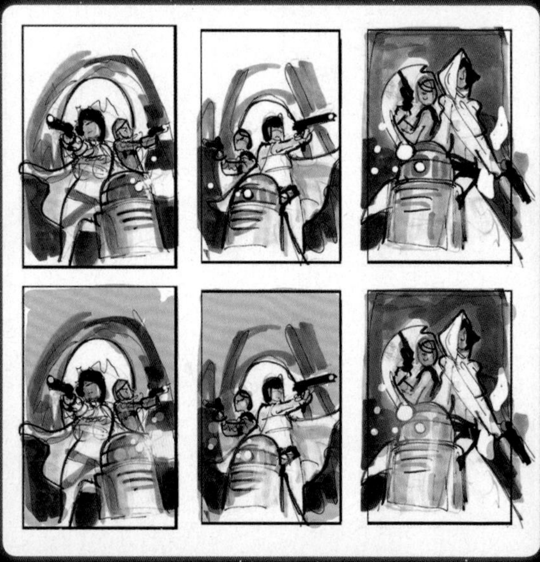

***PRINCESS LEIA* 3**
Cover Sketches

***PRINCESS LEIA* 4**
Cover Sketches

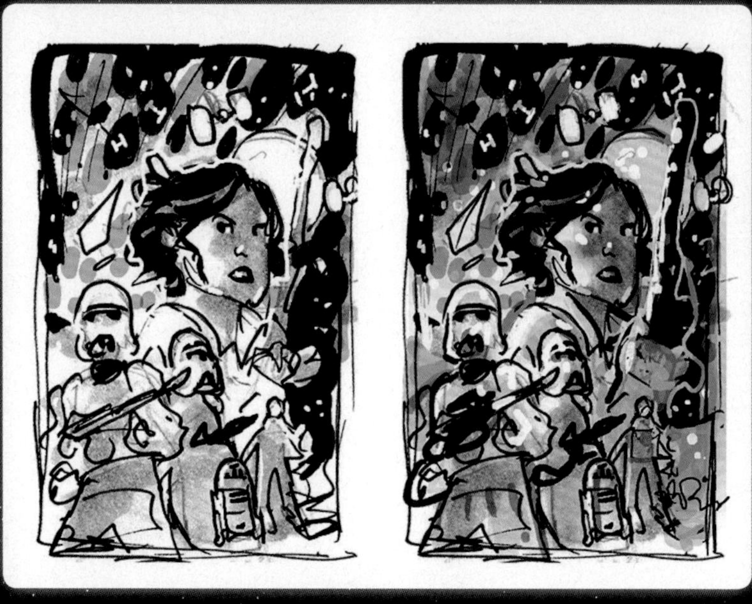

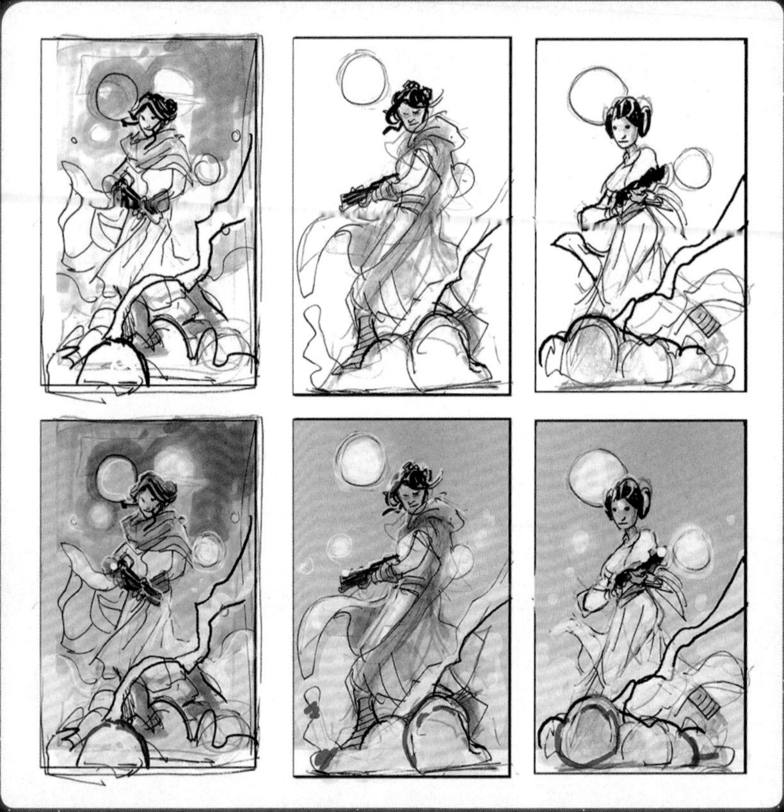

PRINCESS LEIA 5
Cover Sketches

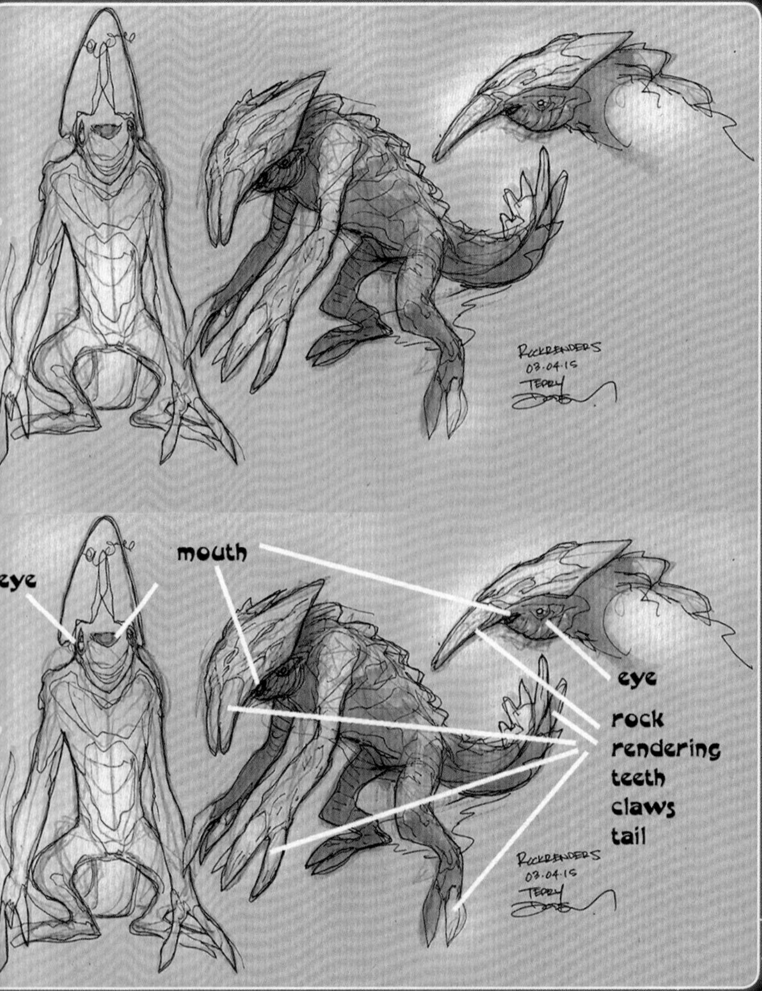
ROCKRENDERS
03.04.15
TERRY
mouth
eye
eye
rock
rendering
teeth
claws
tail
ROCKRENDERS
03.04.15
TERRY

Rock Render Sketches

STAR WARS COMES HOME TO MARVEL!

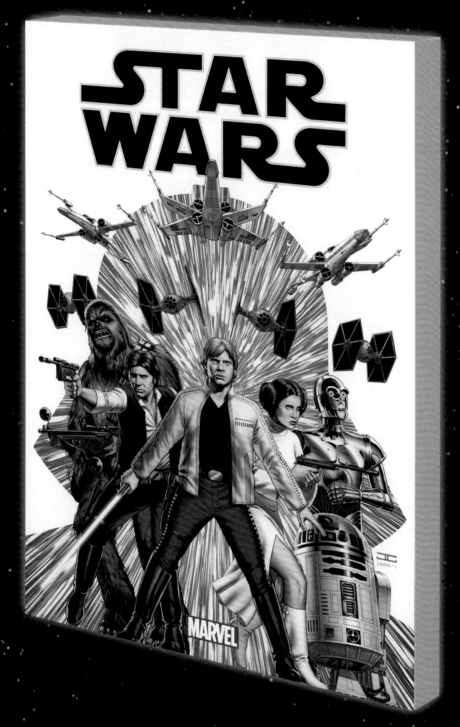

STAR WARS VOL. 1: SKYWALKER STRIKES TPB
978-0-7851-9213-8

AVAILABLE NOW WHEREVER BOOKS ARE SOLD

© & TM 2015 LUCASFILM LTD.

THE ORIGINAL DARK LORD OF THE SITH STARS IN HIS FIRST ONGOING SERIES!

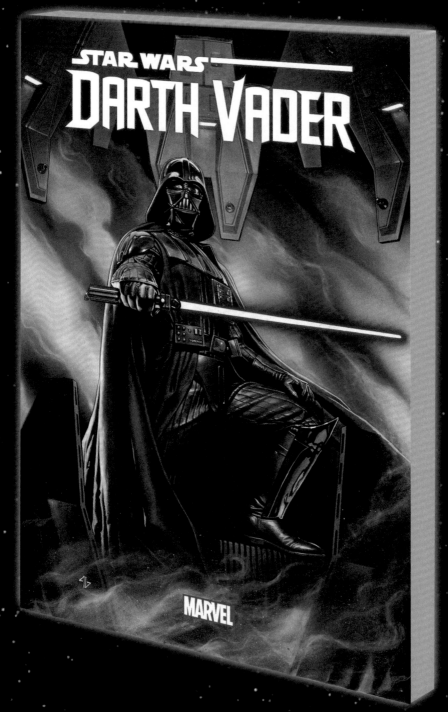

STAR WARS: DARTH VADER VOL. 1 - VADER TPB

978-0-7851-9255-8

AVAILABLE NOW WHEREVER BOOKS ARE SOLD

JOURNEY TO STAR WARS: THE FORCE AWAKENS

AFTER RETURN OF THE JEDI, AN EMPIRE LIES SHATTERED.

Journey to Star Wars: The Force Awakens –
Shattered Empire TPB
978-0-7851-9781-2

AVAILABLE NOVEMBER 2015
Wherever Books Are Sold

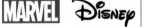

© & TM 2015 LUCASFILM LTD.

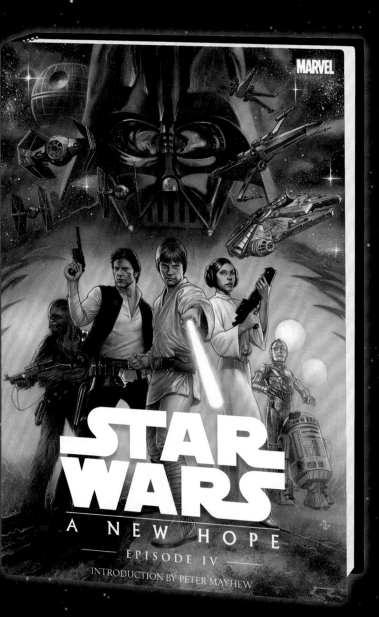

RETURN TO A GAL
THE CLASSIC MARVEL ADAPTATIONS
NOW WITH REMA

STAR WARS: EPISODE IV – A NEW HOPE HC
978-0-7851-9348-7

STAR WARS: EPISODE V
978-0-7851-9367-8

AVAILABLE WHEREVER BOOKS ARE SOLD

MARVEL   Disney   LUCASFILM
© & TM 2015 LUCASFILM LTD.

...XY FAR, FAR AWAY!
...F THE BIGGEST MOVIES IN HISTORY,
...ERED INTERIORS!

MARVEL

...PIRE STRIKES BACK HC

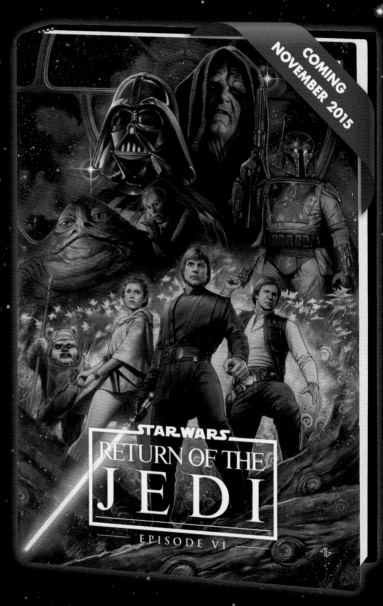

COMING
NOVEMBER 2015

STAR WARS
RETURN OF THE
JEDI
EPISODE VI

STAR WARS: EPISODE VI – RETURN OF THE JEDI HC
978-0-7851-9369-2

RETURN TO THE ORIGINAL MARVEL YEARS WITH THESE DELUXE CLASSIC COLLECTIONS!

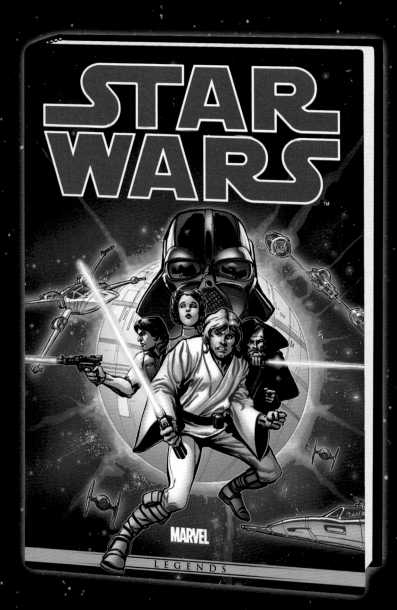

**STAR WARS:
THE ORIGINAL MARVEL YEARS
OMNIBUS VOL. 2
978-0-7851-9342-5**

**STAR WARS: THE ORIGINAL MARVEL YEARS
OMNIBUS VOL. 1**
978-0-7851-9106-3

**STAR WARS:
THE ORIGINAL MARVEL YEARS
OMNIBUS VOL. 3
978-0-7851-9346-3**

AVAILABLE NOW WHEREVER BOOKS ARE SOLD

© & TM 2015 LUCASFILM LTD.

AN EPIC JOURNEY FROM THE BEGINNINGS OF THE OLD REPUBLIC TO THE RISE OF THE EMPIRE AND BEYOND!

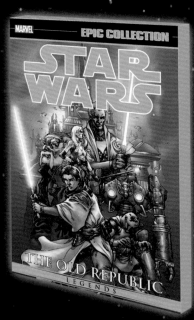

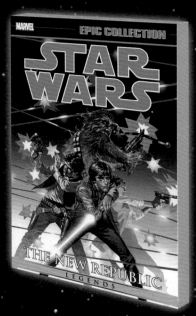

STAR WARS LEGENDS EPIC COLLECTION:
THE OLD REPUBLIC VOL. 1 TPB
978-0-7851-9717-1

STAR WARS LEGENDS EPIC COLLECTION:
RISE OF THE SITH VOL. 1 TPB
978-0-7851-9722-5

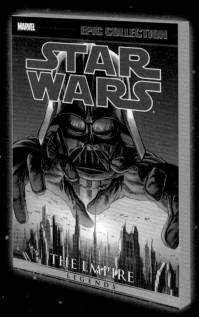

STAR WARS LEGENDS EPIC COLLECTION:
THE EMPIRE VOL. 1 TPB
978-0-7851-9398-2

STAR WARS LEGENDS EPIC COLLECTION:
THE NEW REPUBLIC VOL. 1 TPB
978-0-7851-9716-4

AVAILABLE NOW WHEREVER BOOKS ARE SOLD

© & TM 2015 LUCASFILM LTD.

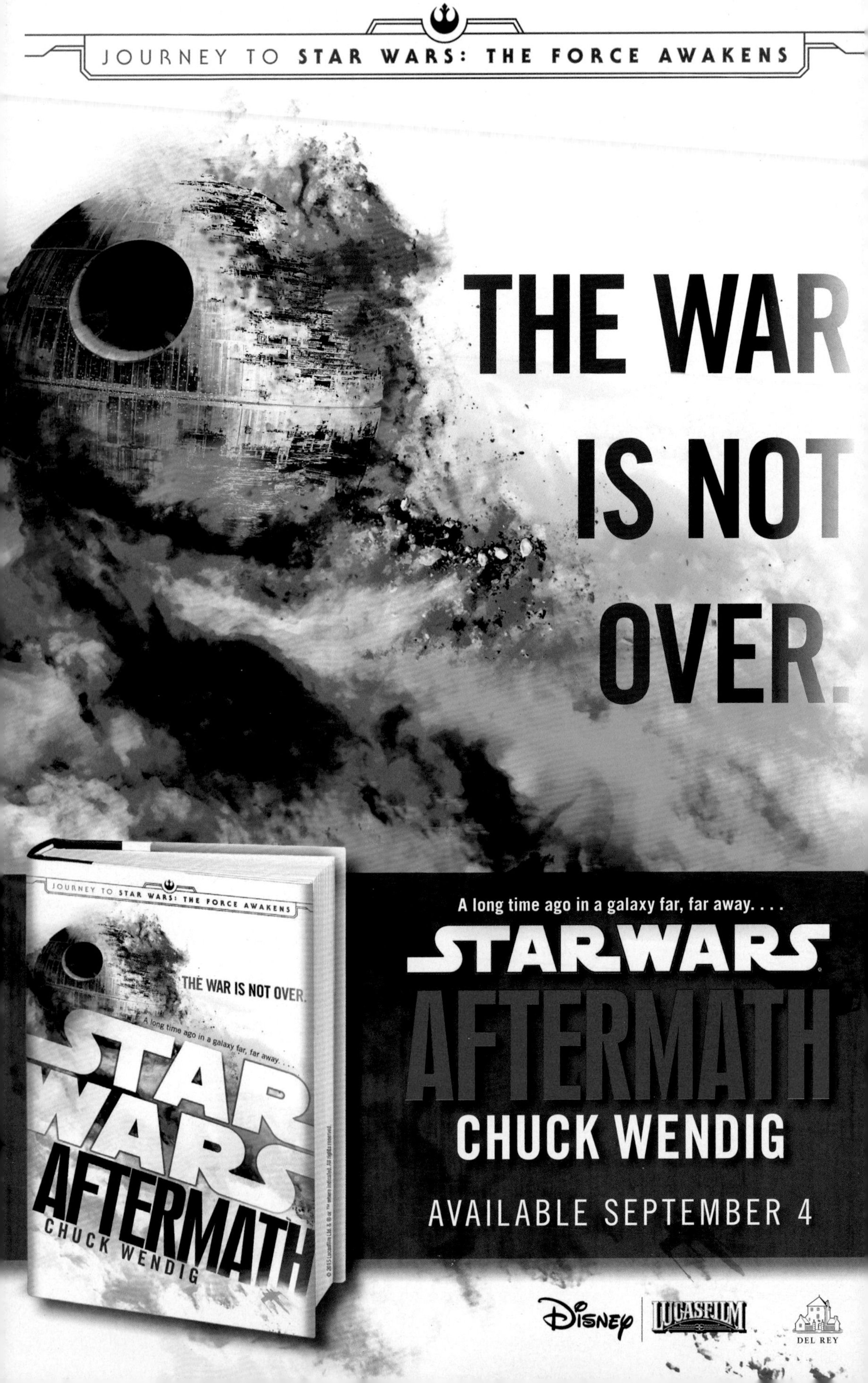
JOURNEY TO STAR WARS: THE FORCE AWAKENS
THE WAR IS NOT OVER.
JOURNEY TO STAR WARS: THE FORCE AWAKENS
THE WAR IS NOT OVER.
A long time ago in a galaxy far, far away. . . .
STAR WARS
AFTERMATH
CHUCK WENDIG
© 2015 Lucasfilm Ltd. & ® or ™ where indicated. All rights reserved.
A long time ago in a galaxy far, far away. . . .
STAR WARS
AFTERMATH
CHUCK WENDIG
AVAILABLE SEPTEMBER 4
Disney
LUCASFILM
DEL REY